Christianity, Wealth, and Spiritual Power in Ghana

Karen Lauterbach

Christianity, Wealth, and Spiritual Power in Ghana

palgrave
macmillan

Karen Lauterbach
University of Copenhagen
Copenhagen, Denmark

ISBN 978-3-319-33493-6   ISBN 978-3-319-33494-3 (eBook)
DOI 10.1007/978-3-319-33494-3

Library of Congress Control Number: 2016953827

© The Editor(s) (if applicable) and The Author(s) 2017
This work is subject to copyright. All rights are solely and exclusively licensed by the Publisher, whether the whole or part of the material is concerned, specifically the rights of translation, reprinting, reuse of illustrations, recitation, broadcasting, reproduction on microfilms or in any other physical way, and transmission or information storage and retrieval, electronic adaptation, computer software, or by similar or dissimilar methodology now known or hereafter developed.
The use of general descriptive names, registered names, trademarks, service marks, etc. in this publication does not imply, even in the absence of a specific statement, that such names are exempt from the relevant protective laws and regulations and therefore free for general use.
The publisher, the authors and the editors are safe to assume that the advice and information in this book are believed to be true and accurate at the date of publication. Neither the publisher nor the authors or the editors give a warranty, express or implied, with respect to the material contained herein or for any errors or omissions that may have been made.

Cover design by Paileen Currie

Printed on acid-free paper

This Palgrave Macmillan imprint is published by Springer Nature
The registered company is Springer International Publishing AG
The registered company address is: Gewerbestrasse 11, 6330 Cham, Switzerland

To the memory of my mother

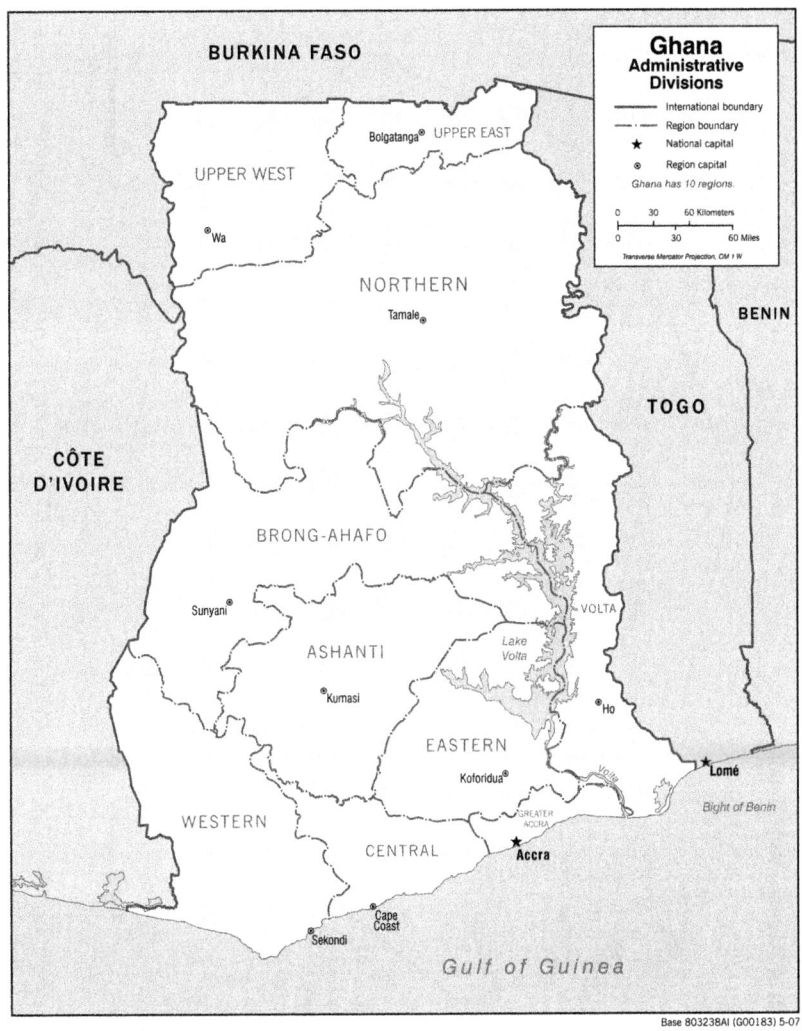

Ghana Administrative regions. *Source:* Central Intelligence Agency Library: https://www.cia.gov/library/publications/resources/cia-maps-publications/Ghana.html

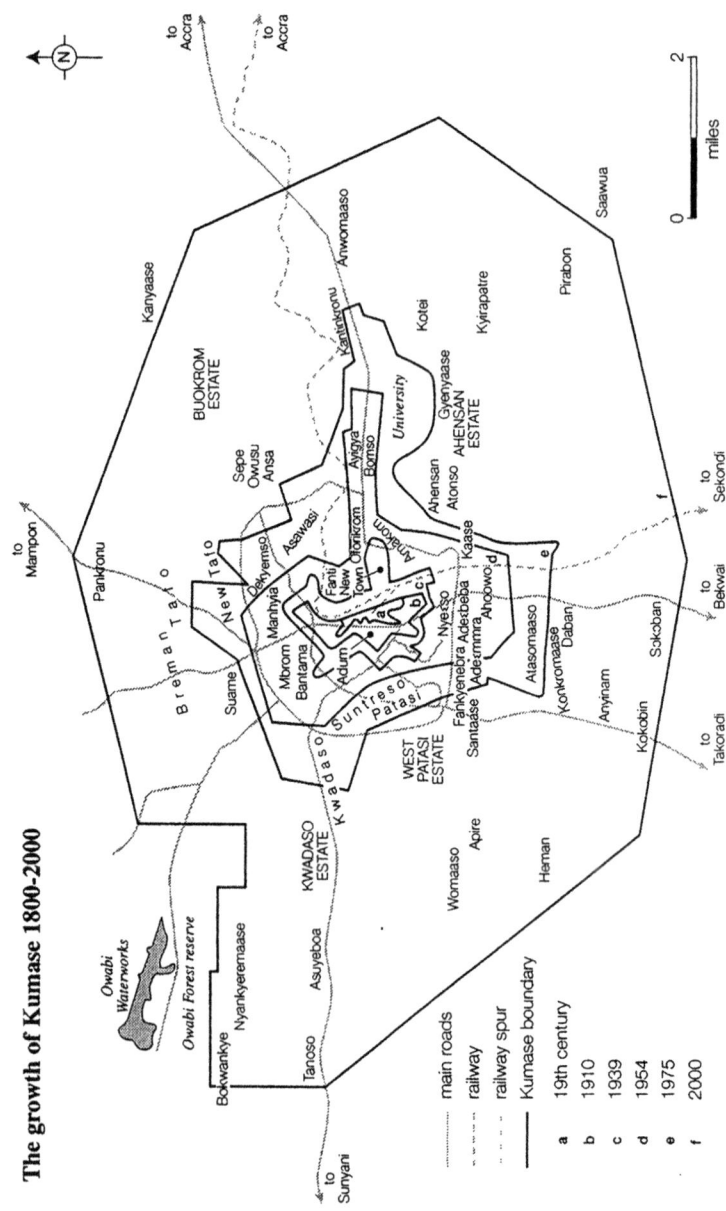

The growth of Kumase 1800–2000. *Source*: T.C. McCaskie. 2000. *Asante Identities. History and modernity in an African village 1850–1950*. Edinburgh University Press for the International African Institute, London, p. 208. The author as well as the International African Institute have kindly permitted the reproduction of the map

ACKNOWLEDGEMENTS

The work that has resulted in the present book has matured over a decade. It began with the writing of my Ph.D. thesis that I defended in 2009. But in many ways that was just the beginning. More research was done, work shared, and comments taken in. Over these years, my fascination with young pastors in Ghana has not decreased and their persistence and enthusiasm still captivate me. It has been a privilege to be able to uncover more layers of what it means to become a pastor and to understand the particularities of this in the Asante context of Ghana.

I am deeply grateful to all the people who contributed to my work while I was in Ghana in 2004, 2005, and 2014: all the pastors, church members, family members, and other people, whom I spoke to and interviewed. I am grateful for the time they spent with me and for the information they shared about their lives. Thanks in particular to Emmanuel Appiah, Sylvia and Emmanuel Owusu-Ansah, Francis Afrifa, and Seth Osei-Kuffour for their openness and willingness to share. I am grateful to Michael Poku-Boansi and Phyllis Kyei Mensah for research assistance and instructive discussions while working in Kumasi and for additional research assistance provided by Ebenezer Kwasi Opuko, James Boafo, Munirat Tawiah, and Naomi Adarkwa. I owe special thanks to George Bob-Milliar for hospitality, friendship, and many long talks.

I have profited immensely from discussions with former colleagues at the Graduate School for International Development Studies and in particular Bodil Folke Frederiksen, Christian Lund, Ebbe Prag, Fiona Wilson, Lene Bull Christiansen, Signe Marie Cold-Ravnkilde, and Roger Leys. I have learned much from inspiring debates with colleagues at the Centre for

Theology and Religious Studies at Lund University (Carl Sundberg, Hans Olsson, Lotta Gammelin, Martina Prosén, and Mika Vähäkangas). I also much appreciate the encouragement and support from colleagues at the Centre of African Studies, University of Copenhagen (Amanda Hammar, Camilla Strandsbjerg, Hannah Elliott, and Julie Sommer von Würden) and in particular the immense and endless support I have received over the years from Niels Kastfelt. Our many conversations have shaped and sharpened my thinking. I owe thanks to David Maxwell for thoughtful comments and encouragement. I thank Ben Jones for always being there to think with me and for our long friendship. I am grateful to the late John Peel for a critical reading of an earlier version of the manuscript, and I am greatly indebted to Tom McCaskie for his willingness to respond to my many questions and share his deep knowledge of Asante society and history.

The Danish Research Council for Development Research, the Nordic Africa Institute, the Swedish Research Council, and Lund Mission Society have funded my fieldwork. I thank Joanna Woods for language proofreading of the book. I am very grateful to the editorial team at Palgrave for much appreciated assistance during the whole process, as well as for the important contributions received during the peer-review process.

Lastly, I thank my family who have been of more importance than they could know.

Karen Lauterbach
Copenhagen
June 2016

Contents

1 Introduction — 1

2 A History of Wealth, Power, and Religion in Asante — 29

3 Wealth and Worth: The Idea of a Truthful Pastor — 63

4 The Craft of Pastorship — 91

5 Performing Spiritual Power and Knowledge — 125

6 The Politics of Becoming a Small 'Big Man' — 151

7 Conclusion — 197

Appendix — 207

Index — 213

Abbreviations

ABC   Alive Bible Congregation
BPMI   Bethel Prayer Ministry International
CCC   Calvary Charismatic Centre
CCG   Christian Council of Ghana
CPP   Convention People's Party
ICBC   International City Baptist Church
IMF   International Monetary Fund
JSS   Junior Secondary School
KNUST   Kwame Nkrumah University of Science and Technology
NDC   National Democratic Congress
NLM   National Liberation Movement
NPP   New Patriotic Party
PNDC   Provisional National Defence Council
SU   Scripture Union

Dollar values in the book are based on the conversion rate of the Ghanaian cedi (new cedi (1967–2007) for 1 September 2005 unless otherwise stated.

Glossary

List of Twi words used in the text (the list is mainly based on McCaskie 1995 and Miescher 2005):

Twi	English
abusua, pl. mmusua	family, kin, matrilineage
ahenkwaa, pl. nhenkwaa	servant of the Asantehene
akonkofoɔ	businessmen in the early colonial period
akwankwaa, pl. nkwankwaa	young man, commoner
anibue	being civilised
Asanteman	the Asante state
ayiyedi	prosperity
bayi	witchcraft
bɔne	evil
krakye, pl. akrakyefoɔ	clerk, scholar
mogya	blood
nkrabea	fate, destiny
ɔbirɛmpɔn, pl. abirɛmpɔn	'big man', accumulator
ɔbosom, pl. abosom	powers of supernatural origin
ɔhemaa, pl. ahemaa	queenmother
ɔhene, pl. ahene	chief, office holder
ɔkɔmfɔ, pl. akɔmfoɔ	priest or fetish priest, one who is possessed by powers of supernatural origin
onyame	creator of the worlds, God
onyame nnipa	'man of God'
ɔsɔfo, pl. asofo	a priest, one who officiates in the service of God or a Fetish, one who performs a religious ceremony

sika — gold, money
sika dwa — golden stool
suman, pl. *asuman* — fetiches, charms, amulets
sunsum, pl. *asunsum* — soul
sunsum sore — spiritual churches
tumi — the ability to bring about change, power

LIST OF FIGURES

Fig. 1.1 Church in class room, Kwadaso, Kumasi　2
Fig. 3.1 Banner announcing prayer meeting, Ahodwo roundabout, Kumasi　83
Fig. 5.1 Hope Palace Chapel, Kwadaso Agric, Kumasi　131
Fig. 6.1 Church in store room, Kwadaso, Kumasi　159
Fig. 6.2 Young pastors in church, Kwadaso, Kumasi　164

CHAPTER 1

Introduction

The church was located in a school building in the Kwadaso area of Kumasi, Ghana. On Sundays, small churches occupied the classrooms of the school where they worshipped alongside one another. Banners hanging outside the school showed where each church was located (Fig. 1.1). When the churches started their services a blend of singing, preaching, and praying filled the air. The sound of drums and tambourines mixed with the loud voices of pastors preaching became a vocal symbol of the prominence and vibrancy of small charismatic churches in Ghana. The interior was sparsely decorated with plastic lace and flowers. The churchgoers were sitting in rows on the benches schoolchildren used during the week. The young pastors, who were leading these small churches, were establishing themselves as men of God not only because of a pastoral calling, but also because they could make use of their spiritual gifts more easily and freely here than while serving under a senior pastor in a larger church.

It was Edward's first visit to Alive Bible Congregation, a small charismatic church that was established in September 2004 by a Ghanaian pastor living abroad. The leadership had been delegated to a pastor in his 40s, who had just come out of Bible school. Edward was in his early 20s, a school leaver and referred to himself as prophet and pastor. Some friends had invited him to the church, and on his first visit in December 2004, the senior pastor gave him the opportunity to preach. At this time, the church had 20 members. Edward joined and left his former church, the Apostolic Church of Ghana, where he was a junior pastor. He now

Fig. 1.1 Church in class room, Kwadaso, Kumasi. *Note*: All photographs are taken by the author in all chapters

referred to himself as 'an associate pastor sort of' and a prophet of God and explained that God spoke through him about the church and the members.[1]

Edward is one among many young people in Ghana who, with the growth of charismatic and Pentecostal Christianity, have embarked on pastoral career trajectories and for whom the process of becoming a pastor is about getting access to and exercising spiritual power. The many small charismatic churches provide a new platform for realising these aspirations. Although Edward joined a very small church, he had the opportunity to preach and hence to show his knowledge of the word of God, which he would not have had in a larger and more established church.

Some months later, in February 2005, the church had moved to a small storeroom located in the same area of Kumasi (see Fig. 6.1) and three young pastors had joined Edward. A Ghanaian colleague and I attended a Sunday service in the church. When we arrived, the grey metal doors that served as an entrance to the storeroom were closed and locked with a padlock. Nobody was around and there were no signs of a church or of a church service about to start. After some 30 minutes, Edward arrived, opened the door, and put a banner with the name of the church outside. He sat down in the back of the storeroom, behind a wooden pulpit with his head bowed, and prayed while we sat waiting. The room was small with no windows. It contained eight blue plastic chairs and a drum besides the pulpit. After some time, two other young pastors arrived as well as a few church attendants, many of whom were children. An hour into the service, the senior pastor turned up and started to preach. He had not been in church for some time, the younger pastors told us, allegedly having gone back to his former church. According to him, however, he did not belong to one specific church, but 'used to move from one church to another because the head pastors in these churches did not treat [him] fairly.'[2]

By September 2005, the young pastors had taken over the leadership of the church and the senior pastor had left. They now referred to themselves as senior pastors and Edward as the head pastor and prophet. The church had moved into the premises of an old restaurant. This location was spacious and served as the young pastors' residence. Despite the new location and the link to a congregation abroad, the church had not grown much in size; the membership remained between 15–30 members and it was a changing and unstable one. Being in this church, however, allowed the young pastors, who were all in insecure positions, to set themselves up as pastors able to mediate spiritual power and in this way also to join power.

After a year or so, most of the young pastors left the church as they disagreed with the founding pastor on doctrinal issues, and he no longer allowed them to use their spiritual gifts in church for deliverance and healing. One of the young pastors, Daniel, went back to his former church, Christ Apostolic Church, and went to University College to study theology. Alongside, he helped a friend establish a Bible school and founded a fellowship himself. He remained within an established structure and hierarchy and at the same time created an independent platform on which he performed and was recognised as a man of God. A decade later, there were no signs of the church. It had collapsed.

THE AIM OF THE BOOK

This book offers a study of pastorship within charismatic churches[3] as pathways to become small 'big men.' By this, I understand processes of pursuing successful careers and attaining power and wealth that resonate with locally and historically embedded understandings of becoming 'big' and being a religious expert. The pastoral careers that I analyse are of middle-level pastors that are establishing themselves as pastors, and I focus both on the social processes of becoming a pastor and the spiritual dimensions of how power and wealth are conceptualised, achieved and legitimised in the particular context of Asante in Ghana. The book works with the premise that the social processes and moral practices at stake resonate with historical experiences and ideas. Based on this, the book offers a reading of how charismatic Christianity engages with contemporary Asante lives and identities, of how historic figures and categories get reshaped and adapted to new circumstances and influences. It combines an analysis that on the one hand historicises current expressions of charismatic Christianity, and on the other hand brings to the fore the role of religion and belief in our understanding of wealth and power more broadly in African societies (McCaskie 1995).

The book has an overarching narrative about the making of middle-level charismatic pastors and tells a story of pastors navigating relations of patronage and entrepreneurship and at the same time proving to the social surroundings that they are truthful pastors. One way of proving to be a truthful pastor is the way in which he achieves wealth and how he uses it. The book integrates the analysis of charismatic Christianity with a historically informed analysis of social mobility and of how people in subordinate positions seek to join power. Rather than focusing on the religious sector—or the church—as an isolated unit, the book analyses how charismatic Christianity is appropriated and made sense of in the local Ghanaian setting, where access to and performance of spiritual power traditionally also played an important role.

Pastorship and Charismatic Christianity

The above depiction of young and up-and-coming pastors, establishing their churches in classrooms and storerooms, is a reflection of the prominence and vitality of Pentecostal and charismatic Christianity in Africa. The Pew Research Centre estimates that Pentecostals in Sub-Saharan Africa constitute around 15 percent of the region's total population (Pew Research Centre 2011).[4] Ghana is the country in West Africa with the largest proportion (75 percent) of its population being Christian (Pew Research Centre 2012), with almost half the Christians being Pentecostals and neo-charismatics.[5] As the figures indicates, this form of Christianity has attracted large numbers of people and has, as noted by Maxwell (2013b), inspired members to give large sums of money to the churches and their pastors. Moreover, adherents spend time in church, not only on Sundays for church service, but also during the week for prayer meetings, Bible study groups, and choir practice. Another salient feature of Pentecostal and charismatic Christianity is the ability to mobilise and engage people in church organisation and various committees, and through this provide access to positions in the church hierarchy.

It is in relation to this tendency that we can understand the emergence of the many small and middle-sized Pentecostal and charismatic churches. Pastors (*asofo*⁶) are in many ways the pivot point of these churches that in Ghana are known as 'one-man churches', meaning a church founded by one person, belonging to one person, and in the control of one person. The pastors have since the 1980s gained prominence and have become new figures of authority and success. In common parlance, people say that everyone can start their own church, all you need is a Bible and a few plastic chairs. No one requires diplomas from Bible schools or formal approvals and registrations. But how does one become a pastor, and why is this middle-level group of aspiring younger pastors finding a pastoral career more attractive than pursuing a civil servant career, finding employment within a growing private sector, or working with an NGO with access to international networks and connections?

The book's focus on young up-and-coming pastors stands in contrast to the picture of the flamboyant mega-star pastors of the large Pentecostal and charismatic churches in Ghana and elsewhere in Africa (Gifford 2004, 2015). The pastors I met in storerooms, garages, and classrooms did not fit into this image. They did not shine and were not rich, and their success depended on a variety of social connections, including family and kin. Maxwell makes a similar and more general comment: '[m]any Africanists may not have heard of these men but they are nevertheless extremely important. In the range of issues they address—moral, material and political—they are the heirs of the community and nationalist leaders of the 1950s' (Maxwell 2000: 471). The focus of this book is not on the famous superstar pastors in Accra, such as Mensa Otabil (founder and leader of The International Central Gospel Church) or Nicholas Duncan-Williams (founder and leader of Christian Action Faith Ministries), but on the middle-level pastor or the small 'big man.' The aim is to revisit how we think about power and being 'big' in Pentecostal and charismatic Christianity, moving the focus away from the Pentecostal 'big man' to the process of achieving 'bigness' and to becoming a small 'big man.'

Notwithstanding the apparent insignificance and smallness of these young pastors, their actions express an eagerness and motivation to succeed, to become successful 'men of God' and through this to escape subordination. Some had little educational background and therefore no qualifications for civil service employment, whereas others had university degrees and jobs. Common to all of them was the fact that by becoming pastors, they acquired status and recognition, not only in church but also more widely in society. In this book, I argue that becoming a pastor is a way to achieve status and join power, because pastors draw on both socio-political and religious criteria for success. They inscribe themselves into a global religious community that has had tremendous impact on the African continent as a whole. At the same time, their trajectories are emplaced within a local political economy that does not leave much space for social mobility and advancement. Pastoral career trajectories thus become a means to achieve social ascension and in the making of these careers, the young pastors draw on criteria of success that are historically embedded in the local Ghanaian context. Their success depends on their positioning in social networks, their ability to accumulate wealth in a legitimate way, as well as their display and possession of knowledge and wisdom. Most crucially, however, becoming a 'man of God' is about proving and performing access to spiritual power.

Small 'Big Men' and Religion in Asante

This book is about women and men seeking a path in life. It lays out the various mechanisms and social processes they draw on and engage in when becoming pastors. It looks in particular at the role of spiritual power in these processes, and at the religious connotations of power and truthfulness. I analyse the making of pastoral careers as a novel form of religious entrepreneurship as well as an expression of cultural creativity that resonates with historical ideas and practices of wealth and power. The book paints a broad picture of pastorship as a way to rise in social hierarchies and as a means through which people in insecure positions escape subordination. Consequently, I view the processes of becoming a pastor as a reflection of broader and changing trends of attaining social status.

An exploration of pastoral careers provides insight into the role of the pastor as more than a religious figure; a pastor is also a public figure of authority. His influence transgresses the field of the church, as well as boundaries of kinship, social status, ethnicity, generation, and gender.

The pastors of this book—who establish their churches in storerooms and garages—represent a larger group of aspiring people that put in play identity, spirituality, and the past in their endeavours to grow (Lauterbach 2010).

The book discusses pastorship with the aim of uncovering the social mechanisms involved in becoming a pastor, as well as the broader socio-political significance of holding religious office. In the analysis, I show that this process involves both apprenticeship and entrepreneurship. By being an apprentice, a young pastor draws on the credibility of a senior pastor, and this permits him or her to invoke the power of God. Concurrently, young pastors who aspire to leadership positions appear to be entrepreneurial and get involved in various networks (congregation, colleagues, and extended family) to realise their aspirations. Pastors are involved in networks in both a horizontal and a vertical sense: in relation to older and more established people and in relation to people who belong to the same layer as themselves. When pastors seek to become 'bigger', they do so not only in the context of the church, but also in a way that is recognised more broadly in society. Although pastors draw on former ideas of wealth, status, and power, they are innovative in the sense that the churches they establish and the hierarchies they are part of are flexible and easy to enter and leave. They create organisational forms where social ascension and status is more accessible.

Understanding the behind-the-scene processes of becoming a pastor contributes to our understanding of other forms of social ascension, as well as the broader patterns of changing power relations and emerging new elites in Ghana. The book argues that new spaces for social mobility occur in the overlapping zones between religion, politics, and social life. While seeing religion as a space that allows for a redefinition and transformation of established ideas and practices, the book also builds on the premise that pastors, as well as other emergent figures of success, are strongly embedded in their social and historical background.

The pastor is a twofold figure. He is a religious leader perceived of as possessing and invoking spiritual power and through this delivering spiritual protection and providing material success. This is a religious figure in a classic Asante sense; the mediator between the spiritual realm and the material world. It is also a religious figure in a Christian sense, one that can interpret the word of God and through this perform wisdom and knowledge.[7] At the same time, a pastor is a leader in a socio-political sense: he is a provider, a protector, and a community builder. Hence, the pursuit of a pastoral career involves claiming authority and generates 'power and flows of patronage which are eminently worth contesting for' (Ranger 1986: 31). The construction of pastorship can be seen as merging these two fields of influence (religious and political office). The book argues that charismatic pastors constitute new versions of older religious leaders and inscribe themselves in the tradition of being a religious figure and a small 'big man' in Asante. At the same time, they are cultural innovators, drawing on both the history of Christianity in Asante and their connections to mainly Nigerian and American charismatic pastors.

Joining Power: Trajectories in Context

Most of the pastors of this book are from Asante[8] in Ghana and many had grown up and were operating in and around Kumasi, the second biggest town in Ghana, and the capital of the Asante kingdom. Kumasi is a fast-growing urban conglomeration with a vast peri-urban zone where newcomers settle (McCaskie 2009; Simon et al. 2004). It is a city that attracts many, mostly young, people with aspirations of making an income and making a life. As in other urban sites, this means pressure on social and physical infrastructure, as well as a fast transformation of the urban physical landscape (see also Esson 2013). What was once known as the Garden City is now by many seen as a site of tensions due to unequal distribution of wealth and resources. At the same time, Kumasi has a history as, and still is, a site of power: economic, political, and spiritual power. Kumasi in this sense is the place where one has the possibility of joining power (McCaskie 2007c).

With a changing economic and political environment during the 1990s and the 2000s (economic recovery and pluralisation of public and political spaces), new trajectories of social ascension were pursued by people who found themselves in insecure positions. They were most often people with no laid out trajectories of how to rise in the social hierarchy, but who were still aspiring to do so. Many were not attracted by the standard career trajectory in the public sector, which had been the emergent sector of the economy in the years after independence. At this time, education was seen as the route to employment in the public sector, which was again the way to achieve social and economic mobility (Arhin 1994: 317; Foster 1965: 196–197; King and Martin 2002: 9; Osei 2004: 431). However, with the decline in the attractiveness of a public sector trajectory, following from financial cuts in the sector, people began seeking more diverse trajectories of gaining social status.

McCaskie analyses two examples of such trajectories: that of Nana Abass who is the founder and priest (ɔkɔmfɔ) of the Medoma shrine in Kumasi and that of a blacksmith and illegal gun producer in Suame Magazine, Kumasi. Nana Abass was destined to become an ɔkɔmfɔ in his early childhood. As a young boy he experienced a number of encounters with *mmoatia* (dwarves, or supernatural beings), but for some time he resisted the calling or his fate. He worked as a taxi driver in Kumasi and converted to Islam to protect himself against the *mmoatia*. He eventually accepted the calling, went through training and initiation by the *mmoatia*, and went back to Kumasi to set up a shrine. His success as an ɔkɔmfɔ was, according to McCaskie, his ability to provide drinking water to the place, besides his spiritual qualifications and performances. This was a way for him to show that he looked after his community and was concerned about the wellbeing of people. Nana Abass has raised a critical voice against charismatic churches with regard to their sectarian touch and pastors' unscrupulous striving for wealth. In this way, he engages in a competition of faith that is about whose god/s are the most honest and efficient. Interestingly, he does that in ways that are similar to how charismatic pastors build themselves up; through spiritual performance and through striking a balance between individual accumulation and redistribution to the community. A last point about Abass worth mentioning is how the fact that he was digging in the ground for water was perceived by some as a way to get access to supernatural powers and by others as a way to show that he was a 'big man' (McCaskie 2008a: 68). Although McCaskie in his analysis does not link these two explanations (being a religious expert or a 'big man'), there is a connection in the sense that being a religious expert and having access to supernatural powers is also an aspect of being 'big.' In other words, there is an overlap or combination of religious office and political office (in some instances political power rather than office), a point that I will come back to with regard to charismatic pastors (see also Ubink 2007).

The second trajectory that I describe here more briefly is that of a gunsmith and illegal trader in weapons, a path that McCaskie also describes as a way to access power and status (McCaskie 2008c). This trajectory is of relevance here not because of its reliance on spiritual power, but because it shares in common aspects of being in insecure positions and of the morality around accumulating wealth. This man had been trained as a blacksmith, had to leave the business because of the economic crisis of the 1980s, and went to Kumasi to do all sorts of small jobs to make an income. He later trained as an electrical repairer in Suame Magazine and eventually went into gun production and arms trading. McCaskie presents discussions he had with this man and other local Asante about the morality of making wealth through criminal activities. These discussions reveal a distinction between stealing from the rich and taking from the poor, where the former is seen as 'little thieves stealing from very big thieves' and the latter is described as 'deeply immoral' (McCaskie 2008c: 448). McCaskie compares this moral distinction to '*nkwankwaa* talk' of the 1880s and 1950s, and thereby draws a connection between the contemporary trajectories of a desperate youth and earlier subordinate groups that also expressed social critique through their practices.

The above trajectories can be related to the young pastors in the storeroom churches in at least two ways. First, a shared experience of subordination and insecurity, although dealt with in dissimilar ways, frames how young people seek their pathways in life. Second, the trajectories are all about how people who are seeking a space to grow deal with wealth. The important question is whether wealth is accumulated and redistributed in a morally acceptable way. These trajectories therefore point to the similarities between pastors and other groups of aspiring people that very much revolve around the establishment of one's public position and the cultivation of 'an image as a local "big man", giving out cash, arbitrating disputes, dispensing advice and bribing neighbourhood police' (McCaskie 2008c: 433).

In order to historicise the way pastoral careers are made sense of, I also draw on Asante political and religious historic figures as well as earlier Asante upward socially mobile groups such as the *nkwankwaa* (youngmen) and the *akonkofoɔ* (young businessmen in the early colonial period). These groups expressed a critique of the established holders of power, challenged moral views on wealth, and through this came to legitimise more individual forms of accumulation and consumption of wealth. My point is to draw attention to the forerunners of the present-day figures of success in Asante and to highlight how the tensions and debates around wealth and power are tensions that have for long been part of the shaping and shaking up of Asante and Asante identities (McCaskie 2000).

In her work on the Asante National Liberation Movement in the 1950s, Allman discusses the history of the Asante youngmen as a social group and the relation between this group and the ruling elite. She points out that 'the youngmen had been a potent and active political force since at least the mid-nineteenth century, when they were known as the *nkwankwaa* ... The sense of the term was not that the *nkwankwaa* were literally young, but that they existed in often uneasy subordination to elder or chiefly authority' (Allman 1993: 29). This is relevant for the focus of this book, since Allman's observation points to the long history in Asante of tensions between holders of power and subordinate groups that has played out differently at various moments in time. My point is that the group of charismatic pastors that has appeared in Asante (and elsewhere in Ghana and Africa) since the 1980s can be seen as a variation of former groups of people in insecure positions that aimed at joining power and escaping subordination.

In this way, the book argues that pastoral careers are not only responses to changing socio-economic conditions (such as the economic hardships of the 1980s and the ensuing neo-liberal era), but influenced by local and historically rooted norms, beliefs, and ideas. I furthermore argue that it is the combination of claiming access to divine power and operating within and between different social, economic, and political spheres that influences one's ability and success in becoming an important 'man of God' (*Onyame nnipa*). What is striking is not so much that becoming a pastor is a way through which to gain and exercise some sort of power, but more that this power is recognised and regulated by one's social surroundings and is rooted in existing social and cultural categories and configurations. The role of pastors is related to ideas around access to spiritual power and mediation between the spiritual and the material world. Historically, mediators between these spheres (such as a chief [*ohene*] and a priest [*ɔkɔmfɔ*]) have had an ascribed status. The craft and politics of pastorship is about invoking spiritual power, which enables one to gain influence in ways that transcend the spiritual or religious sphere.

Religious Institutions, Ideas and Innovators: Resonance or Response?

As follows from the above, this book builds on the premise that new religious institutions and ideas resonate with historic figures, moral practices, and values, and that they at the same time are expressions of improvisations and adaptations of them. Asking questions around how people draw on ideas from the past to render things of the present meaningful is one way of drawing out elements of continuity and change. As also argued by Barber this is about understanding 'by what specific methods people simultaneously improvise and make things stick, and why they do it' (Barber 2007b: 37).

Christianity in Asante, and in Africa more generally, has taken its form through processes of appropriation and encounters between missionaries and local adherents, of which some became pastors and priests (see for instance Greene 2002; Maxwell 2006a, 2013a; Peel 2000). Local constructions of religious narratives and ideas came out of these encounters. I see the ways in which pastors become small 'big men' and establish their careers as building on notions of status, wealth, and power that were shaped in Asante before the introduction of Christianity and the emergence of Pentecostal and charismatic Christianity, but that are also shaped by these. The trajectories are appropriations and adaptations of new religious and cultural influences and they are at the same time cultural improvisations of the past; they are 'neither a replica of the old nor a replica of the new' (Greene 2002: 5). However, as Greene also points out, these appropriations took place at different scales and with different intensity and we therefore need to pay attention to 'the range of cultural responses' that these encounters produce, rather than seeing them in the singular (Greene 2002: 5). Moreover, Peel analyses the idiom of 'making country fashion' as a way to dissolve the distinction between the religious and the non-religious in his study of the encounter between the Yoruba and Christian missionaries. In this way he draws everyday routines and practices that are part of and infused in the broader Yoruba understanding of religion into the analysis (Peel 2000: 88 ff.) I am inspired by these approaches when analysing pastoral careers in Asante because they offer a broad and embedded view of religion and religious encounters.

For new churches and pastors to be legitimate, there has to be resonance with former practices and experiences. New institutions require a stabilising principle and as Douglas puts it there 'needs to be an analogy by which the formal structure of a crucial set of social relations is found in the physical world, or in the supernatural world, or in eternity, anywhere, so long as it is not seen as a socially contrived arrangement' (Douglas 1986: 48). An exploration of the phenomenon of pastorship in charismatic churches in Asante thus calls for drawing on the social history of pre-colonial and colonial Asante and at the same time looking at these institutions as fields of cultural and social improvisation (see also Jones 2009: 10).

Religion as Response: The 'Social Malaise' Argument

This leads on to another premise of the book, namely that the rise of new religious movements is not necessarily a reaction to certain moments in time such as modernity or neo-liberalism or contexts of 'social malaise.' Although present in much recent scholarship that seeks to explain the rise of charismatic Christianity in Africa, this is not a new argument. In the following quote, Baëta reacts to the argument that the rise of African Independent Churches (in Ghana known as spiritual churches—*Sunsum sorè*) was a response to the anxieties brought about by colonial impact, modernity, and Western influence:

> It appears to me that in recent studies of new cults and other movements of a religious nature among African peoples, the presumed background element of psychological upheaval, tensions and conflicts, anxieties, etc., due to 'acculturation, technology and the Western impact' has tended to be rather overdrawn. Here is a typical judgment in this connection ... Whether there is more anxiety in Ghana now than at any time previously, or than in most other countries of the world at present, must probably remain a matter of opinion. After all, people have seen some very rough times here, e.g. slaving era, and the 'Western impact' has been with us already for the best part of half a millennium. (Baëta [1962] 2004: 6)

This 'social malaise' argument was (and still is) prevailing in studies of religious movements in Africa. The assumption is that the popularity of religious movements is a reaction to structural change in society, a change that brings fragmentation and chaos as well as hopes and aspirations (Meyer 1998c: 759). Comaroff and Comaroff (2003) argue that there is a conjuncture between the rise of millennial capitalism and a growing occurrence of occult economies and hereby sees a new Protestant Pentecostal ethic as a response to a new spirit of capitalism and neo-liberal ethic. Religious mobilisation is in this frame of understanding a response either in terms of providing security and order or in terms of permitting to contest new and suppressing powers. The causality is often unquestioned, and consequently, religion is seen as a response or an instrument. As Baëta some 50 years ago questioned the relationship between the hardships of a certain period in time and the rise of a particular religious movement, Marshall criticises the tendency to 'domesticate modernity' and to see new religious movements as responses to globalisation and socio-economic crises (Marshall 2009: 22).

At the same time, there is a different literature that is more concerned with *how* religious practices are part of people's lives and self-understandings (Coleman 2011: 36) and in this approach religion is 'perhaps above all, a site of *action*, invested in and appropriated by believers' (Marshall 2009:

22). There is a need to question the taken for granted assumption of connections between certain developments of time and the rise of religious movements, and instead 'treat them as problematic, as needing explanation, just as all other kinds of social and political implications of religious movements need explanation' (Ranger 1986: 51).

The point is that we cannot simply set up a causal line of argumentation, but that it rather is the interplay and affinities between the conditions through which religious phenomena emerge and the phenomena itself as a mode of action that must be explored through ethnographic fieldwork and reflection (Ranger 2007). Religious institutions and ideas have an affinity with social, political, and economic interests and practices (Weber [1930] 2001; Gerth and Wright Mills 1991: 63). What is important is not that a particular cult arose or faded in a specific moment in time, but as Ranger puts it: '[t]he point is much more that through all these periods African religious movements were flexible and responsive, reflecting a great variety of aspirations and interests, and engaged both in micro and macro politics' (Ranger 1986: 49).

Rupture and Continuity

The above discussion relates to debates about continuity and rupture that feature prominently in scholarship on Pentecostal and charismatic Christianity. Rupture and ideas of breaking with the past have been central in studies of Pentecostalism and in the anthropology of Christianity (Robbins 2004, 2014). In African contexts, it is in particular questions of making distance to traditional religious beliefs and cultural practices that have received attention, the argument being that by doing so, Pentecostal Christianity reinforces the role of, for instance, witchcraft and evil spirits (Meyer 1998a; van Dijk 1997; Lindhardt 2015). Rupture is a prominent feature in the rhetoric of many Pentecostal and charismatic churches and implies that those who are 'born-again' should distance themselves from both the immediate past (one's personality and the kind of life one has led) and the ancestral past (relations to ancestors) (Lauterbach 2005; Meyer 1998a).

Conversion in itself is an act of rupture and of transforming one's self. The Pentecostal narrative is that through accepting Jesus Christ as a personal saviour, converts start living new lives that correspond to Pentecostal ethics around, for instance, alcohol, sexuality, and family life. In his work on the Church of Pentecost in Ghana and London, Daswani (2013, 2015) points out that rupture as an ethical practice is a dialectical process in which church members reflect upon and dispute the ideology of rupture. This implies that rupture is not exclusive, but situated within a continuum of reproduction and freedom. Likewise, Lindhardt has made the important observation that 'scholars tend to find both more continuity and more discontinuity with existing religious traditions' in studies of Pentecostal and charismatic Christianity (Lindhardt 2015: 163). This is important because it invites us to go beyond the binary of change and continuity that to some degree has disrupted the debate.

The powerful discourse and imagination of rupture and breaking with the past has led many scholars to put particular emphasis on the transformative character of Pentecostalism as a process of individualisation linked to modernity (Asamoah-Gyadu 2005a; Engelke 2004; Marshall 1993; Meyer 1998a; Laurent 1999, 2003; van Dijk 1997). The focus has been on how '[b]ecoming a Christian would thus involve completely reordering all other forms of identification and all other relationships' (Asamoah-Gyadu 2005a: 136) and on how conversion to Pentecostalism is a way to escape social bonds and hierarchies. Engelke (2010) provides a critical discussion of this focus on rupture. He sees the close linking of rupture with modernity as problematic because it takes away the attention from what (other) histories and traditions people relate to and draw on. Moreover, he argues that there is too strong a focus on discourse to the detriment of analysing practice: 'What people say is often striking, but it needs to be accompanied by a focus on what they do' (Engelke 2010: 179) (see also Haynes 2012: 133–134). I follow Engelke's call for differentiating between an official religious discourse and the social practice of religious actors. The rhetoric on rupture is undoubtedly distinctive, but it does not tell us much about church members' and pastors' relationships to family and kin, speaking more to ideas of a generalised condition or experience of modernity. One needs to think of the multiple factors that may influence these social relationships (education, employment, migration to mention a few). Focusing too closely on the Pentecostal break with the past distracts us from observing some of the broader trends of continuity and change with regard to social mobility, joining power, and accumulating wealth, and of how religion plays out in a particular historical, political, and social context. I wish to draw attention to continuity and change not only within a religious context, but also in relation to how a religious figure and spiritual power is understood in broader socio-political terms and in relation to the past. I accentuate context and continuity by pointing out that the Asante context (and Southern Ghana) is a predominantly Christian area, and a context in which belief in evil forces and witchcraft has existed alongside Christianity. Most pastors come from Christian families and have often grown up in a mission church or in a classical Pentecostal church, which implies that becoming a pastor in a charismatic church might not represent that much of a break in social terms.

Status, Wealth, and Power in Asante

In this book, I interpret pastoral career trajectories in the light of what it means to be a 'big man' and a religious expert in an Asante context and argue that it can be understood as means of claiming and achieving status, wealth, and power. Status is the recognition that follows being a pastor; wealth is related to how being in religious office permits one to accumulate and distribute wealth, and power is about how pastors are in positions to bring about change and build up positions of authority. These perspectives are interlinked and reflect the Asante historical context where for instance economic wealth, access to spiritual power and political office were closely related (McCaskie 1995; Wilks 1993).

Becoming a pastor entails being recognised as a religious mediator widely in society and not only within one's church, which permits social mobility. Part of my argument is that this is so because of the role religious experts have had in Asante historically, but also because having access to spiritual power was not restricted to the traditional priest, but was accessible more broadly. Status is built up by claiming access to the spiritual realm, by being able to perform spiritually and exercising religious authority. However, recognition also depends on pastors' ability to be truthful and to do what they speak.

In Asante the accumulation, distribution, and display of wealth was and is seen as an avenue to status and power. In order to achieve status as a 'big man of God' pastors must display wealth (such as money, cars, clothing, housing, followers, and size of church), and this wealth is understood as being a blessing from God. Wealth is a way to display and prove one's spiritual capabilities. At the same time, wealth has to be accumulated and redistributed in a morally acceptable way, which means that there has to be a balance between accumulating for the individual and redistributing to the community. A premise of the book is that pastors invoke and build on ideas of wealth that resonate with an Asante experience, and that this overlaps with the focus on wealth and prosperity in the charismatic churches.

One of the questions that I address is to what extent and in what ways charismatic Christianity introduces new perceptions of wealth. I argue that within charismatic Christianity in Asante, wealth is understood as more than money; it is richness in both a material and a spiritual sense. For pastors, wealth also means control over people, over an institution, over international relations as well as possessing the capacity to heal and be in contact with God. Achieving wealth means that pastors have proven their abilities to perform as religious experts, and that God has rewarded them with wealth. However, wealth in itself does not bring power and status; wealth needs to be displayed, recognised, and legitimised (Gilbert 1988: 307).

The book also discusses how claimed spiritual power is invoked in mundane social relations. This follows an understanding of power that is more than influence and control over others in an institutional setting, but also includes 'extra-human agency' (Arens and Karp 1989: xv). Arens and Karp propose to understand power as a cultural construct, where power is not only something being exercised, but also something with a culturally informed rationale. Power takes various forms, has multiple sources and needs to be legitimised (Arens and Karp 1989: xv–xvii).

In an article on the history of power in Asante, Akyeampong and Obeng have drawn attention to forms of power that did not lie within the realm of the state. Through this they shed light on the 'complex negotiations that surrounded power relations in Asante society' and argue that '[p]ower was thus rooted in the Asante cosmology, and individuals and groups that successfully tapped into this power source translated this access into authority if they controlled social institutions' (Akyeampong and Obeng 1995: 483). This, in my view, is where the key lies to understanding religion and power in contemporary Asante. Their analysis points to the broadness of the Asante concept of power and at the same time to its accessibility to those on the ground: 'power was available to anyone who knew how to make use of *Onyame*'s[9] powerful universe for good or evil' (Akyeampong and Obeng 1995: 483). This implies that the spiritual realm is a source of power in the Asante context. Akyeampong and Obeng moreover distinguish between authority (political power) and *tumi* (the ability to bring about change). The first is the monopolisation of power, whereas access to *tumi* originates in the spiritual world and is more broadly accessible to those who have knowledge.

In a retrospect of 40 years in Asante studies, McCaskie recapitulates what he sees as central to the working dynamic of Asante society:

> ... I believe the web forged by three centuries of tumi and all of its ramified manifestations still defines, structures, and binds Asante culture. "Joining power" remains a sure path to self-realisation and success in Asante society, and the door to the career open to talent—best smoothed, of course, by connections—has been held ajar, but carefully policed, throughout Asante history. (McCaskie 2007c: 151)

In the above, McCaskie suggests that the aspirations to and processes of 'joining power' is the central clue to understanding Asante society both historically and presently. Power is in this understanding about political dynamics, cultural norms, and individual trajectories. It is not political power *strictu sensu*, nor restrained to being about control over material resources or pure self-interest. It is power in its transitive form, an embedded and encompassing form of power. It is more broadly about the dynamics of realising social aspirations, attaining status, and gaining wealth.

Implicit in the idea of joining power is the understanding that power is not something that lies within the individual or something that an individual has. In the Asante understanding, power is something that lies outside the individual and something that transgresses the realm of the physical world (it is also metaphysical). By using McCaskie's metaphor of joining power, I wish to bring forth the idea that power is something that a person joins, draws upon and taps into that exists outside of the person. Power exists in both a physical and metaphysical sense, but also very much in a historical sense. Therefore, when people join power they draw on a pool of power anchored in the Asante past. Power is something that exists out there, and one needs to get access to it, master it, and use it.[10] This means that it is not only the ability to exercise control over others that matters, but just as much the ability and knowledge to get access to the source or pool of power (Akyeampong 1996; Akyeampong and Obeng 1995; McCaskie 1995).

Moreover, access to and engagements in social networks are important to the dynamics of pastoral careers (where they come from, how they are promoted, how they eventually start on their own, whom they relate to, and who assist them). Founding and leading a 'one-man church' does require relations to other churches and pastors (to both senior pastors and pastors at the same hierarchical level). Besides, if a pastor does not succeed within one church (getting the right promotion or possibility to grow) and instead creates a new church, it implies being involved in a new set of social relations or adjusting existing ones. This is to say that a pastoral career is not only about individual self-promotion or about having a personal calling, but it is also an investment in social relationships, which serve as the foundation for being able to operate as a figure of authority and to impose oneself as a 'man of God.' In other words, pastors operate in a web of social relations.

My analysis of pastorship consists of several layers of social relationships: the immediate religious environment, relationships with the extended family as well as wider social relations. The immediate religious environment comprises how pastors operate in the church in relation to other pastors (senior or junior), and in relation to church members or the congregation. How do they legitimise or prove their spiritual power? What kinds of performances are involved, and how do the church members take part in this? The extended family layer focuses on where pastors come from, their relationships to home and with extended family members, as well as how they take up new roles, responsibilities, and privileges after becoming pastors. Pastors are also engaged in wider social networks nationally and transnationally. These relations are crucial for their work as pastors; they get inspiration, training, and resources from these relations. Such networks provide opportunities to travel and to preach in other churches, which is a way to gain standing in pastoral networks.

The above reflections point to my understanding of religious institutions and actors as being linked up with other institutions and actors, and not as self-contained places. In this I draw on Jones who, in his work on Pentecostalism and social change in rural Uganda, makes the point that it is 'important to understand that religious identities are necessarily played out in wider social circuits' (Jones 2009: 160). In the chapters that follow, I approach pastorship as being constructed and made sense of in relation to broader social networks and in ways that have resonance with Asante experience and the past, rather than approaching pastorship as something that builds up and unfolds only in church.

Religion and Politics: Processes of Becoming Small 'Big Men'

I employ the metaphor of the small 'big man' in the book to indicate that I see pastorship as a process of achieving 'bigness', a process that involves pastors and their social surroundings. The idea is not to employ the term 'big man' as a labelling for a certain type of leadership figure, but to cast light on the social processes of becoming bigger.

In the classical literature on 'big men,' the accumulation and redistribution of wealth (or 'the art of redistribution') is central. In order to be legitimate, a 'big man' must redistribute the accumulated wealth, which gives political capital, which again permits him to accumulate further: '*il faut avoir du pouvoir politique pour être riche, il faut être riche pour le conserver*' (Médard 1992: 172). A related aspect is the strategy of straddling various positions (or accumulating positions), which means that there is changeability of accumulated resources. This also indicates that the role of the 'big man' is not only political, but also economic, social, and religious. Médard argues that straddling is not only about accumulating positions, but also about strengthening the positions one already has (Médard 1992: 176).

I argue, in the same vein, that becoming a pastor is about operating in and between various fields simultaneously. Achieving recognition as a pastor in a church or a religious community implies gaining respect within domains other than the church, for instance, within families, kinship, and community groups. In her work on 'big men' and avenues to power in Northern Ghana, Lentz questions the use of the straddling image when discussing how 'big men' become 'big' in more than one field. She argues that it upholds an idea and image of separate fields of action (Lentz 1998: 61).[11] She instead suggests to focus on the complementarity and combination of different registers of power rather than the accumulation of positions per se. Taking this critique into account, I argue that pastors combine different registers of power to achieve 'bigness' (Lentz 1998: 48).

I seek to move beyond a depiction of pastors as small 'big men' that 'are persistent performances of the patrimonialist narrative as a form of static normative labelling' (Gould 2006: 923). Pastors are not 'big men' in the sense of Médard (1992), as they are not 'trapped' in and only relying on clientilistic relations, but are able to move beyond and recreate relationships that permit them to grow. These relationships unfold both at a horizontal and vertical level, which means that they are both egalitarian and hierarchical (see also Peel 2000: 53). Moreover, with regard to redistributing wealth, pastors perform both by redistributing wealth themselves, and by making people receive wealth as a blessing from God. The themes of 'sowing and reaping' and 'receiving God's blessing' are religious forms of redistribution. While it is God who provides, the pastor is the one who enables or mediates the provision and transaction. The kind of 'big man' that I deal with here transgresses the material focus and the strict patron-client relations of Médard's 'big man.'

This book positions itself in this debate by focusing on the tension between a reproduction of hierarchical power relations and the simultaneous potential to transgress hierarchical power structures. African Pentecostalism is, in the words of Maxwell (2006a: 3), 'a religious movement animated by a dialectic between primitive egalitarian ideals on the one hand and hierarchy and authoritarianism on the other' (see also Soothill 2007).

A Note on Methodology

The fieldwork on which this book is based was organised around following pastors rather than churches. I followed the social networks of pastors and talked to their colleagues, former colleagues, mentors, friends, family members and church members. The focus was on people rather than institutions, and on how crucial decisions in their lives were taken and made sense of (Rathbone 1996: 2). I interviewed 40 pastors. Some interviews focused on various aspects of pastorship as such, and others were of a more biographical character. I interviewed some pastors several times and was able to follow a few over a period of ten years. I think this offers the most useful way of piecing together the particular and contingent nature of what is involved in becoming a pastor and becoming bigger.

The material consists of 106 interviews, participation in 35 church services and events in 15 different churches, collection of audio-visual material (videos and cassettes) from church services, religious booklets and magazines, newspaper articles, questionnaires, archival files from the Ghana National Archives in Kumasi and the archives of the Manhyia Palace, pastors' Facebook pages as well as numerous conversations and email correspondences with pastors. The material was collected during 2004, 2005, and 2014.

I did the major part of my work in Kumasi. As I studied pastors and not churches per se, I did not concentrate on one particular area of Kumasi or on one particular church. I went wherever the pastors were living and preaching. I did a few interviews in Accra mainly with church members and pastors I got connected to through Ghanaians in Denmark, as well as with scholars working on Ghanaian Pentecostalism. Moreover, part of my material was collected in Sunyani and Techiman, both in the Brong-Ahafo region of Ghana.

The Book

The remainder of the book consists of six chapters. Chapter 2 provides a historical analysis of wealth, power, and religion in Asante and how the meaning of these categories has changed over time. The chapter is organised around two historic figures: the 'big man' (*ɔbirɛmpɔn*) and the religious expert (*ɔkɔmfɔ*). The chapter moreover provides an account of the introduction of Christianity in Asante as well as the growth of the Pentecostal and charismatic movement in Kumasi. The third chapter focuses on the idea of a truthful pastor and relates this to wealth, both to historic understandings of wealth as well as the Pentecostal doctrine on wealth (prosperity gospel). The discussion is organised around two sets of schisms, on the one hand a schism between accumulation for the individual or to the benefit of the community, and on the other hand a schism between being a true or a false pastor. Chapter 4 is concerned with the internal dynamics of pastorship and offers an analysis of the social processes involved in becoming a pastor. It provides an account of the various facets of becoming a pastor: the pastoral calling, training and Bible School and moreover analyses how a call to become a pastor is narrated, how it is approved and validated by the social surroundings. Chapter 5 is on performing spiritual power and knowledge. Spiritual power is shown and performed at church services, through prayers and performance of miracles, deliverance, and divination. The performance of spiritual power is a contested field in which accusations of relying on evil forces are made. In Chap. 6, I analyse pastoral trajectories and show that the process of becoming a successful pastor involves apprenticeship as well as entrepreneurship. I argue that young pastors seek relationships that, on the one hand, provide protection and legitimacy, and on the other hand, permit them to gain and exercise authority. I also discuss how pastors' authority influences their family relations. In the concluding chapter, I return to the overall discussion of the study of pastorship as a commentary on recent and historical trajectories of religious and social change in Asante. I argue that the craft of pastorship represents new ways of building up status, wealth, and power that also draw on vernacular understandings of these concepts. I further argue that one-sided analytical approaches (that focus mainly on rupture and response) are not satisfactory in explaining the attractiveness of becoming a charismatic pastor in Kumasi. It is in the conjuncture and interplay between material conditions, historic ideas of figures of authority and wealth and a new religious doctrine and practice that the craft of pastorship emerges.

Notes

1. Interview with Edward Owusu-Ansah, Kumasi, 13 December 2004.
2. Interview with James Abu, Kumasi, 13 February 2005.
3. In this book I most often use the term charismatic Christianity, but sometimes also refer to Pentecostal and charismatic Christianity. By charismatic churches, I mean the newer and independent churches that are sometimes referred to as neo-Pentecostal/charismatic churches (Meyer 2004). The latter broad labelling (Pentecostal and charismatic) refers to both the classical Pentecostal churches, introduced by missionaries, and to the newer independent charismatic churches, but does not include the charismatic movement within other Christian denominations such as the Catholic Church. When using this term I refer to the broader movement, but also to the blurred boundaries between the various categories. Some of the pastors figuring in this book came out of classical Pentecostal churches, created independent charismatic churches, but still move in and out of these different kinds of churches. The focus of the book is on young pastors in charismatic churches. This term encompasses the broad range of independent churches as well as more loosely organised fellowships. The pastors themselves use the term charismatic rather than Pentecostal. When I refer specifically to older generations of Pentecostal churches I write classical Pentecostal churches. See Omenyo (2013) on the categorisation of Ghanaian Pentecostal and charismatic churches as well as some recent figures.
4. This figure does not include charismatics within other Christian denominations or independent charismatic churches.
5. In Ghana 8,000,000 out of 17,352,722 Christians are counted as Pentecostals and neo-charismatics (*World Christian Database*, country information on Ghana, (accessed 4 March 2015)).
6. The Twi word *ɔsɔfo* (pl. *asɔfo*) means a priest, one who officiates in the service of God or a Fetish or who performs a religious ceremony. The word was in use before the introduction of Christianity, but has been adapted by Christianity. It is worth emphasising that the term *ɔsɔfo* does not represent an isolated vocabulary specific to Ghanaian Pentecostalism. It is part of a terminology that has a history beyond Pentecostalism and is rooted in Asante experience

(McCaskie, personal communication; McCaskie 1995: 290). See also Sackey (2000).
7. There are certain similarities with prophets, evangelists and missionaries who were also to some extent capable of achieving symbolic and political transformations and change. This is further elaborated in Chap. 2.
8. Asante was an independent Akan kingdom founded in 1701. Today part of the geographical region is administratively called the Ashanti region and other parts of the former kingdom are included in the Brong-Ahafo region. Asante exists today as a traditional state in Ghana. I use the term Asante throughout the book, whenever possible, because it alludes to the broader understanding of the historic polity of Asante, and because I draw on a specific Asante cultural and historic repertoire such as ideas of wealth and truthfulness. When referring to specifically colonial or postcolonial administrative regions or titles I use Ashanti (Boone 2003: 146, fn. 5). See Rathbone (1991: 335) for a comment on defining Asante.
9. The Supreme Being.
10. T.C. McCaskie, personal communication, 5 March 2014.
11. In her critique Lentz also questions Weber's distinction between traditional, rational and charismatic authority and the ideal types they represent. Her point is that these types of authority coexist and intersect (1998: 59).

References

Akyeampong, E. (1996). *Drink, power, and cultural change. A social history of alcohol in Ghana, c. 1800 to recent times.* Portsmouth: Heinemann.

Akyeampong, E., & Obeng, P. (1995). Spirituality, gender, and power in Asante history. *International Journal of African Historical Studies, 28*(3), 481–508.

Allman, J. (1993). *The quills of the porcupine: Asante nationalism in an emergent Ghana 1954–1957.* Madison: University of Wisconsin Press.

Arens, W., & Karp, I. (1989). Introduction. In W. Arens & I. Karp (Eds.), *Creativity of power. Cosmology and action in African societies.* Washington: Smithsonian Institution Press.

Arhin, K. (1994). The economic implications of transformations in Akan funeral rites. *Africa, 64*(3), 307–322.

Asamoah-Gyadu, J. K. (2005a). *African Charismatics. Current developments within independent indigenous pentecostalism in Ghana.* Leiden: Brill.

Baëta, C. G. ([1962] 2004). *Prophetism in Ghana. A study of some 'Spiritual' Churches.* Achimota: Africa Christian Press.

Barber, K. (2007b). Improvisation and the art of making things stick. In E. Hallam & T. Ingold (Eds.), *Creativity and cultural improvisation*. Berg: Oxford and New York.

Boone, C. (2003). *Political topographies of the African state. Territorial authority and institutional choice*. Cambridge: Cambridge University Press.

Coleman, S. (2011). Prosperity unbound? Debating the 'sacrificial economy'. In L. Obadia & D. C. Wood (Eds.), *The economics of religion: Anthropological approaches* (Research in Economic Anthropology, Vol. 31). Bingley: Emerald Group Publishing Limited.

Comaroff, J., & Comaroff, J. (2003). Second comings: Neo-protestant ethics and millennial capitalism in Africa, and elsewhere. In P. Gifford (Ed.), *2000 years and beyond. Faith, identity and the 'common era'*. London and New York: Routledge.

Daswani, G. (2013). On Christianity and ethics: Rupture as ethical practice in Ghanaian Pentecostalism. *American Ethnologist, 40*(3), 467–479.

Daswani, G. (2015). *Looking back, moving forward. Transformation and ethical practice in the Ghanaian Church of Pentecost*. Toronto, Buffalo, London: University of Toronto Press.

Douglas, M. (1986). *How institutions think*. New York: Syracuse University Press.

Engelke, M. (2004). Discontinuity and the discourse of conversion. *Journal of Religion in Africa, 34*(1/2), 82–109.

Engelke, M. (2010). Past Pentecostalism: Notes on rupture, realignment, and everyday life in Pentecostal and African Independent Churches. *Africa, 80*(2), 177–199.

Esson, J. (2013). A body and a dream at a vital conjuncture: Ghanaian youth, uncertainty and the allure of football. *Geoforum, 47*, 84–92.

Foster, P. J. (1965). *Education and social change in Ghana*. London: Routledge & Kegan Paul.

Gerth, H. H., & Wright Mills, C. (Eds.) (1991). *From max weber. Essays in sociology*. London: Routledge.

Gifford, P. (2004). *Ghana's new Christianity. Pentecostalism in a globalising African economy*. London: Hurst & Company.

Gifford, P. (2015). *Christianity, development, and modernity in Africa*. London: Hurst and Company.

Gilbert, M. (1988). The sudden death of a millionaire: Conversion and consensus in a Ghanaian Kingdom. *Africa, 58*(3), 291–314.

Gould, J. (2006). Strong bar, weak state? Lawyers, liberalism and state formation in Zambia. *Development and Change, 37*(4), 921–941.

Greene, S. E. (2002). *Sacred sites and the colonial encounter. A history of meaning and memory in Ghana*. Bloomington: Indiana University Press.

Haynes, N. (2012). Pentecostalism and the morality of money: Prosperity, inequality, and religious sociality on the Zambian Copperbelt. *Journal of the Royal Anthropological Institute, 18*(1), 123–139.

Jones, B. (2009). *Beyond the state in rural Uganda*. Edinburgh: Edinburgh University Press for the International Africa Institute.

King, K., & Martin, C. (2002). The vocational school fallacy revisited: Education, aspiration and work in Ghana 1959–2000. *Journal of Educational Development, 22*(1), 5–26.

Laurent, P.-J. (1999). Du rural à l'urbain. L'eglise des Assemblées de Dieu au Burkina Faso. In R. Otayek (dir.), *Dieu dans la cité. Dynamiques religieuses en milieu urbain ouagalais*. Bordeaux: CEAN.

Laurent, P.-J. (2003). *Les pentecôtistes du Burkina Faso, Mariage, pouvoir et guérison*. Paris: IRD Éditions et Karthala.

Lauterbach, K. (2005). Notions of the past among young Pentecostals in Ouagadougou. In Per Hernæs (Ed.), *The 'traditional' and the 'modern' in West African (Ghanaian) history: Case studies on co-existence and interaction*. Trondheim: Department of History, Norwegian University of Science and Technology.

Lauterbach, K. (2010). Becoming a pastor: Youth and social aspirations in Ghana. *Young: Nordic Journal of Youth Research, 18*(3), 259–278.

Lentz, C. (1998). The chief, the mine captain and the politician: Legitimating power in Northern Ghana. *Africa, 68*(1), 46–67.

Lindhardt, M. (2015). Continuity, change or coevalness? Charismatic Christianity and tradition in contemporary Tanzania. In M. Lindhardt (Ed.), *Pentecostalism in Africa. Presence and impact of pneumatic Christianity in postcolonial societies*. Leiden and Boston: Brill.

Marshall, R. (1993). 'Power in the name of Jesus': Social transformation and Pentecostalism in Nigeria 'Revisisted'. In T. Ranger & O. Vaughan (Eds.), *Legitimacy and the state in twentieth-century Africa*. Oxford: Macmillan Press.

Marshall, R. (2009). *Political spiritualities: The Pentecostal revolution in Nigeria*. Chicago: University of Chicago Press.

Maxwell, D. (2000). Review article in defence of African creativity. *Journal of Religion in Africa, 30*(4), 468–481.

Maxwell, D. (2006a). *African gifts of the spirit. Pentecostalism & the rise of a Zimbabwean transnational religious movement*. Oxford: James Currey.

Maxwell, D. (2013a). Freed slaves, missionaries, and respectability: The expansion of the Christian frontier from Angola to Belgian Congo. *Journal of African History, 54*(1), 79–102.

Maxwell, D. (2013b). Social mobility and politics in African Pentecostal modernity. In R. Hefner (Ed.), *Global Pentecostalism in the 21-century*. Bloomington, IN: Indiana University Press.

McCaskie, T. C. (1995). *State and society in pre-colonial Asante*. Cambridge: Cambridge University Press.

McCaskie, T. C. (2000). *Asante identities: History and modernity in an African village 1850–1950*. International African Institute, London: Edinburgh University Press.

McCaskie, T. C. (2007c). Asante history: A personal impression of forty years. *Ghana Studies, 10*, 145–161.
McCaskie, T. C. (2008a). Akwantemfi–'In mid-journey': An Asante shrine today and its clients. *Journal of Religion in Africa, 38*(1), 1–24.
McCaskie, T. C. (2008c). Gun culture in Kumasi. *Africa, 78*(3), 433–454.
McCaskie, T. C. (2009). 'Water wars' in Kumasi, Ghana. In F. Locatelli & P. Nugent (Eds.), *African cities: Competing claims on urban spaces*. Brill: Leiden.
Médard, J.-F. (1992). Le "big man" en Afrique: esquisse d'analyse du politicien entrepreneur. *L'Année Sociologique, 42*, 167–192.
Meyer, B. (1998a). 'Make a complete break with the past', memory and post-colonial modernity in Ghanaian Pentecostalist discourse. *Journal of Religion in Africa, 28*(3), 316–349.
Meyer, B. (1998c). Commodities and the power of prayer: Pentecostalist attitudes towards consumption in contemporary Ghana. *Development and Change, 29*(4), 751–776.
Meyer, B. (2004). Christianity in Africa: From African independent to pentecostal-charismatic churches. *Annual Review of Anthropology, 33*, 447–474.
Omenyo, C. N. (2013). Trans-national protestant missions: The Ghanaian story. *Swedish Missiological Themes, 101*(1), 41–66.
Osei, G. M. (2004). The 1987 junior secondary-school reform in Ghana: Vocational or pre-vocational in nature? *International Review of Education, 50*(5–6), 425–446.
Peel, J. D. Y. (2000). *Religious encounter and the making of the Yoruba*. Bloomington: Indiana University Press.
Pew Research Centre (2011). *Global Christianity. A report on the size and distribution of the world's Christian population*. Pew: Pew Forum on Religion & Public Life.
Pew Research Centre. (2012). *The global religious landscape. A report on the size and distribution of the world's major religious groups as of 2010*. Pew: Forum on Religion & Public Life.
Ranger, T. (1986). Religious movements and politics in Sub-Saharan Africa. *African Studies Review, 29*(2), 1–69.
Ranger, T. (2007). Scotland yard in the bush: Medicine murders, child witches and the construction of the occult: A literature review. *Africa, 77*(2), 272–283.
Rathbone, R. (1991). Discussion. 'The youngmen and the porcupine'. *Journal of African History, 32*(2), 333–338.
Rathbone, R. (1996). *Have you heard my message to my fathers? The private conscience and public lives of two remarkable Africans*. Inaugural lecture. London: School of Oriental and African Studies.
Robbins, J. (2004). The globalization of Pentecostal and charismatic Christianity. *Annual Review of Anthropology, 33*, 117–143.

Robbins, J. (2014). The anthropology of Christianity: Unity, diversity, new directions: An introduction to supplement 10. *Current Anthropology, 55*(S10), S157–S171.
Sackey, B. M. (2000). Recognising other dimensions of epistemology: Conceptualisation of Abosom ("Deities") in Ghanaian experience. *Research Review (Institute of African Studies, University of Ghana, Legon), 16*(1), 13–30.
Simon, D., McGregor, D., & Nsiah-Gyabaah, K. (2004). The changing urban-rural interface of African cities: Definitional issues and an application to Kumasi, Ghana. *Environment and Urbanization, 16*(2), 235–248.
Soothill, J. E. (2007). *Gender, social change and spiritual power. Charismatic Christianity in Ghana.* Brill: Leiden.
Ubink, J. (2007). Traditional authority revisited: Popular perceptions of chiefs and chieftaincy in peri-urban Kumasi, Ghana. *The Journal of Legal Pluralism and Unofficial Law, 39*(55), 123–161.
van Dijk, R. (1997). From camp to encompassment: Discourses of transsubjectivity in the Ghanaian Pentecostal diaspora. *Journal of Religion in Africa, 27*(2), 135–159.
Weber, M. ([1930] 2001). *The protestant ethic and the spirit of capitalism.* London and New York: Routledge.
Wilks, I. (1993). *Forest of gold: Essays on the Akan and the kingdom of Asante.* Athens, OH: Ohio University Press.

CHAPTER 2

A History of Wealth, Power, and Religion in Asante

How did one become a 'big man' in Asante and how have social mobility and the signs of social status changed over time? This chapter first explores the socio-economic and political structures of Asante society and how status, wealth, and power have been achieved and how these categories have changed meaning over time. Second, the chapter examines how religious ideas, practices, and office have been constituted and have changed. What was the role of religious specialists? How was spiritual power constituted and achieved and how have the relations between the religious and the mundane been understood over time? The chapter reviews these themes from the perspective of aspiring groups in Asante and I discuss the circumstances that have enabled such groups to gain status over time. These groups are innovators and entrepreneurial and at the same time aim at being recognised as people with status and power according to established norms. The chapter also discusses two particular established social categories: 'big men' (*abirɛmpɔn*[1]) and religious specialists (*akɔmfoɔ*[2]). Ultimately, the chapter seeks to look at the historical resonances of the figures of *abirɛmpɔn* and *akɔmfoɔ* in charismatic Christianity as well as to draw parallels to earlier groups of aspiring people. The book argues that charismatic pastors achieve status, power, and wealth when becoming pastors and that these positions are recognised (and debated) widely in society. In order to get a fuller and deeper understanding of the social principles and mechanisms around this, we need to understand the particular expressions and importance of social promotion, titles, and

© The Author(s) 2017
K. Lauterbach, *Christianity, Wealth, and Spiritual Power in Ghana*,
DOI 10.1007/978-3-319-33494-3_2

becoming a 'big man' in pre-colonial Asante and the linkages with ideas around belief and spiritual power.

I explore these questions by looking into how religious leaders and specialists draw upon and tap into systems of social stratification and by analysing how norms related to both political and religious office are improvised and reproduced. To what extent do the figures of ɔbirɛmpɔn and ɔkɔmfɔ represent present-day political and religious figures and how have these figures changed over time? One argument of the chapter is that contemporary religious figures do not constitute an isolated social category. They draw on a broader repertoire of norms and ideas that are not limited to the religious field.

Wealth and 'Big Men' in Pre-colonial Asante

In pre-colonial Asante,[3] social recognition and status were dependent on one's ability to accumulate wealth and display it in public. Even though there were restrictions on the wealth of the ɔbirɛmpɔn in the nineteenth century (for instance, death duties and social restrictions on spending and distribution), a 'big man' had to display his wealth publicly. The tensions around the sources and the distribution of power in pre-colonial and colonial Asante have been discussed by, among others, Berry (2001) and Akyeampong and Obeng (1995). As referred to in the previous chapter, Akyeampong and Obeng argue that the notion of power was rooted in Asante cosmos, and that it was accessible to all if they had the knowledge of how to access and use it. Hence, there were metaphysical underpinnings to the state and power. This argument further points to the reading of Asante state power as being "less concentrated and all-encompassing in precolonial Asante than previous scholarship has suggested" (Berry 2001: 1).

In the same vein, McCaskie (1995) argues that the political economy of pre-colonial Asante not only should be understood in economic terms, as wealth also had socio-political and ideological aspects to it. Wealth—as measured in gold, people, land, and food—was part of the experience and knowledge of Asante on how to obtain success and progress, "hence, the accumulation of wealth as imperative and as yardstick, and the deeply resonant meaning of wealth as symbol and as mnemonic, were abiding and central figures of Asante life, history and self-knowledge" (McCaskie 1995: 37). The process of accumulating wealth was to a large extent controlled by the state and because the Asante state (*Asanteman*) and its political power was highly centralised it was possible, at least in some periods of time, to exercise extensive control.

The Asante state was founded at the beginning of the eighteenth century in the forest region of Ghana by Osei Tutu (the first Asantehene [1701–1717]).[4] The state was based on a military coalition between a number of Akan states that defeated the Denkyira.[5] The coalition was later transformed into a polity with the Asantehene as the supreme political authority (Wilks 1993: 112). An important figure in relation to the foundation of the kingdom was Komfo Anokye (ɔkɔmfɔ, a priest).[6] He assisted Osei Tutu in founding the kingdom by mediating the appearance of the Golden Stool (*sika dwa*), which was (and is) the symbol of political authority as well as of the soul (*sunsum*) of Asante (McCaskie 1986b: 318–319). The Golden Stool therefore symbolises an integration of the supernatural and political authority. It is the symbol of the highest political authority (the physical symbol of political office) and is, at the same time, a symbol of the supernatural; its origin is supernatural and its appearance was facilitated by an ɔkɔmfɔ. As McCaskie writes: "Precolonial Asante had been forged around an ideology that combined the materialism of the state and the religio-spirituality of the Asante people in the superordinate symbol of the Golden Stool" (McCaskie 1986a: 16). As mentioned earlier, this integration of the political and the spiritual is key to our understanding of the role of present-day charismatic pastors in Asante.

In the first half of the nineteenth century, the Asante state was a relatively closed system and its power unchallenged. The state controlled and monopolised the accumulation of wealth in order to maintain social and political order (Arhin 1990: 525) and upward social mobility could only be achieved within the state (McCaskie 1995: 38, 52).[7]

In Asante, status was achieved by becoming office holder and eventually through promotion by being awarded the title ɔbirɛmpɔn ('big man').[8] The ɔbirɛmpɔn was both a provider and a protector: an entrepreneur who gathered followers, secured access to gold, and established villages; the fact that the accumulated wealth was seen as belonging to the community put certain social restrictions on its use (Austin 2003: 23–24). As McCaskie summarises: "To be an ɔbirɛmpɔn—at the level of social thought—was all at once to preside over society and to be responsible for its maintenance and continuity" (McCaskie 1983: 27). Moreover, the recognition coming with the title was also an acknowledgement of the person having contributed to the collective wellbeing of Asante society. Extreme individual consumption was seen as anti-social and as "an act of theft from the future wellbeing of Asante society" (McCaskie 1995: 47). This indicates that the meaning of wealth and its accumulation was a social matter rather than an individual one.

The strong control of the state began to be questioned during the reign of Asantehene Kwaku Dua Panin (1834–67). After 1831, new opportunities for trading with the Fante on the coast emerged, and this meant new possibilities of obtaining wealth. This trade permitted non-office holders to accumulate wealth, and therefore the accumulation of wealth was not, to the same degree as before, dominated by the state (McCaskie 1983: 35).[9]

During the reigns of the Asantehenes Kofi Kakari (1867–74) and Mensa Bonsu (1874–83), Asante as a closed system ended. This was caused by a combination of the external influences and the failure of the system itself. The state functioned more and more by force and less by consensus. The increasingly authoritarian nature of the state and its use of force to, for example, collect taxes led many to flee from Asante to the Gold Coast Colony, and some of these people later came to represent a challenge to the established system.

Religion in Pre-colonial Asante

The Asante believed in the existence of a God creator (*Onyame*) and a number of smaller gods or supernatural powers beneath the *Onyame*. These smaller gods or supernatural powers were called *abosom* (sing. *ɔbosom*) and got their power (*tumi*) from *Onyame*. Below this level were the fetishes (*asuman*) (McCaskie 1995: 276; McLeod 1981: 57). People worshipped the gods and consulted them for advice and healing, and by bringing offerings. The gods communicated by possessing people. Sometimes possession of a person was understood as a sign that the person was to become a priest (*ɔkɔmfɔ*). The *ɔbosom* used the *ɔkɔmfɔ* to communicate with the Asante; which means that the *ɔkɔmfɔ* was understood to be a mediator, and a channel of communication between the highest spiritual power and the people. The functions of the *akɔmfoɔ* were located in the "cognitive flux between order and anxiety" and they were expected to bridge this flux (McCaskie 1986b: 333–34). It was their role to give advice, to find the causes of illness and misfortune, and to help with protection and healing (McLeod 1981: 61).

The training of an *ɔkɔmfɔ* took seven years, and during this time he/she was living with an established *ɔkɔmfɔ*. The training consisted of learning to control the state of possession, dancing in order to become possessed, and herbal treatment. After the period of training the ɔkɔmfɔ had to become possessed at a ritual attended by his mentor and other priests. This ritual was a test (McLeod 1981: 59–60). McLeod notices that "[t]oday this training is usually paid for by the priest's matrilineal kin, and large thanks-offerings may be made to the instructing priest. The family will expect to profit later from the money the god brings" (McLeod 1981: 60). This is important to keep in mind, as it shows the relation between family and priest, and especially how the family helps finance the priest's training and later expects to get something in return. As we shall see later, a similar relation of reciprocity exists to some extent between charismatic pastors, their family, and their congregation (as it does no doubt also within other religions).

The akɔmfoɔ were perceived as being in opposition to the state since their power, which originated in the supernatural realm, was the inverse of the secular power of the state (McCaskie 1995: 333–34). But the state also depended on religious specialists, as they were supposed to provide order and impede unrest. According to McLeod, some chiefs tried to control the akɔmfoɔ by testing their skills in making prophecies and by exercising control over new gods. At the end of the nineteenth century (and Asante independence) some people used priesthood to oppose the rule of Asantehene Mensa Bonsu by claiming to be incarnations of Komfo Anokye (the priest who assisted the first Asantehene). McLeod writes:

> The incident is obscure, but it appears that those involved were declaring their complete separation from the usual political process and appealing to a different view of the Asante state. The use of the names of famous priests for this purpose seems, therefore, to indicate a pre-existing tension between state and priesthood (McLeod 1981: 65).

Even though akɔmfoɔ mediated strong powers this did not necessarily entail secular influence. There was no consolidated priesthood, and the priests were functioning rather independently of each other (McCaskie 1995: 123; McLeod 1981: 64). This fragmentation of the priesthood could have been caused by the control of the state, as well as a highly competitive market (McCaskie 1995: 124). An ɔkɔmfɔ was in some ways seen as a threat to the state and the holders of political office, as he was speaking on behalf of, and with the powers of, a hidden authority. Chiefs also had a religious role as they were seen as being the link and mediator between people and their ancestors (Adubofour 1994; Akyeampong and Obeng 1995; Asamoah-Gyadu 2005b; Busia 1951). Busia notes that when a chief is enstooled "his person becomes sacred" (1951: 26). He acts as the medium through which people can get power from God (*Onyame*) or be protected from evil spirits.

WEALTH, STATUS, AND POWER: ASANTE COLONISED, C. 1900–1950s

The British exiled the Asantehene in 1896 and made Asante a protectorate. But it was not until after the Yaa Asantewa War of 1900–1901 that Asante formally settled under colonial rule as a Crown Colony (Arhin 1995: 102; McCaskie 2000: 10).[10] Asante was reorganised under a chief commissioner and provincial and district commissioners. The chiefs occupied central positions in the political system of the colony and were members of the legislative and provincial councils (Boone 2003: 148). The colonial administration established the Council of Chiefs in Kumasi to take care of customary matters. The council was under the supervision of the Chief Commissioner of Ashanti. The Asantehene Prempeh I returned from exile in the Seychelles in 1924 and was installed as *Kumasihene* in 1926. In 1935 the Ashanti Confederacy Council was established by the colonial authorities, and the *Kumasihene* was reinstated to the former position as Asantehene (Arhin 1976/77: 462; Arhin 1995: 104; McCaskie 2007a: 151).

Capitalisation, Cash, and Cocoa

Concurrent to the implementation of colonial rule, changes in the economy and agricultural production took place, and new possibilities for social mobility occurred. There was an increasing degree of individual accumulation of capital and wealth. New social groups and leaders emerged who were less bound to traditional leaders (Arhin 1976/77: 457). The British introduced a uniform currency, which made it easier to measure wealth in the form of cash, and there was less restraint on money-making (Arhin 1976/77: 455).[11] The colonial regime permitted "a regime of commoner enterprise and competition with the *ohene* [chief] for wealth", as well as individual wealth seeking (Arhin 1976/77: 458). The forms of wealth changed; it was no longer slaves, gold, and ornaments, but savings in the bank, the construction of big houses, and cars. That said, there were unsuccessful attempts by the Council of Chiefs (1908) and later by the

Kumasihene (1930) to control accumulation of wealth by proposing a reintroduction of death duties.

The boom in rubber production at the end of the nineteenth and at the beginning of the twentieth centuries marked the start of cocoa farming in Asante (Berry 2001: 5).[12] According to Austin, economic behaviour at the beginning of the twentieth century focused more on accumulation of wealth than it did on survival. There were no severe food shortages as cocoa farming mostly was combined with food crop production (Austin 2003: 4). Also, scarcity of land and labour was seldom a problem, whereas capital and credit were in short supply. This led to extended money-lending (Austin 2003: 5) and a situation with 'pressure of cash' (Arhin (1976/77) (see also McCaskie 2000). The success of cash crop production of cocoa between 1900 and 1930 entailed a widespread use of cash. There was a need for cash because of a high demand for imported goods and the increasing monetisation of land and labour.

This capitalisation of the economy also influenced social life. It changed certain social obligations; gifts, marriages, and funeral rites were monetised (Arhin 1976/77: 460). Austin remarks that the production of cocoa was an individual enterprise and therefore altered extended family relations; "it was the individual and the conjugal family, not the matrilineal segment, that was the basic work unit whether in agriculture or outside"(Austin 2003: 24). In the same vein, Busia quotes a farmer saying "*Cocoa See abusua, paepae mogya mu*", meaning "Cocoa destroys kinship, and divides blood relations"(Busia cited in Arhin 1976/77: 459–460, fn. 32). This saying refers to the change in family relations and social obligations that came with cocoa production and the introduction of the cash crop economy.[13]

It has been debated to what extent colonial rule and the changing socio-economic landscape led to more opportunity for social mobility and individual accumulation of wealth. As mentioned above, some argue that the capitalisation of the economy led to new opportunities of acquiring cash and consuming in a way that escaped certain social bonds of obligation. This change also led to the emergence of new social groups of businessmen and educated clerks. Others have argued that the resources of the new economy were controlled by those who were in power in pre-colonial times. Austin, for example, argues that the introduction of cocoa farming did not entrain drastic forms of social mobility, as those who engaged in cocoa production were those who had already accumulated some wealth (Austin 2003: 21). Thus, the elite (mainly chiefs and office holders) had the capital to invest in, for instance, cocoa production, and this wealth was therefore kept by those already possessing it. Consequently, social mobility related to the change in the economy is understood as being less important than the retention of wealth and power among the traditional elite.

With the decline of slavery and pawning[14] at the beginning of the twentieth century, non-wage labour became scarce and wage labour was increasingly used (Austin 1987: 263). People tended to work on their own farms rather than comply with family or stool obligations (Austin 1987: 266). By 1938 many of these wage labourers were the so-called cocoa migrants who came from the north and from the surrounding French colonies (Arhin 1995: 103). The pressure of cash led to political unrest (Arhin 1976/77: 466–68). There were, for instance, several collective protests by cocoa-farmers against low cocoa prices; the so-called cocoa hold-ups (see Austin 1988).

Emerging Social Groups: The Akonkofoɔ

In 1901, with the British annexation, many of those who had fled to the Gold Coast Colony returned to Asante as businessmen (Arhin 1986: 26). The colonisers viewed them as progressive. As a group, they (or those coming after) became known as *akonkofoɔ*[15] (McCaskie 1986a: 7). The new lifestyle of the *akonkofoɔ* was according to Arhin inspired by the colonies on the coast; "[t]he *akonkofo* believed that they had, and were believed to have, acquired a complex of ideas of *anibue*, 'being civilised', from the coast. At the core of this complex of ideas was belief in the coastal version of the British way of life ..." (Arhin 1986: 26). Among the Fante, education played a much more important role in achieving status, whereas among the Asante an office holder had more status than someone with education (Arhin 1983: 2), and among the Fante it was easier for non-office holders (for instance, traders) to achieve wealth and to gain power. There was a mercantile class that fostered an entrepreneurial spirit (Arhin 1983: 15).

The *akonkofoɔ* became a distinct social group in the colonial period, after the exile of Prempeh I and under protection of the British colonial administration (Arhin 1986: 25). Upon their return to Asante, they introduced and practised new ideas of accumulation and wealth. They were the new and progressive Asantes, who defended the "individual's right to accumulate and to dispose capital" (McCaskie 1986a: 7). The *akonkofoɔ* had broken with the past in the sense that they tried to escape the moral constraints embedded in ideas of wealth and accumulation. At the same time, they were still drawing on the social norms of the nineteenth century and behaved like a new type of *abirɛmpɔn*. The *akonkofoɔ* represented a new development in Asante and a "very confused 'individualism'" (McCaskie 1986a: 9). Many *akonkofoɔ* converted to Christianity "some doubtless as believers, many as a mark of 'modernity'" (McCaskie 1986a: 12). The *akonkofoɔ* were generally against the power of the Golden Stool and in favour of colonial rule. Colonial power was seen as bringing both progress and Christianity, and had in addition permitted the *akonkofoɔ* to pursue their careers as merchants, traders, and men of property. They viewed British rule as protecting their private property against the chiefs and guaranteeing material progress (Arhin 1986: 27).

Their favourable attitude to colonial rule was limited to matters of wealth and the protection of individual enterprise and property. Likewise, their criticism of traditional authority was limited to the issue of personal accumulation of wealth (Arhin 1986: 28). Most *akonkofoɔ* were illiterate and can in many ways be seen as the forerunners of the Asante Kotoko Society (the latter claimed distinction on the basis of literacy, whereas the former on signs of wealth) (Arhin 1986: 29).

Another group seeking social mobility was the royal *nhenkwaa* (servants of the Asantehene). The *nhenkwaa* was a special social class in Kumasi. They were known both for their arrogance, greed, and pride, but also for their ambition for social promotion (the '*nhenkwaa* ethic'). They were particularly envious of the *abirɛmpɔn* and of office holders. With British colonialisation and the Asantehene's exile they became a fragile class with no place in Asante society (McCaskie 1986a: 11). They had been under the protection of the Asantehene, which had also served as their access to wealth and success. The *akonkofoɔ* and this group can be seen as somewhat overlapping and both were new models of *ɔbirɛmpɔn* (McCaskie 1986a: 10–12). Individuality and individual accumulation of wealth was becoming the norm: "Money, and there could never be enough of it at the cognitive level, was the key to individual success" (McCaskie 1986a: 15).

Money and Mobility

With the rise of Western-type education and the creation of a new civil administration other types of employment emerged; such as civil servants, white collars, teachers, lawyers, pastors, and journalists.[16] Moreover, people went to work in cocoa farms, and at the newly established railways and roads that were to connect Asante with the coast. This was a way to enter the "[c]olonial regimes of mobility and money" (McCaskie 2000: 124). People engaged both in spatial and social forms of mobility.

These new types of work permitted people to earn money for individual accumulation and consumption. As they often entailed being away from one's home town or village, it also meant getting away from control of the elder generation and discovering new ways of life. In his work on Asante lives in the twentieth century, McCaskie portrays young people who express an ambivalent attitude towards the new regime of money and mobility. On the one hand, there was the attraction towards consumption of "the sweet things of life" and, on the other hand, there was a view that the "unrestrained pursuit of the money needed to acquire them was a social evil that destroyed lives, families and communities" (McCaskie 2000: 126).

The point is that this was a time of rapid social change. Ideas about community, authority, religion and wealth were challenged and new ideas around progress, individuality and money were introduced. The introduction of the cash economy signified both a change in material conditions and a change in ideas about wealth, money, and consumption. Still, these new ideas drew upon pre-colonial conceptions that were "reconfigured and mobilised to join with innovation in meeting the challenges posed by colonial capitalism" (McCaskie 2000: 132–33). Along the same lines, Austin draws attention to the significant continuity in Asante history with regard to attitudes towards accumulation and wealth. In the nineteenth and the twentieth centuries, the goal was not only to strive but more importantly to achieve. He notes:

> Riches were celebrated, but what was admired [-] rewarded by the state, praised by the powerful and the powerless, hallowed posthumously [-] was the self-acquisition of wealth: materially successful endeavour. It was, precisely, a moral economy of accumulation (Austin 2003: 23).

And these ideas of wealth, consumption and display were still linked to the figure of the 'big man'. My point here is that these ideas are what underpin the potential success and legitimacy of charismatic pastors; pastors challenge existing hegemonic ideology and at the same time base their behaviour and legitimacy on the idea of the 'big man'.

Religion and Colonialism: Institutions and Innovators

Colonial rule was, moreover, the time when Christian missionaries got a foothold in Asante and people began to convert to Christianity. The introduction of Christianity meant exposure to new ideas and worldviews. The period was moreover marked by a rise in anti-witchcraft shrines.

Christianity

Pre-colonial Asante was a relatively closed ideological and social system and influence from outside was controlled by the state and largely avoided (McCaskie 1995: 100). Hence, the first missionaries had difficulties working in Asante and it was not until Asante came under British rule that missionaries were able to build mission stations and people started to convert to Christianity.[17]

Rev. Thomas Birch Freeman was the first Christian missionary to establish a Wesleyan-Methodist mission in Kumasi in 1839. Christian missionaries were met with suspicion by the Asante state because of association with the colonial regime and because they were seen as seeking "[i]deological access to Asante social formation" (McCaskie 1995: 136). The Wesleyans were permitted to set up a mission station, but not a school, and they only made very few converts. The mission station was closed again in 1872 (Akyeampong 1999: 281; Obeng 1996: 102). According to McCaskie, the combination of a strict doctrine and focus on personal salvation posed a major challenge to the advancement of Christianity in pre-colonial and colonial Asante:

> The insurmountable stumbling block to Wesleyan-Methodist progress in Asante was the mission's espousal of an inflexible doctrine that married together the concepts of a grace and salvation personally achieved through faith, and an emancipation and advancement socially inculcated through education (McCaskie 1995: 137).

It was not until 1896 (with British colonisation) that the missions became more permanently installed in Asante (first the Basel mission, followed by the Wesleyans and the Catholics), and only after 1908 that people converted to Christianity in significant numbers (Obeng 1996). The introduction of Christianity mainly took place under the reign of the Asantehene Agyeman Prempeh I, who himself converted to Christianity in 1904 while in exile in the Seychelles islands (Akyeampong 1999).

In the beginning it was mainly non-Asantes, or migrants to Kumasi, who converted. But with the Christian churches' creation of schools, clinics, and hospitals, more people were inclined to convert. The Asantes were, according to Allman and Tashjian (2000: 26–34), in many cases converting to escape the power of their chiefs or to obtain "worldly gain", which produced a tense relationship between Christians and chiefs. Some converts refused to obey traditional rulers and to participate in traditional religious activities, which on the other hand made chiefs reluctant to allow missionary activity (Obeng 1996: 110).

In November 1908, T.E. Fell (provincial commissioner of Western Asante) wrote a letter to the chief commissioner (F.C. Fuller) in Kumasi about three youngmen (Kwoku Boanu, Kwasi Amponsa and Kwasi Boanu) from Tepa who "allege they were recently baptised in Kumase by the Rev Bauer of the Basel Mission" and as a consequence refused to obey the instruction of the chief. He further explained that "[t]hese youngmen used to carry water for a certain Fetish, a work they now refuse to do". T.E. Fell had informed the chief of Tepa that if these youngmen had become Christians, he could not oblige them to take part in work for fetishes, "although they must do all other kinds of work which may be required of them". Earlier the same month, T.E. Fell had addressed Rev. N.V. Asare of the Basel Mission about the same youngmen, and because the chief of Tepa had doubts about the sincerity of the youngmen's alleged conversion, Fell inquired as to whether they had been baptised or not. In his response to Fell, Asare recounted that he had passed through Tepa to investigate the case and that he had talked with the chief and found out that the young boys had signed up with the Wesleyans in Kumasi. He continued: "Even in my presence one of them behaved so unbecoming on the street whilst I was addressing the people". He then assured him that the youngmen were not affiliated with the Basel mission and "we therefore know nothing about them". At the end of the letter, Rev. Bauer added a small note saying that they only baptised people after they had been instructed for between one and one and a half years. The letter ends with the following remark: "I often met with such fellows, who behaved worse than heathen, but had tickets from the West & boasted themselves to be Xians".[18] The case illustrates how Christianity and conversion was used by some to avoid submission to traditional authorities, but also that both chiefs and missionaries were careful about distinguishing 'true converts' from 'rascals'. At the same time, the case shows how the colonial authorities approached the question of conversion to Christianity in relation to submission to traditional authorities. They allowed Christians to refrain from participating in any activities that were related to fetishes or traditional religious practices, but at the same time underlined that this did not permit Christians to refrain from their other obligations in their communities.

There were cases of chiefs complaining that their wives had converted without their consent, and that they were losing authority when their subordinates converted to Christianity. In their studies on how Christian missions have influenced social values in colonial Asante, Allman and Tashjian (2000: 205–206) focus especially on welfare and educational programmes, as well as on the promotion of the Christian ideal of family, motherhood and marriage. They give the example of a young woman who went to a Methodist school for the training of young Asante women. She married a catechist, they had two children and lived together, "and [she] relied on none of her matrikin, male or female, in the raising of her children" (Allman and Tashjian 2000: 199). However, in other cases, the pattern was not as radical, and converts would for instance never live with a husband, but instead stay in the matrilineal family house (Allman and Tashjian 2000: 200).

Anti-witchcraft Movements

The significance and reasons for the rise of anti-witchcraft movements and its relation to social change in colonial Asante and in the Northern Territories have been debated by Austin (2003) and Allman and Parker (2005). Austin situates anti-witchcraft shrines in the new context of cocoa farming and the altered social relations this led to and questions the assumption that "this nervous individualism was necessarily a novelty of the cocoa era" (Austin 2003: 20). Allman and Parker argue that the new context of cocoa production and the ensuing opportunities, inequalities, individualism, and changed kinship and gender relations "were increasingly being expressed in the idiom of *bayi* [witchcraft]" (Allman and Parker 2005: 142) and hence the growth in anti-witchcraft shrines. These debates, as well as earlier work, are centred around the tension of whether the rise in anti-witchcraft shrines were merely due to social instability or because of growth in wealth and in particular possibilities of individual accumulation.

The early literature on anti-witchcraft movements in colonial Asante (and more generally in the Akan region) was also concerned with the question of whether accusations of witchcraft was a religious response to rapid social change and to anxieties brought about by colonialism. Some have argued that anti-witchcraft cults emerged primarily after the implementation of colonial rule, and therefore to some extent were a response to the changes brought about in this period (Field 1968; Ward 1956). Others like Goody have argued that the coming of colonialism did not mean a rise in either the practice of witchcraft or in the number and significance of anti-witchcraft cults. He challenges the causal link between social change, social malaise and increase in religious activity (and echoes Baëta's argument referred to in Chap. 1):

> Clearly there is a situation of rapid change. But to view this process, as sociologists have tended to do, as leading to anomie (normlessness) is in fact to make a value judgement regarding the course of that change on what would appear to be inadequate evidence (Goody 1957: 362).

As explained by Allman and Parker (2005: 116) Goody's argument was that the anti-witchcraft cults were a continuation of earlier religious traditions.[19]

Goody furthermore draws attention to the sometimes diffuse and transient character of some of the shrines: "they are constantly coming into being … whether such creations [new shrines] become widely employed, and enter into the circulation of shrines, is quite another matter. These shrines are always waxing and waning in importance" (Goody 1957: 359). Goody explains this partly by people's pragmatic and eclectic attitude vis-à-vis the shrines: "If one shrine appears to be effective, they take it up. If it fails them, they drop it. The next man's shrines, whatever 'faith' he may profess, are as good as one's own; better, if they are more successful" (Goody 1957: 359). Interestingly, Goody includes shrines that do not last in his discussion (for a similar point on spiritual churches see Baëta [1962] 2004). Goody also points to the relation between wealth and religious innovation and asserts that an increase in religious activity may be due to an increasing availability of wealth rather than social tensions and instability (Goody 1957: 361) (see also Allman and Parker (2005: 133)).

Many of the anti-witchcraft shrines were established at the same time as the first cocoa boom (1910–1925) (Austin 2003; Allman and Parker 2005). Austin argues that most envy and conflict arose over profits and the inheritance of cocoa farms. Cocoa production was based on individual entrepreneurship and there were no traditional social obligations attached to the money gained from this production. This created some room for individual accumulation relieved of kinship solidarity and obligation (Austin 2003: 19–20, 2005: 38–39, 45). Cocoa farmers paid for protection against witchcraft because they felt vulnerable to the envy and jealousy of their family members. Envy and jealousy was understood as arising when people acquired wealth, because it had to be at the cost of others (Austin 2003: 18–19). The owners of cocoa trees wanted to protect themselves against misfortune and as failure was understood to have a cause, "witchfinding was big business" (Austin 2003: 20–21).

Spiritual Churches, the Prophet Movement and Early Pentecostalism

Another factor that was of importance to the spread of Christianity in Ghana was the spiritual churches (*Sunsum sorè*). The movement has been labelled a prophet movement, because of the central role of the prophet and 'the cult of the person' (Baëta [1962] 2004: 6). Central to the spiritual churches was also a search for 'practical salvation' and not only spiritual salvation, expressed for instance in finding solutions to practical problems in everyday life (Asamoah-Gyadu 2004). Baëta describes the leaders of the spiritual churches as kings. They were often dressed like kings, and in some churches the titles of the traditional chieftaincy system were applied. In one case the founder and leader of a church was called the king and his wife the queen mother (Baëta [1962] 2004: 39, 57). The leader was also seen as the bearer of a 'call'. Baëta sees the spiritual churches as drawing both from Methodism and Catholicism, on the one hand, and from the Akan chieftaincy system on the other (Baëta [1962] 2004: 57).[20]

A number of prophets (Sampson Opong, Wade Harris and others) who worked more independently, but also for the Christian missions, also played a role for the spread of Christianity (Allman and Parker 2005: 135–136). According to Larbi (2001: 32) these prophets attracted many members to the already established churches (for example the Catholic, Methodist, and Anglican churches), but were at the same time the forerunners of the Pentecostal/charismatic movement (Asamoah-Gyadu 2005a: 19–21). Prophet Wade Harris from Liberia had a big influence in the coastal towns, where he demonstrated God's power through conversion, healing, and prophecy (Asamoah-Gyadu 2005a: 19). Another prophet, who operated in Asante, was Sampson Opong (or Samson Opon), who before his conversion to Christianity was known as Opon Asibe Tutu (McCaskie 1976). In the late 1910s he became member of the African Methodist Episcopal Zion Church and later had a successful career as a preacher and prophet, but before that he had been a worker on cocoa farms and involved in criminal activities (McCaskie 1976: 34). These prophets were seen by the local authorities with some scepticism as they were a challenge to their power (Allman and Parker 2005: 136).

Another prophet operating in the 1930s was Peter Anim, who established a church of his own (Faith Tabernacle Church, later Apostolic Church, Gold Coast). In 1931 the Assemblies of God arrived in the Northern Territories, and in 1937 the missionary James McKeown arrived from the Apostolic Church in the UK. He founded what was later to become The Church of Pentecost.

INDEPENDENCE AND ASANTE NATIONALISM

The 1950s and 1960s were marked by Ghana's independence and the emergence of the nationalist movement in Asante. In 1954, the National Liberation Movement (NLM) was founded partly based on the Asante Youth Association (AYA) created in 1947. Some of the founders of the NLM were the so-called youngmen (*nkwankwaa*). They were not literally young, but subordinated to chiefly authority and other senior people in society (Allman 1990: 268).[21] The *nkwankwaa* were a group of young aspiring Asante that sought economic and political power not through traditional trajectories (chiefly offices), but through education and work. They have been seen as the first mass politicised generation, who were characterised as the Asante *petit bourgeoisie*. Most were from well-off families, but they did not have aspirations of succeeding in chiefly office (Allman 1990, 1993: 32; Wilks 1975: 535–543). They rather attempted to rise in society through education, employment, and political engagement.

The *nkwankwaa* had positions in the new colonial bureaucracy such as clerks, teachers, journalists, and accountants, and were moreover engaged in small-scale trading. Their goal to achieve political power was pursued through participation in the NLM. The NLM was in opposition to Kwame Nkrumah and the Convention People's Party (CPP), and looked to the Asante chiefs for legitimisation and support. They believed that the support of the chiefs would also give them the support "of the spirits and ancestors of the entire nation" (Allman 1990: 272). The *nkwankwaa* were the only group who could mobilise people and form an opposition. And they had:

> aspirations which had been historically thwarted by the pre-colonial Asante state, by the structure of indirect rule and now by the bureaucratization and centralization of the CPP—as general Asante aspirations (Allman 1990: 274).

Similarly, McCaskie argues that the NLM used the Asantehene and the idea of the Asante nation to promote the interests "of the new model of ɔbirɛmpɔn and the business class against the presumed 'socialism' of Nkrumah" (McCaskie 1986a: 17–18). However, the support of the chiefs also had a price, as the *nkwankwaa* now relied on "those very powers who had historically thwarted their bid for political power within Asante" (Allman 1990: 276). The chiefs and the Asante elite gradually took over the leadership of the NLM and, in 1956, transformed the movement into a parliamentary political party and the social and political hegemony in Asante was somewhat re-established. The *nkwankwaa* joined the CPP and eventually, the CPP defeated the NLM (McCaskie 1986a: 17–18). The Asante members of the CPP combined features of the nineteenth and twentieth centuries' 'big men' and some of the successful ones became "the very model of a new model ɔbirɛmpɔn" (McCaskie 1986a: 17–18.).

The *nkwankwaa* as a social group is worth paying attention to because they challenged established norms around the accumulation of wealth as well as established holders of power, and in this way aspired to escape positions of subordination. According to Müller (2013), the *nkwankwaa* moreover challenged chiefly authority through the religious realm by their involvement in neo-indigenous religious movements. They were in this way seen to pose a threat to the spiritual underpinning of chiefly office. The *nkwankwaa* also used religion to legitimise the private accumulation of wealth (Müller 2013: 138). Charismatic pastors draw on some of the same social and cultural mechanisms as they also represent a group of aspiring individuals that build up their status through the accumulation and distribution of wealth, but also through the manifestation and demonstration of spiritual power. However, the public support of charismatic pastors is not unanimous, but is much debated and contested as will be discussed in Chap. 3.

At the same time, in both the *akonkofoɔ*'s and the *nkwankwaa*'s striving to create an autonomous space and through their attempts to carve out possibilities for social mobility lie also a formulation of a social critique directed towards the holders of power that defended values that put social constraints on accumulation and use of wealth. As mentioned in the introductory chapter, McCaskie compares contemporary dissatisfaction with political rulers that do not deliver with former '*nkwankwaa* talk' as a form of social critique and class consciousness. Of particular relevance here is the distinction between 'stealing from the rich' and 'stealing from the poor' and the related discussion of accumulating for oneself or accumulating for the benefit of the community (McCaskie 2008c: 447–448). Common to these different social groups is the fact that social critique is expressed in ethical debates of how one acquires and uses wealth.

Similarly, McCaskie links the career of the above-mentioned prophet Sampson Opong (Opon Asibe Tutu) to the broader social context of Asante in the early twentieth century. He contends that behind or underneath the Christian motivations for his activities were other reasons that had to do with suppression from chiefly rule in Asante, namely "the yearnings, bitterness, and necessarily partial and confused social critique of a frustrated, seemingly intelligent, but illiterate man" (McCaskie 1976: 34). The point is that Christianity and a career as a prophet was a way for Sampson Opong to escape subordination, realise social aspirations, and express social critique. At the same time, his religious activities and appearance resonated with traditional religious priests and he became a recognised religious figure. These are examples of a strong conjunction between social context (suppression and aspiration) and religion historically in Asante, which implies that we can not only perceive of these prophets as forerunners of charismatic Christianity. They were also Asante people who used a religious platform to engage with and challenge the ruling and emerging elites in Asante. This point does not imply that religion is instrumental (only), but it suggests and underlines that a career as a prophet was a way out of subordination that was acknowledged by the social environment.

Religion and Politics: 1950s–Present

In 1957, Ghana became independent with Nkrumah as President (1957–66). Although the ideology of Nkrumah and the CPP was socialist and he had a strong pan-Africanist vision, his political rhetoric was also influenced by Christianity (Gifford 1998: 58). Iijima (1998: 171) asserts that Nkrumah had a particular charismatic style of leadership, which resembled the leadership of prophets in the spiritual churches. Also, General Acheampong (1972–78) made reference to religion during his political office. According to Pobee (1987: 58), Acheampong used religion both to mobilise supporters and to legitimise his own position as head of the country when he came to power after a military coup in 1972. During the 1960s and 1970s, both religious language and religious movements played a role in national politics. Organisations such as the Christian Council of Ghana (CCG) and the Ghana Bishop's Conference of the Catholic Church played a mediatory role in conflicts between the government and students, university teachers and nurses (Pobee 1987: 59; Gifford 1998: 70). As Pobee (1992: 6) argues, "religion has been a factor of Ghanaian traditional politics and that it is still a factor of modern and contemporary politics".

In the early 1980s, the Ghanaian economy was in a critical state, a situation which was further aggravated by the Nigerian expulsion of undocumented migrants, of which many where Ghanaians. This situation created, according to Adubofour, "a national spiritual awareness which caused many to seek God's blessing for themselves and Ghana as a whole" (1994: 349). Moreover, many thought that the problems of Ghana were because "God had withdrawn his blessings from Ghana" (McCaskie 2008b: 323). It was also at this time that the charismatic movement started to grow. One pastor noted that the charismatic movement did not become popular because of the economic hardship, but rather because God was their only source.[22]

Rawlings came to power by a *coup d'état* first in 1979 and again in December 1981 and with him came a time of revolution and attacks on the elite and those who had hitherto been holders of power. However, after 1983, Rawlings and the PNDC (Provisional National Defence Council) turned towards the IMF (International Monetary Fund) and the World Bank, which entailed structural adjustment programmes with cutbacks in the public sector and privatisation (Gifford 1998: 59). In 1992, presidential elections were held, and Rawlings was elected president of the country. Relations between the mainline churches and the PNDC were tense. In 1989 the government issued a law (Religious Bodies Registration Law/PNDC Law 221) that obliged all churches to register with the Ministry of the Interior, so the churches would be accountable to the government (Gifford 1998: 69). This was also seen as an attempt to 'divide and rule' the churches so their influence could be controlled. The mainline churches refused to sign, as did some of the charismatic churches.[23] The

CCG and the Catholic Bishops took part in political debates on various issues through pastoral letters and joint memoranda, for example a memorandum to the PNDC in 1992 against the violation of human rights and for the release of political prisoners (Gifford 1998: 68, see also Nugent 1995: 187–189). The relationship between the PNDC and the mainline churches should, as noted by Gifford (1998: 70), be understood in the light of the elite/populist divide in Ghanaian politics. Rawlings presented himself as a populist and disdained those belonging to the elite, such as doctors, lawyers, and journalists. The leaders of the mainline churches also belonged to this elite. The PNDC was also initially critical vis-à-vis the new churches (of a Pentecostalist/charismatic orientation), of which some came from the USA. These churches were seen as dismissing African culture and not obeying political authority and, as a result, the activities of the Mormons and the Jehovah's Witnesses were banned (Nugent 1995: 188).

It was, however, the Pentecostal churches that later contributed to the legitimisation of Rawlings' political power. After Rawlings was elected president in 1992 he asked the Christian churches to organise a thanksgiving service. The mainline churches refused, but the Pentecostal churches agreed and prayed for Rawlings (Gifford 1998: 86). In the 2000 elections, the position of the Pentecostal and charismatic churches was somewhat equivocal. Pastors like Duncan-Williams (Action Chapel International) and Agyin Asare (World Miracle Church International) supported the NDC. However, after the defeat of the NDC candidate (John Atta Mills), Agyin Asare turned to the winner of the presidential elections, Kufuor, and prayed at his thanksgiving service (Gifford 2004: 179).

Economic decline, structural adjustment and political instability in the 1980s also changed the conditions for becoming 'big' in Ghana. New criteria for achieving status and success emerged. The rising groups of the 1950s such as university professors, teachers and civil servants, who had a stable income and status, experienced a new economic context that would also influence their social standing. They became the 'respectable poor' and tried to find a new balance between their status and decreased income (Nugent 1995: 4, 27). In particular, Rawlings' hostile attitude towards the elite and their wealth meant that "'big men' who had grown used to flaunting their wealth woke up to discover that conspicuous consumption attracted hostile scrutiny rather than admiration" (Nugent 1995: 58). However, as the political regime changed in the 1990s, so did the attitude towards possessing wealth, and new groups of people who had acquired wealth over a short period of time, rather than over decades as earlier, emerged (Nugent 1995: 204). As Nugent further notes, it was again possible to display wealth without the discontent of the government; the 'sociability of wealth' had been restored. What mattered was to show that wealth was acquired in a legitimate way, and that taxes were paid (Nugent 1995: 204). As will be discussed more in the following chapter, the view that it was again morally acceptable to accumulate wealth was also vividly debated within the Christian churches. These debates as well as the focus on wealth in the charismatic sector contributed to the renewed 'sociability of wealth,' although the accumulation of wealth of certain pastors also generated (and still does) much controversy.

Pentecostalism and Charismatic Christianity in Ghana

There are, according to Asamoah-Gyadu (2005a: 18–29), three waves of Pentecostal Christianity in Ghana. The first wave, the *Sunsum sorè*, or spiritual churches, was, as mentioned above, born out of the activities of a number of prophets at the beginning of the twentieth century. The second wave consists of the so-called classical Pentecostal churches that were introduced by foreign missionaries. The classical Pentecostal churches consist of churches such as the Assemblies of God, the Church of Pentecost, the Apostolic Church, and the Christ Apostolic Church. The forerunners of the movement were prophets like Wade Harris, Sampson Oppong and John Swatson, who attracted many members to the already established churches (for example the Catholic, Methodist, and Anglican churches) (Larbi 2001). The early Pentecostal movement was a break with the more established Christian churches (called mainline or Orthodox churches in the Ghanaian context) in particular in their emphasis on healing and the role of the Holy Spirit.

The third wave, which is the focus of this book, is the so-called neo-Pentecostal or charismatic churches. According to Asamoah-Gyadu (2005a), this movement manifested itself in three different ways: in new indigenous or independent churches or 'ministries', in transdenominational fellowships, and in charismatic groups within mission churches (see also Gifford 2004; Quampah 2014). The term 'charismatic movement' is used more broadly to include charismatic groups outside the Pentecostal sector, such as the Catholic Church.[24]

The charismatic churches in Ghana rose significantly from the 1960s. The rise mainly took place in para-church evangelical associations, such as fellowships, prayer groups, and music teams. An example of a tremendously powerful and influential fellowship is the Scripture Union (SU).[25] SU operated in educational institutions and organised, for instance, Sunday school and youth work. Many charismatic pastors have had high positions in SU as it provided opportunities for young pastors to practise and to test their leadership ambitions. The educational background of some of the young charismatic pastors that rose in the 1980s is, according to one pastor, what separated them from the classical Pentecostal churches. This pastor explains that many of the young charismatics did not feel at home in the classical Pentecostal churches because they had a higher level of education than many with leadership positions in the classical Pentecostal churches.[26] There was also a generational factor that influenced the attraction of the new churches to young people. Many of the classical Pentecostal churches had more strict rules with regard to worship and how people were allowed to dress, so many young people found the new charismatic churches more in line with their own aspirations and as a less restricted space. The charismatic movement in Ghana was from the early days influenced by American missionaries like Kenneth Hagin and Morris Cerullo as well as missionaries from Nigeria.

The majority of the charismatic churches are organised under the National Association of Charismatic and Christian Churches (NACCC, founded in the late 1990s), but some belong to the Ghana Pentecostal Council (GPC), which is a body that organises the classical Pentecostal churches and which was founded in the late 1970s. There are smaller churches that do not belong to any of these councils, but work independently. Alongside these councils there exist a number of pastoral associations that are concerned with the training and guidance of pastors (Quampah 2014).

Within the Catholic Church, which is the single biggest church in Ghana, the charismatic movement is organised in the Catholic Charismatic Renewal. Already in 1972, a 'Centre for Spiritual Renewal' was established in Kumasi. The Catholic Charismatic Renewal movement organised various National Leaders Conferences (e.g. in 1986 and 1992), which were attended by up to 2500 participants (Larbi 2001: 84–87).

Kumasi: 'The Spiritual Capital of Ghana'

In the 1960s, the religious landscape of Asante and in particular Kumasi was still characterised by Christian denominations that had been established by missionaries in the beginning of the century. At the time, most Christian Asante belonged to Methodist, Catholic or Anglican churches in which they had often grown up. Their religious lives were "embedded in the easy sociability of modified tradition, a round of weekly Sunday services punctuated by church meetings, festivals, christenings, confirmations, weddings and funerals" (McCaskie 2008a: 57). Being a Christian had since colonial times been associated with being educated, being modern, and being elite. Throughout the 1980s and until presently this landscape and constellation of Christian denominations has changed dramatically. As McCaskie remarks: "even the most casual observer can sense the ways in which Christianity has become more salient in Kumasi life" (McCaskie 2008a: 57–58).

As has been described in detail by Adubofuor (1994), the charismatic movement in Kumasi started in the 1950s with the proliferation of Scripture Union within educational institutions (mostly secondary and tertiary school). Later on in the 1960s, Town Fellowships and other para-church movements emerged. Initially, the fellowships were joined by well-educated people, but with the Town Fellowships the "educationally underprivileged and non-professional literates" would also take part (Adubofuor 1994: 81). The foreign influence derived from international evangelists such as Benson Idahosa from Nigeria and Morris Cerullo from the USA is still very much present today. During the 1960s and 1970s, Kumasi witnessed a growth and transformation of the charismatic movement; "Kumasi emerged as a "spiritual Capital"—the epicentre of charismatic activity in Ghana" (Adubofuor 1994: 318–319). In the 1980s, the number of crusades, conventions, and other events grew significantly (Adubofuor 1994: 348). The first of the independent charismatic churches in Kumasi were founded in the 1980s and they were in many cases offspring of the classical Pentecostal churches such as the Church of Pentecost and the Assemblies of God.[27]

Today the presence of the charismatic churches in Kumasi can be observed on at least two levels. On the one level, there are large and well-established churches such as Calvary Charismatic Centre and Family Chapel International. These churches, which both come out of the Assemblies of God, have large church buildings and various branches around Ghana and abroad. In these churches, there are two or three services on a Sunday that attract between 1000 and 2000 people. The general picture is one of a rather detailed and hierarchical organisational set-up, with well-defined roles for each participant and heavily centred on the founder and leader of the church. In 2005, Calvary Charismatic Centre had a specific Sunday service for students. For this purpose it operated a bus service from the university campus, as well as other educational institutions, to provide means of transportation for the students. This church was also the first in Kumasi to do their church services in English, which was by many seen as impossible because of the cultural awareness of people in Asante.[28]

On another scale, there are the many small churches that meet on Sundays in school buildings, canteens, storerooms or under canvas roofs.[29] Typically, they have been established more recently and gather from around 100 down to 10 church members. The pastors take along drums, tambourines and large banners. The rooms are decorated with artificial flowers, white lace curtains and in some cases a pulpit from which the pastor can preach. The pastors of these many small churches come from one of the bigger churches, come from a Bible school, or just start a church themselves.

There is also a difference between the Kumasi-based charismatic churches and those with headquarters in, for instance, Accra or Nigeria. The former group of churches is seemingly the more successful in terms of attracting members and constructing large church buildings. The pastors from the Kumasi-based churches are well known locally and have local influence. According to Samuel Brefo Adubofuor,[30] the success of the locally-founded churches should be seen in light of earlier pastoral networks within, for example, the 'Faith Convention'. The 'Faith Convention' was founded in Kumasi in 1981 with the aim of coordinating the many activities of the new charismatic fellowships and ministries (Adubofuor 1994: 345–348). This created a platform whereby the churches could promote themselves, put on joint events and from where their leaders could exercise influence. The movement was managed by a group of people, including Gregory Ola Akin of Harvesters Evangelistic Ministry, Alfred Nyamekye of House of Faith, Douglas Frimpong of Christian Outreach Ministries, Koranteng of the Presbyterian Church, Samuel Otoo of Redemption Hour Faith Ministries and Ransford Obeng of the Calvary Charismatic Centre.[31] Most of these are today important and influential charismatic church leaders in Kumasi (Adubofuor 1994: 347). The Faith Convention became very popular in Kumasi, and attracted many young people who had been called by God. Those behind the Faith Convention started a Bible School to teach these young people, who later started their own churches. The Faith Convention also moved beyond Kumasi and had meetings in Sunyani and Koforidua, but not in Accra. As one of the pastors involved explains: "Accra was more difficult for us because it was as if we were entering other people's territory".[32]

The charismatic movement in Kumasi is not a mere subdivision of the Accra-based churches, but is in many ways a separate category with its own history. One pastor, who was part of the early charismatic movement in Kumasi, explains that the Accra-based churches were more focused on Bible teachings on themes such as success and prosperity, whereas the charismatic churches in Kumasi were concentrating on deliverance, healing and miracles. He said: "In Kumasi our influences were in-bred ... Most of us came from backgrounds where people had to struggle to survive so one's whole life was about praying to touch God and so I think that gave an expression to prayer and deliverance in those days".[33] In relation to these early differences in the charismatic movement in Accra and Kumasi, it is worth noting that some of the most controversial charismatic pastors today are Kumasi-based, such as Daniel Obinim of The International God's Way Church and Ebenezer Opambuor Adarkwa Yiadom (or Prophet 1) of Ebenezer Miracle Worship Centre in Kumasi. They are often accused of using black magic and of being under the spiritual protection of traditional priests.[34]

The more well-established charismatic churches in Kumasi are today recognised and accepted both by the traditional and the religious elite. When the current Asantehene (Otumfour Osei Tutu II) celebrated his 60th birthday in 2010, he held a thanksgiving service in the Calvary Charismatic Centre (CCC). The Asantehene is a member of the Anglican Church, so this was seen as a sign of acknowledgement by the founding pastor of CCC: "He came along with all the chiefs because the Asantehene moves with more than forty chiefs. For them to come here shows their acceptance of the charismatic movement. Now they accept the charismatic movement".[35] At the same time, the charismatic pastors also accept the faith of the traditional leaders, which they earlier saw as un-Christian or related to evil forces because of traditional rituals such as the pouring of libation. There is also collaboration between Christian leaders of different denominations, who are organised in the Kumasi Minister's Council. One leading charismatic pastor said: "In this city, anybody who is a servant of God is a servant of God. There is no discrimination ... There is quite a measure of unity, unity in diversity in this city … We always choose an Orthodox[36] to head with a Pentecostal or charismatic pastor assisting. They are our senior brothers. We honour and respect them".[37] When the city holds conventions and other programmes it is organised by this council, as for instance in 2014, when Reinhard Bonke visited Kumasi.

History and Religious Change

This chapter has provided not an extensive history of Asante or of religious change in Asante, but a descriptive analysis of important moments of change and of significant figures. These moments and figures illustrate how ideas and practices of status, wealth and power were established and changed throughout the last two centuries in Asante. The aim has been to lay the foundations for the argument I make in this book: that charismatic pastors in Asante build on the historic figures of *akɔmfoɔ* and *abirɛmpɔn*, but also draw on more recent figures from the prophet movement to establish themselves as pastors and become new versions of 'big men'. This has historically been linked to the accumulation, distribution and display of wealth. When the circumstances under which someone became a 'big man' changed, especially around the turn of the last century, so did the possibilities of social ascension. The groups of young people with social and political aspirations, such as the *akonkofoɔ*, challenged existing ideas around wealth and redistribution. It became morally acceptable to accumulate wealth for the individual, and wealth was no longer seen as exclusively belonging to the community. They represented a new type of *ɔbirɛmpɔn*. The point is that although times have changed, people who seek to 'join power' and accumulate wealth still make reference to and draw on the ideas associated with the *ɔbirɛmpɔn* and in this way charismatic pastors draw on these historical repertoires of cultural norms and meaning when they seek to become 'big'.

With regard to the study of charismatic Christianity and history more generally, there are two points I would want to raise in conclusion to this chapter. First, I offer an approach to the study of religious change that is historically based. When studying religion and the links to the social world, it is fruitful to approach the historical background and context more broadly than merely the history of one particular religion (as a closed unit of analysis). I do not therefore distinguish too sharply between a certain religion and related social sets of ideas and practices. Also, drawing on history does not mean that religious ideas and practices that were formed in the past are only something of the past. Allman and Parker (2005: 8) argue that African traditional religion is historical, but all too often portrayed as timeless and thereby seen as inherently traditional.[38] This point is also (and particularly) valid with regard to studies of charismatic Christianity in Africa. By portraying this strand of Christianity mainly as a modernity marker, much of the literature at the same time portrays it as ahistorical and timeless, and consequently, the historical resonances are treated in a superficial manner (Engelke 2004; Gifford 2004; Meyer 1998a).[39] Moreover, the literature often presents the historical repertoires that charismatic Christianity draws on as restricted to the history of religion (for instance Akan cosmology, spiritual churches, the prophet movement, earlier Christian churches) (Adubofour 1994; Asamoah-Gyadu 2005a, b; Larbi 2001). And again, these religious movements are analysed as timeless and as a form of baseline against which to understand contemporary religion. We need to understand the current Christian landscape and for instance pastoral careers not only in relation to the historical dynamic of other religious movements but also in relation to the cultural, ideological, political and social baggage and, in the Asante context, analyse "significant moments and areas in which the ideological wheel of accumulation, wealth and belief turned" (McCaskie 1986a: 19).

This leads to my second point about history and resonance that draws on Douglas' argument that there has to be resonance, resemblance and similarity between new institutions and the society in which they arise. Douglas (1986: 45) writes that "[t]o acquire legitimacy, every kind of institution needs a formula that founds its rightness in reason and in nature". This is partly a cognitive and partly a social process. The point is that new institutions need a stabilising principle. The following quote from Douglas takes us back to the first point about understanding charismatic Christianity and pastors in relation to their broader socio-historical context:

> Many of the philosopher's problems about the social origins of religious belief come from treating religion as something that goes on in church. The parallel mistake would be to isolate the ancestor cult from the whole social complex (Douglas 1986: 50).

How does charismatic Christianity resonate with the past and how does the past provide a frame for making sense of new religious ideologies? In this book, the past is understood as both part of and shaping the enabling circumstances that make it worthwhile, meaningful and attractive to engage in a pastoral career. Still, when context changes, people also change their ways of going about things, and the analytical work lies in tracing these changes both diachronically and synchronically to understand how aspiring political and religious figures achieve and maintain power.

Notes

1. ɔbirɛmpɔn (pl. abirɛmpɔn) means a 'big man', and also implies rule, power, and wealth. According to McCaskie "[i]t was a hereditary title held by the heads of territorial chiefdoms, and also conferred upon the very wealthiest accumulators" (McCaskie 1995: 275).
2. The literal meaning of ɔkɔmfɔ (pl. akɔmfoɔ) is one who is possessed by ɔbosom (pl. abosom, powers of supernatural origin). An ɔkɔmfɔ is a mediator between the highest spiritual power, and the people. The term ɔkɔmfo is often translated as priest or fetish priest, but according to McCaskie this is misleading. Rather, "an ɔkɔmfɔ was also ɔsɔfo … an ɔkɔmfɔ might conduce manifestation of an ɔbosom, but he could not command it" (McCaskie 1995: 290). The term ɔsɔfo (a priest) is widely employed also in a Christian charismatic context.
3. Geographically, pre-colonial Asante covered most of modern Ghana and the eastern parts of the Ivory Coast. This is also referred to as the Asante empire or Greater Asante (Arhin 1995: 98).
4. The historiography of the origins of the Asante kingdom is quite extensive, see among others Arhin (1983, 1990), Austin (2005), McCaskie (1983, 1995, 2007b), McLeod (1981), Wilks (1975, 1993: 91–126), and many more. I am aware that this short summary does not do justice to the nuances and details of this literature.
5. Denkyira was an Akan state that together with the Adanse, Akyem, Asante, and Asen (Assin) constituted the cradle of the Akan (Wilks 1993: 91).
6. Whether this is merely a myth or whether Komfo Anokye existed as a historical figure has been debated, see among others McLeod (1981: 65) and McCaskie (1986b: 319). The significance of Komfo Anokye can, according to McCaskie (1986b: 320), be seen as "his cognitive 'necessity' as metaphor", and McCaskie thereby distinguishes between his significance as a historical fact in a specific moment in time and as a metaphor that comprises all time.

7. The state, for instance, controlled the distribution and the outflow of gold. This was necessary because gold was "the supreme embodiment of wealth as well as the measure of authority" (Arhin 1995: 99, see also Wilks 1993: 136).
8. Wilks understands *abirɛmpɔn* more as a class of entrepreneurs and developers, who were into agricultural production and exploitation (Wilks 1993: 96–97). However, for the purpose of this book it is of more relevance to approach the social category of *ɔbirɛmpɔn* as a route to social promotion and thus highlight the opportunities of mobility, rather than describe them as a distinct class as such.
9. The influence of the coast is important in understanding the changes that took place in Asante from the mid- nineteenth century as it provided new and alternative views of the world: "This was the intensely competitive, free-market and highly individualistic (Christian) capitalism of the area of the southern Gold Coast presided over by the British" (McCaskie 1983: 36).
10. Colonial Ashanti comprised the Ashanti and Brong-Ahafo regions of modern Ghana. The term Ashanti is also used for the present day Ashanti region.
11. In pre-colonial Asante, three modes of currencies existed: first pieces of iron, and later (eighteenth and nineteenth centuries) cowries and gold dust. The last two forms co-existed (Arhin 1995: 98–99).
12. Cocoa production took off on the Akuapim ridge (now Eastern region) at the end of the nineteenth century, and expanded to the Akyem Abuakwa district and further (Austin 1987: 260). See also Hill ([1963] 1997).
13. To the contrary Boone argues that cocoa production in the 1930s was predominantly based on the *abusua* (2003: 149–152).
14. Slavery and pawning were officially banned in Asante in 1908.
15. *Akonkofoɔ* is a term used about Asante businessmen from the beginning of the twentieth century. The term carries "implications of wealth, of capitalist individualism, and of 'modernity'" (McCaskie 1995: 71). See also McCaskie (1995: 291).
16. See Miescher (2005: 84–114) for an analysis of the *akrakyefoɔ* (clerk, scholars) as up-coming, middle figures in the 1930s–1950s. These people were neither part of the traditional elites, nor the lawyer-merchant class (elite intelligentsia). Still, they had social, political, and economic aspirations. Often they were Standard VII

school leavers and worked as clerks, cocoa brokers, storekeepers, teachers, and pastors.
17. See also Peel (1987: 108).
18. ARG 1/30/2/6, Rev. N. V. Asare to T. E. Fell, 8 November 1908 and T. E. Fell to The Chief Commissioner Kumase, 27 November 1908.
19. This debate relates to a larger and more recent debate on whether an increase in religious movements can be explained as a reaction to rapid social change caused by modernity and neo-liberalism (see Chap. 1, Comaroff and Comaroff (2003) and Coleman (2011)). It is interesting to note that this discussion, at least in a Ghanaian context, was part of academic debates in the 1940s–1960s (Field 1940; Goody 1957; Baëta [1962] 2004).
20. See also Sundkler ([1948] 1961) on Bantu prophets as chief-like leaders. Obeng (1996) has made a similar point about the adaptation of Asante social structures in Asante Catholicism.
21. See also Rathbone (1973).
22. Interview Victor Osei, Kumasi, 4 December 2014.
23. Interview Victor Osei, Kumasi, 4 December 2014.
24. As already mentioned, I use the term charismatic churches or charismatic Christianity as this was the term used by the people I interviewed.
25. The SU was established in Ghana by a UK-based branch. It celebrated its hundred years of existence in Ghana in 1990. SU was regarded as a conservative evangelical movement (see Adubofuor 1994: 58–92; Asamoah-Gyadu 2005a: 103–105 for more information on SU in Ghana).
26. Interview Victor Osei, Kumasi, 4 December 2014.
27. Though it is not the focus of this book, it is important to recognise the role Muslims play in the history of the region. Most Muslims were located in the Zongo and were not originally from Kumasi. Many originated from the North and were involved in trade. See Schildkrout (1974) for a history of the political role of Muslims in Kumasi.
28. Interview Ransford Obeng, Kumasi, 9 December 2014.
29. These small-scale churches are not particular to the religious landscape of Kumasi, but are present in other cities in Southern Ghana as well.
30. Personal communication, Christian Service College, Kumasi, 7 September 2005 and 12 September 2005.

31. Interview Ransford Obeng, Kumasi, 9 December 2014.
32. Interview Ransford Obeng, Kumasi, 9 December 2014.
33. Interview Victor Osei, Kumasi, 4 December 2014.
34. In one among many examples, Obinim recently claimed that he could transform himself into an animal and visit people at night, which was contested as un-Christian by other pastors. (GhanaWeb 8 March 2016: http://www.ghanaweb.com/GhanaHomePage/religion/I-will-chase-Obinim-out-of-Ghana-Owusu-Bempah-421796 (accessed 14 March 2016)).
35. Interview Ransford Obeng, Kumasi 9 December 2014.
36. A mainline church such as the Anglican Church, the Methodist Church or the Catholic Church.
37. Interview Victor Osei, Kumasi, 4 December 2014.
38. See also Ranger and Kimambo (1976) who advocated for studying the history of religion in Africa in relation to political, social, and economic history. The work of particular Africanist historians follows the approach of this pioneering work and to which the critique of Allman and Parker does not apply (see for instance McCaskie (1995) and Peel (2000)).
39. See also Maxwell (2006b) for a discussion of this.

References

Adubofour, S. B. (1994). *Evangelic Parachurch movements in Ghanaian Christianity: c. 1950—Early 1990s*. Unpublished Ph.D. thesis, University of Edinburgh, Edinburgh.

Akyeampong, E. (1999). Christianity, modernity and the weight of tradition in the life of *Asantehene* Agyeman Prempeh I, c. 1888–1931. *Africa, 69*(2), 279–311.

Akyeampong, E., & Obeng, P. (1995). Spirituality, gender, and power in Asante history. *International Journal of African Historical Studies, 28*(3), 481–508.

Allman, J. (1990). The youngmen and the porcupine: Class, nationalism and Asante's struggle for self-determination, 1954–57. *Journal of African History, 31*(2), 263–279.

Allman, J. (1993). *The quills of the porcupine: Asante nationalism in an emergent Ghana 1954–1957*. Madison: University of Wisconsin Press.

Allman, J., & Parker, J. (2005). *Tongnaab. The history of a West African god*. Bloomington and Indianapolis: Indiana University Press.

Allman, J., & Tashjian, V. (2000). *"I will not eat stone". A women's history of colonial asante*. Portsmouth: Heinemann.

Arhin, K. (1976/77). The pressure of cash and its political consequences in Asante in the colonial period. *Journal of African Studies, 3*(4), 453–468.

Arhin, K. (1983). Rank and class among the Asante and Fante in the nineteenth century. *Africa, 53*(1), 2–21.

Arhin, K. (1986). A note on the Asante Akonkofo: A non-literate sub-elite, 1900–1930. *Africa, 56*(1), 25–31.

Arhin, K. (1990). Trade, accumulation and the state in Asante in the nineteenth century. *Africa, 60*(4), 524–537.

Arhin, K. (1995). Monetization and the Asante state. In J. Guyer (Ed.), *Money matters. Instability, values and social payments in the modern history of West African communities*. Portsmouth, NH: Heinemann and James Currey.

Asamoah-Gyadu, J. K. (2004). Foreword. In C. G. Baëta (Ed.), [1962] 2004. *Prophetism in Ghana a study of some 'spiritual' churches*. Achimota: Africa Christian Press.

Asamoah-Gyadu, J. K. (2005a). *African Charismatics. Current developments within independent indigenous pentecostalism in Ghana*. Leiden: Brill.

Asamoah-Gyadu, J. K. (2005b). "Christ is the answer": What is the question? A Ghana airways prayer vigil and its implications for religion, evil and public space. *Journal of Religion in Africa, 35*(1), 93–117.

Austin, G. (1987). The emergence of capitalist relations in South Asante cocoa-farming, c. 1916–33. *Journal of African History, 28*(2), 259–279.

Austin, G. (1988). Capitalists and chiefs in the cocoa hold-ups in South Asante, 1927–1938. *The International Journal of African Historical Studies, 21*(1), 63–95.

Austin, G. (2003, May 8). *Moneylending and witchcraft: The moral economy of accumulation in colonial Asante*. Paper presented for the Modern Economic History Seminar, LSE.

Austin, G. (2005). *Labour, land and capital in Ghana: From slavery to free labour in Asante, 1807–1956*. Rochester, NY: University of Rochester Press.

Baëta, C. G. ([1962] 2004). *Prophetism in Ghana. A study of some 'Spiritual' Churches*. Achimota: Africa Christian Press.

Berry, S. (2001). *Chiefs know their boundaries. Essays on property, power, and the past in Asante, 1896–1996*. Portsmouth: Heinemann.

Boone, C. (2003). *Political topographies of the African state. Territorial authority and institutional choice*. Cambridge: Cambridge University Press.

Busia, K. A. (1951). *The position of the chief in the modern political system of Ashanti*. London: Oxford University Press.

Coleman, S. (2011). Prosperity unbound? Debating the 'sacrificial economy'. In L. Obadia & D. C. Wood (Eds.), *The economics of religion: Anthropological approaches* (Research in Economic Anthropology, Vol. 31). Bingley: Emerald Group Publishing Limited.

Comaroff, J., & Comaroff, J. (2003). Second comings: Neo-protestant ethics and millennial capitalism in Africa, and elsewhere. In P. Gifford (Ed.), *2000 years*

and beyond. Faith, identity and the 'common era'. London and New York: Routledge.
Douglas, M. (1986). *How institutions think*. New York: Syracuse University Press.
Engelke, M. (2004). Discontinuity and the discourse of conversion. *Journal of Religion in Africa, 34*(1/2), 82–109.
Field, M. J. (1940). *Social organisation of the Ga people*. London: Crown Agents.
Field, M. J. (1968). Some new shrines of the gold coast and their significance. *Africa, 13*(2), 138–149.
Gifford, P. (1998). *African Christianity. Its public role*. London: Hurst & Company.
Gifford, P. (2004). *Ghana's new Christianity. Pentecostalism in a globalising African economy*. London: Hurst & Company.
Goody, J. (1957). Anomie in Ashanti? *Africa, 27*(4), 356–363.
Hill, P. ([1963] 1997). *The migrant cocoa-farmers of southern Ghana*. Oxford: James Currey Publishers.
Iijima, M. (1998). Developing charisma: Nkrumah as a "cargo" benefactor in Ghana. *African Study Monographs, 19*(4), 171–185.
Larbi, E. K. (2001). *Pentecostalism. The eddies of Ghanaian Christianity*. Accra: Centre for Pentecostal and Charismatic Studies.
Maxwell, D. (2006b). Writing the history of African Christianity: Reflections of an editor. *Journal of Religion in Africa, 36*(3–4), 379–399.
McCaskie, T. C. (1976). Social rebellion and the inchoate rejection of history: Some reflection on the career of Opon Asibe Tutu. *Asante Seminar, 4*, 34–38.
McCaskie, T. C. (1983). Accumulation, wealth and belief in Asante history. I. To the close of the nineteenth century. *Africa, 53*(1), 23–43.
McCaskie, T. C. (1986a). Accumulation: Wealth and belief in Asante history: II the twentieth century. *Africa, 56*(1), 3–23.
McCaskie, T. C. (1986b). Komfo Anokye of Asante: Meaning, history and philosophy in an African society. *Journal of African History, 27*, 315–339.
McCaskie, T. C. (1995). *State and society in pre-colonial Asante*. Cambridge: Cambridge University Press.
McCaskie, T. C. (2000). *Asante identities: History and modernity in an African village 1850–1950*. International African Institute, London: Edinburgh University Press.
McCaskie, T. C. (2007a). The life and afterlife of Yaa Asantewaa. *Africa, 77*(2), 151–179.
McCaskie, T. C. (2007b). Denkyira in the making of Asante, c. 1660–1720. *Journal of African History, 48*(1), 1–25.
McCaskie, T. C. (2008a). Akwantemfi–'In mid-journey': An Asante shrine today and its clients. *Journal of Religion in Africa, 38*(1), 1–24.
McCaskie, T. C. (2008b). The United States, Ghana and oil: Global and local perspectives. *African Affairs, 107*(428), 313–332.

McCaskie, T. C. (2008c). Gun culture in Kumasi. *Africa, 78*(3), 433–454.
McLeod, M. D. (1981). *The Asante*. London: British Museum Publications Ltd.
Meyer, B. (1998a). 'Make a complete break with the past', memory and postcolonial modernity in Ghanaian Pentecostalist discourse. *Journal of Religion in Africa, 28*(3), 316–349.
Miescher, S. (2005). *Making men in Ghana*. Bloomington & Indianapolis: Indiana University Press.
Müller, L. (2013). *Religion and Chieftaincy in Ghana. An exploration of the persistence of a traditional political institution in West Africa*. Munster: Lit Verlag.
Nugent, P. (1995). *Big men, small boys and politics in Ghana*. London: Pinter.
Obeng, J. P. (1996). *Asante Catholicism: Religious and cultural reproduction among the Akan of Ghana*. Leiden: Brill.
Peel, J. D. Y. (1987). History, culture and the comparative method: A West African puzzle. In L. Holy (Ed.), *Comparative anthropology*. Oxford: Basil Blackwell.
Peel, J. D. Y. (2000). *Religious encounter and the making of the Yoruba*. Bloomington: Indiana University Press.
Pobee, J. S. (1987). Religion and politics in Ghana, 1972–1978. Some case studies from the rule of General I. K. Acheampong. *Journal of Religion in Africa, 17*(1), 44–62.
Pobee, J. S. (1992). *Religion and politics in Ghana. A case study of the Acheampong Era 1972–1978*. Accra: Ghana University Press.
Quampah, D. (2014). *Good pastors, bad pastors. Pentecostal ministerial ethics in Ghana*. Eugene, Oregon: WIPF & STOCK.
Ranger, T. O., & Kimambo, I. N. (Eds.). (1976). *The historical study of African religion*. Berkeley, CA: University of California Press.
Rathbone, R. (1973). Businessmen and politics. *Journal of Development Studies, 9*(3), 390–401.
Schildkrout, E. (1974). Islam and politics in Kumasi. An analysis of disputes over the Kumasi Central Mosque. *Anthropological Papers of the American Museum of Natural History, 53*(2), 111–138.
Sundkler, B. G. M. ([1948] 1961). *Bantu prophets in South Africa*. London: Oxford University Press.
Ward, B. E. (1956). Some observations on religious cults in Ashanti. *Africa, 26*(1), 47–61.
Wilks, I. (1975). *Asante in the nineteenth century. The structure and evolution of a political order*. London: Cambridge University Press.
Wilks, I. (1993). *Forest of gold: Essays on the Akan and the kingdom of Asante*. Athens, OH: Ohio University Press.

CHAPTER 3

Wealth and Worth: The Idea of a Truthful Pastor

This chapter[1] is concerned with the ideological and moral underpinnings of what it takes to become a truthful pastor. I distinguish between the social process of being recognised and legitimised as a pastor and the ideological and moral aspects of being a truthful one. I deal with the social aspects of pastorship in the succeeding chapter and return to the spiritual underpinnings of pastorship in Chap. 5. I am interested in the cognitive framework around attaining wealth and how this relates to ideas of being a truthful pastor. I use the concepts wealth and truthfulness (*nokware*) as sets of ideas that both have a specific historic resonance in Asante and that are also defined and expressed within Christian ideological frameworks. More concretely, I analyse the affinity between the ideas of wealth in charismatic and Pentecostal doctrine and ideas of wealth and truthfulness in a local historical context as well as how pastors draw on these ideological repertoires.

There is a historic tension in Asante between accumulating wealth for the individual or to the benefit of the community (McCaskie 1986b, 1995, 2008a). In pre-colonial Asante 'big men' (*abirɛmpɔn*) were responsible for the maintenance and continuity of society and therefore had a responsibility to redistribute accumulated wealth. The Asante state imposed restrictions on the use of wealth, but there were also moral standards as to how wealth was to be redistributed. Moreover, wealth was a sign of worth and the public display of it was the manner in which the status and title of 'big man' was proved and approved.

In this chapter I argue that present-day charismatic pastors manoeuvre within this tension between accumulation for the individual and the com-

© The Author(s) 2017
K. Lauterbach, *Christianity, Wealth, and Spiritual Power in Ghana*,
DOI 10.1007/978-3-319-33494-3_3

munity. On the one hand, pastors focus strongly on prosperity and economic success (as a sign of God's blessing) in their preaching. On the other hand, they also draw attention to their role as providers and caretakers of the community, for instance, by praying for the wellbeing of society, engaging in social development projects and contributing to their home communities. Gyekye (1987: 132) notes that the Akan concept of 'good' is concerned with the welfare and the wellbeing of the community, which explains why the tension between accumulation to oneself or the community is central in Asante morality. He moreover argues, and this is important with regard to the public criticism of charismatic pastors, that 'Akan social thought attempts to establish a delicate balance between the concepts of communality and individuality', which implies that the two poles do not exclude one another (1987: 161). At the moral level, pastors need to accommodate and relate to this tension in order to be truthful mediators between the spiritual and the material world. Another concern with regard to wealth is how wealth is accumulated, which informs debates around the moral legitimacy of wealth.

I argue that the ideas of wealth within Pentecostalism and charismatic Christianity are attractive for both pastors and church members and that is what makes the charismatic churches dynamic. There is a dual driving force in the religious ideas about wealth: on the one hand, these ideas are conducive to a certain form of entrepreneurship and on the other hand, they relate to more established ideas around social mobility, status, and legitimacy in Asante. The aim is, therefore, not to ask how Pentecostal ideology is an expression of and a reaction to the times of post-colonial modernity and neo-liberalism (Comaroff and Comaroff 2000; Meyer 1998a), but rather to approach the relation between religious ideas and social change as non-mechanical and as a mediation of local history and broader ideological and economic influences (Gerth and Wright Mills 1991: 63; Haynes 2012; Lambek 2002: 51). Or to use the words of Weber, I am interested in 'the manner in which ideas become effective forces in history' (Weber [1930] 2001: 48).

Wealth and Charismatic Christianity in Public Debate

Tensions around the accumulation and use of wealth are reflected in contemporary public debates on charismatic pastors and their role in Ghanaian society. There are two basic positions in this debate: one that hails money and wealth, and perceives it as a sign of God's blessings and spiritual power and authority, and another that conceives of the role of religion/Christianity as being to provide a moral code of behaviour and to contribute to the welfare and wellbeing of society. These positions are often portrayed as being promoted by charismatics on the one hand and traditionalist and adherents to mainline Christian churches on the other. But as the following discussion will show, this tension is also prevailing within the charismatic sector as well as more widely in society. Therefore, I propose that the tension around accumulation and redistribution of wealth and *nokware* is one that charismatic pastors relate to and seek to balance in order to appear as truthful. Charismatic pastors seek to redefine the moral codex around wealth (as did the *akonkofoɔ* in the early twentieth century) and at the same time, they are deeply aware of the importance of contributing to the wellbeing of society.

The following newspaper article reports how a high-ranking Methodist minister attacked the charismatic churches publicly by accusing them of being to the detriment of Ghana's social and economic wellbeing and 'exploiting the poor':

> 'Charismatic churches exploiting the poor–Dickson'. A renowned Methodist Minister and one time Chairman of the Christian Ghanaian Council of Ghana, the Rt. Rev. Prof. Emeritus Kwesi A. Dickson, has expressed grave concern about the manner some charismatic and upcoming churches in the country are overly exploiting a cross-section of Ghanaians purported to be members of their congregations. He said these so-called churches are causing serious harm and doing the nation a complete disservice by keeping their members all day long in prayer camps, denying them the opportunity to pursue vital productive economic activities and services that could enhance their livelihood. He noted that these pastors who manage to lure these members from the orthodox churches because of the 'miracle and prosperity gospel' they preach to extract a lot of money from the poor without providing any kind of social services to benefit these members in return ... Prof. Dickson indicated that most of these churches, whose pastors are self-ordained and proclaimed, veer off the normal and true cause of evangelism as they have no laid down regulations to practically guide their conduct and their religious approach to worship ... He describes them as a machinery for money making; the pastors are barely cheats and a liability to our society. (*The Daily Dispatch*, 7 September 2005)

The above quotation is an example of the public criticism of charismatic churches and their pastors in Ghana. The debate touches in particular on the churches' focus on, and display of, money and wealth, as well as their religious foundation, authenticity and lack of order and regulation. The Methodist minister quoted here summarises the controversy of the so-called one-man churches by attacking their focus on prosperity and describing the pastors as self-ordained. Hence, in his view, such churches have no authority and legitimacy and misrepresent Christianity.

This tension is also played out within and between religious institutions and actors. In an article on the shrine priest Nana Abass, referred to earlier in this book, McCaskie describes how the priest through his activities in the local community stresses his contribution to its wellbeing, progress, and development (McCaskie 2008a: 66). Through this, Nana Abass also criticises charismatic pastors and their focus on prosperity. Nana Abass sees these pastors as seeking wealth for themselves to the detriment of church goers and this represents a threat to the social cohesion of society more generally. Behind this view lies an understanding of prosperity (*ayiyedi*) as not only being about possessing wealth, but also about how one uses it: 'It meant "security" and "welfare" in the sense of an expenditure for others rather than only on oneself' (McCaskie 2008a: 66). This tension is central to the public criticism of charismatic pastors, but it is also part of the moral framework that pastors position themselves within in their efforts to prove themselves to be truthful pastors.

WEALTH AND *NOKWARE*

The process of becoming a small 'big man' and establish oneself as a pastor is related to the Akan concept *nokware*. *Nokware* translates to truthfulness and is a matter of sincerity in dealing with oneself and with others; 'being of one mouth' or 'being of one voice' (Wiredu 1998: 234). McCaskie, moreover, points out that the term is to be understood 'in the transitive sense of *acting* honestly, truthfully, or with probity' (1995: 252), or doing what one says, hence the strong focus on the correspondence between speech and act. Wiredu puts a stronger emphasis on the relation between one's thinking and one's saying and thereby downplays the importance of how this is reflected in action or behaviour (Wiredu 1998: 234). Consequently, the legitimacy of a position as pastor depends on whether one is thought of as acting truthfully and hence in accordance with a moral set of criteria.[2]

The idea of a truthful pastor is linked to the concept of wealth, both in its historic Asante understanding and in its more recent Pentecostal and Christian interpretations. One way in which a pastor is recognised as being truthful is related to his or her ways of dealing with wealth; the way wealth is accumulated, consumed, distributed, and displayed publicly. In the case of pastors, this for instance relates to how and whether they act according to the principles they preach in church.

There is both a material and a spiritual side to being truthful. Realising *nokware* is therefore about being successful in both a metaphysical sense and a material sense. Pastors are successful on the one hand through proving and mediating spiritual power and on the other hand through gaining material wealth. Worldly success and wealth is linked to belief and the spiritual sphere and realising *nokware* involves both (the worldly and the other-worldly do not exclude one another). There is strong resonance between the Asante understanding of *nokware* and the Pentecostal focus on prosperity as a sign of God's blessing.

When pastors talked about or defined *nokware* they did so in a way that related both to the Asante understanding of the term and by making reference to Christianity. One pastor explained it this way: 'letting yr [your] yes be yes and no be no concerning yr private, social, financial and marital life. Yr walk and talk must synchronize.'[3] This definition very much reflects the understanding of the term outlined above, but also includes the aspects of life where one shows oneself to be a good Christian. Another pastor defined *nokware* in three senses: first, as being truthful to God; second, as being truthful to members of the church; and third, as being truthful to oneself, including members of your family.[4] This pastor relates truthfulness strongly to the religious sphere and in this way delimits the social relationships in which being truthful is most important.

Some pastors deliberately distinguished themselves from pastors who had a strong focus on prosperity in their preaching, and instead explained that prosperity came through experiencing Christ as the anointed: 'And what does the anointing? It brings yokes, it removes burdens, it brings joy and gladness and there is also prosperity within the anointing.'[5] Therefore the aim is to teach and preach about experiencing Christ and not about prosperity. The same pastor also explained that he could not go and preach in someone else's church and ask for offerings: 'I don't want somebody to go behind me and say that this man came to our church and he collected money from me.' At the same time, he stresses the principles of sowing and reaping (that I discuss below) and sees this differently as it is giving to God. What seems to be important here with regard to truthfulness is that as a pastor, he is not seen as taking other peoples' money, and there has to be a purpose in the giving, which could be to give to God or to help people in need. Yet, the ideas around *nokware* and wealth have been shaped by a history of other social groups that negotiated and claimed rights for self-determination of their accumulated wealth.

Ideas of Wealth and Social Entrepreneurs in Asante

As discussed in Chap. 2, a new group of social entrepreneurs (*akonkofoɔ*) emerged in Asante in the first half of the twentieth century. They were progressive businessmen, who represented at new type *ɔbirɛmpɔn* and 'had shaken off the constraints of the historic ideology surrounding accumulation, wealth and belief, but they were still enmeshed—as their descendants are—in the received (if modified) cultural imagery of behaving like a "big man", an *ɔbirɛmpɔn*' (McCaskie 1986a: 8).

Also, the royal *nhenkwaa* represented new ways of dealing with wealth and changing ideas around accumulating for the individual. One way was to accumulate as much and as rapidly as possible without bearing notice of the historical rules and moral principles around it; they were like 'an *ɔbirɛmpɔn* divorced from historic belief and culture' (McCaskie 1986a: 11). Similar points of criticism are being posed against charismatic pastors, as for instance the statement by the late Rev. Prof. Emeritus Kwesi A. Dickson referred to above. One issue of concern is the way 'rapid money' is (and was) seen as wealth with negative connotations or wealth that was not accumulated according to morally acceptable norms.

Another way was represented by those *nhenkwaa* who were able to adapt to the new economic circumstances and to the new holders of power. They maintained striving for wealth and status, but managed to modify their ideal to a new model *ɔbirɛmpɔn* with fewer restrictions on the use of acquired wealth as well as new cultural criteria of wealth (Arhin 1976/77; McCaskie 1986a: 12).

A point worth paying some attention to regarding the above-mentioned social groups is that they formed and challenged existing ideas around wealth in times of rapid socio-economic and political change. Their behaviour and cultural perceptions around wealth were shaped as a reaction against the Asante state's social and moral sanctions on wealth as well as the new socio-economic opportunities for attaining and consuming wealth. Inherent to this is the above-mentioned continuous tension in Asante around accumulation of wealth for the individual or the community (McCaskie 1995; Skinner 2009). This tension is also central in pastors' efforts to build themselves up as truthful pastors and in the way they are debated publically and present themselves publically.

Ideas of Wealth in Ghanaian Christianity

It is in relation to wealth, money and prosperity that charismatic pastors are criticised in public debate. As mentioned above, they are accused of stealing from the poor when imposing tithing and encouraging members to contribute financially to the church. The criticism revolves in particular around the flamboyant appearance and lifestyle of some pastors, because of which they are perceived as collecting money mainly for their own personal consumption. In order to be seen as truthful and legitimate, pastors have to show publicly not only that they are rich, but also that they share and distribute their wealth. The perceived immorality has to be overcome by showing that the money is redistributed and used for the wellbeing of the community. But they also seek to justify themselves through reformulating religious ideas around wealth. Pastors legitimate their wealth by ideologically showing that it is a sign of God's blessing and hence provide a moral acceptance of it. So they both relate to Asante experience by showing that they care for the community and do not steal from the poor, which, in an Asante context, is problematic (McCaskie 2008c: 448) and they also relate to a Christian frame of understanding that promotes an ascetic lifestyle and hence seek to re-legitimise the use and display of wealth.

I suggest that charismatic pastors' rhetoric and behaviour with regard to wealth can (also) be seen as a reaction to the mainline churches and the classical Pentecostal churches' stance on accumulating, using, and displaying wealth. Several people told me that with the emergence of the charismatic churches it had again become legitimate to gain and use wealth. In the mainline churches, there was a much more ascetic (or classical Protestant) view on wealth. Here abundant wealth and a flamboyant lifestyle were not in compliance with Christian values. These values were on the other hand characterised by 'a retreat from the world and an anti-material or "holiness" stance' (Soothill 2007: 37). Within these churches, piety was related to material asceticism (Bonsu and Belk 2010: 309).

One pastor explained how earlier on (he referred specifically to the 1980s and 1990s) being a Christian meant having a pious lifestyle, 'a lifestyle of living so simple and living a life associated with nothing, and the way you dress and talked became different from society.'[6] It is interesting that he defines this style of living as being an exception and as 'different from society' because it indicates that it was in opposition to the more general focus on wealth and money in Asante that had been prominent since the early twentieth century. Moreover, he links the mainline churches' view of wealth with ideas of money as 'the root of all evil' and continues, 'So anything that brought you so much money, they thought will bring you to evil'. In the pastor's way of explaining this, he touches upon and links the mainline churches' ideas of wealth and ideas of abundant wealth as associated with evil, which was also a topic in Asante with the rise of the anti-witchcraft cults as discussed, among others, by Austin (2003) and referred to in Chap. 2.

With the growth of the charismatic movement, this ideology was challenged. Wealth in its broadest sense was (again) something one could display publicly and it was seen as a sign of God's blessing and not as sinful; it was made spiritually legitimate to accumulate wealth.[7] The pastor referred to above points in particular to the problem that the mainline churches did not 'emphasise on the attitude by which one gets the money' and this criticism was backed up by others. Here we touch upon one of the central themes of this chapter, namely the relation between wealth and *nokware* (truthfulness). Wealth and richness is legitimate if it has been accumulated and used in a morally acceptable way, and it is moreover necessary in order to progress in life and to avoid poverty. The cultural criteria of wealth were still building on many of the same symbols prominent in colonial Asante such as big houses, cars, clothing, but also on relations to 'big' pastors abroad, and appearing in public space (on television or radio for instance).

The prosperity gospel becomes the ideological framing that is referred to when legitimising the accumulation and use of wealth. It is of particular significance that it is a religious frame of reference that is drawn upon. Referring to wealth as sign of God's blessing is a way for pastors to prove that wealth is acquired in a truthful way, but it is also contested and put into question by the more established religious elite.

Prosperity Gospel

Prosperity gospel (or faith gospel) is, in brief, about seeing wealth and richness as a sign of God's blessings (Gifford 2001: 62–65; Meyer 1998c). In Gifford's words: 'A believer has a right to the blessings of health and wealth won by Christ, and he or she can obtain these blessings merely by a positive confession of faith' (Gifford 1998: 39).[8] A common way of explaining the appeal of the charismatic churches is that people come to church to seek success in life—such as in business, marriage, education, to get a visa and travel—and to 'switch from low status to high status religious groups ... establish social and economic connections as well as meet people of similar moral or religious conviction' (Ukah 2005: 268). The focus on success and prosperity is, in other words, what makes charismatic churches attractive and as being in consonance with many people's aspirations for a modern lifestyle and material wealth (Meyer 1998c: 762).

I shall elaborate on and discuss two central ideas of the message on prosperity; namely the idea of 'giving and receiving' and the idea of 'refusal of poverty' (see also Lauterbach 2006). Before doing that I will discuss more in depth how the literature on charismatic Christianity in Africa has approached wealth. Studies of wealth and prosperity within charismatic Christianity have mainly focused on the part of the religious message that touches upon money and commodities: monetary and material wealth, gift-giving and the symbolic function of wealth in the sense that money serves as a symbol of success (Bonsu and Belk 2010; Gifford 2004; Meyer 1998b, c; van Dijk 1999). Moreover, as Haynes points out, this scholarship has emphasised wealth in the prosperity gospel as being for individual consumption rather than for redistribution in the community (Haynes 2012: 133), which is linked to the aforementioned discussion of 'making a complete break with the past' and social rupture (Meyer 1998a).

The way wealth is perceived in this scholarship is narrow in the sense that it merely looks upon wealth as money and commodities and does not take into account other less material aspects of wealth. Notwithstanding the strong rhetorical emphasis on material richness as a sign of God's blessing, I argue in the following analysis that wealth is more than money both in the religious message and in church members' and pastors' practice. I suggest to broaden out the concept of wealth in order to get a more nuanced and historicised understanding of how wealth is perceived within these churches and how practices around wealth take form. Wealth, in this understanding, also includes aspects such as people, time, institutions, and relations. This way of approaching wealth is based on the works of Guyer (1995), McCaskie (1983, 1986a, 1995), Lonsdale (1992) and Berry (1995) among others, and suggests that wealth is more than things and money. The church is understood as an arena for negotiating claims to wealth, and one's success as a pastor depends on mobilising supporters and establishing a congregation (Berry 1995: 307). In other words, wealth is also in people, in social relations and, moreover, wealth has a cultural meaning that changes over time. Wealth is closely linked to social identity and to the making of social relations since wealth is also about displaying it, claiming it, and recognising it.

However, we should not forget that prosperity gospel, as it is understood and practiced in Kumasi, is a local interpretation of a more global religious ideology, and it is through this work of interpretation that prosperity in the charismatic sense has resonance in an Asante context.

Principle of Giving and Receiving

The Christian principle of giving and receiving (sowing and reaping) is referred to again and again by pastors as the underlying rationale behind receiving the blessings of God: the more one gives in church the more one receives from God.[9] Pastors teach church members how to learn to give freely and spontaneously. One pastor said while preaching:

> God gives in the first place and we give back and it comes back multiplied. Then it becomes easy to give … We surrender things to God, submit our entire life and possessions to the Lord and it comes back to us multiplied. People who spend more time with the Lord, they get more time back to work.[10]

This principle builds on the unique relation between man and God (you give as an individual person and God gives back to you as an individual). All that members give in church is seen as something they give to God, which means that giving to the church or the pastor is the same as giving to God. This relation is what Ukah terms 'an economic transaction between believers and God' (2005: 261) mediated by the religious leadership. However, it is worth noticing that receiving the blessings of God (although this might be imaginary) would not necessarily come through the church or the pastor. So the relations of exchange are not reciprocal (at least not in an ideological sense). The language used to explain the principles of giving and receiving is often an economic one. Giving is talked about as an investment and receiving as the fruits one harvests from that investment.

But church members were not only asked by pastors to give money to God and they not only expected to get commodities in return. They were also asked to give their time and to give their loyalty. As one pastor instructed: we have to give 'our life, our time, our talents and abilities, our possessions: monies, clothes, cars, houses'.[11] Giving in church is understood broadly and this also links up to the broad definition of wealth. Time and presence can be seen as something to give, in the same way as money and other commodities. If church members give their time by being present in the church, they at the same time contribute to making the pastor look wealthy and as someone who has a large flock and who has control over people. Along the same lines, Ukah refers to members of the Redeemed Christian Church of God in Nigeria being asked to 'increase their expenditure, time, conviction and commitment in the cause of the church' (2005: 258).

Francis Afrifa, who at the time was a young independent pastor in Kumasi, was a guest preacher in the Atonsu/Gyinyase branch of Family Chapel International. In his sermon he talked about giving and ended by encouraging church attendants to pledge cement bags to finalise the construction of the church. He said:

> Noah offered. What have you given to this church? Since we started this building, how much have you given? Noah gave an offering, and God was moved. God took away curse ... Its time you spend time with God. Give time. Give money, give, give, give, give. Who gave food to the pastor at Christmas? The pastor's gift is to understand the principles of giving and receiving ... You are not travelling because you have not sown financially. You have died spiritually because you haven't spent time with God ... Give, give, give, give your time, money, *sika*, and resources. Be blessed and lifted up. He is about to favour you. Who wants to buy cement for the church? It's an opportunity to be blessed.[12]

After the sermon people got up, stood in the front of the church and pledged how many cement bags they would give. The residing pastor and his wife were the first to rise up and they offered two bags of cement (which was double from the week before where they had offered one bag, I was told). They were then prayed for by the pastor. The pastor prayed and laid his hand on everyone who had pledged cement bags while saying 'break it; it's a financial break through'. Around 20 bags of cement had been pledged. To my surprise my research assistant, who was a Catholic and had a critical attitude towards the charismatic churches, also stood up, pledged a bag of cement and received the pastor's blessing.

This event is not about a pastor collecting for individual consumption. Francis was not preaching in his own church but was, as mentioned, a guest preacher in a branch church of Family Chapel International, which was led by one of his friends.[13] The incentive for this pastor to get people to give is not so much about him getting richer in a material sense, but rather to show that by invoking the word and the power of God, he was able to make people give. By proving his ability to collect, he also shows that he is a powerful preacher, he can control people, and that is how he builds up a position as a powerful 'man of God' (*Onyame nnipa*). Moreover, it is important to note that he collected money for finalising the construction of the church. This is to the benefit of the church community and also legitimises his call for offerings.

Clearly, money plays a significant role, both as a powerful symbol of wealth and as necessary to run a church. For instance, at a Sunday service at Family Chapel International, church members and leaders gave money to the musicians who were responsible for the worship. They put notes on the musicians' foreheads or in a basket. At the end of one service, the head pastor rose from his big chair at the side of the stage and threw a bunch of cedi notes at the musicians.[14] This flashing of money and material wealth can both be interpreted as religious re-legitimisation of possessing wealth and individual consumption (in contrast to the values of the mainline churches) and at the same time as the use of money to show recognition to specific people.

For our understanding of the prosperity gospel, it is therefore fruitful to link the focus on money in churches to the longer historical trend of capitalisation and monetisation in Ghanaian society and more particularly in Asante, where cash was required for consumption (McCaskie 2000: 132–133), and at the same time recognise that control over people and over institutions also plays a role in the ways in which pastors build up and display wealth. There is, moreover, a connection between material richness and spiritual richness. The display of wealth is a way to prove one's spiritual capabilities and access to spiritual power.

Refusal of Poverty

The idea of 'refusal of poverty', as expressed by charismatic pastors, is that no one is destined to be poor ('you don't need to be poor'), and that by being with the right people and 'claiming what belongs to you', one can escape poverty (see also Gifford 2001). Victor Osei, founder and leader of Family Chapel International, said at a church programme entitled 'Break in, Break free, Break through': 'To break in, is to take everything that belongs to you. You need to take it, you need to do something actively.'[15]

In this statement, he clearly calls for personal advancement, progress, and success and links this to personal action. To 'take everything that belongs to you' does not necessarily imply that one does not share or redistribute, but rather that it is seen as morally acceptable to be successful and to have wealth. The statement is also linked to the idea of 'refusal of poverty' and to the Asante concept *anibue* (enlightenment) (Skinner 2009). Victor Osei and other pastors talked about the importance of knowing the Bible and at the same time the importance of working hard to achieve success.

On another occasion, Victor Osei talked about the problem of having the wrong 'spirit' or mentality. He shouted:

> I can do all things, I can do all things, I can do all things, I can do all things. I can do, because you are 'I can do' person. The problem with many Christians is, that they depend on lack. Most people are programmed to fail in life. You are programmed to fail and your friends, they will cause you more failure. Walk with 'I can do' people. Move from area of lack and change to possibility. Change your mentality. People work for it ... If you sit there you will die. People work hard for money. Success is like a beautiful woman. If you tell her, it won't change her. You have to convince money to be at your side. Success brings forth success. Richer gets richer and poorer gets poorer. Make friends with money. Seek it. If you are stupid your money will be taken from you.[16]

Victor Osei talks about attitude and mentality with regard to being successful and about associating oneself with the right kind of people. Getting rich is not only about praying, going to church, and 'sowing financially', but also about one's mentality and about being with the right people. It is an active refusal of being poor. While I was visiting the church in 2005, Victor Osei was offering classes every Tuesday evening on how to start a small business. Being from an elite family himself, and with a father who had been a wealthy businessman in Kumasi and closely related to the Asantehene, he had a flair for wealth and was discretely associated with the Asante aristocracy, and hence with wealth and power.

The refusal of poverty and striving for progress can also be linked to the above-mentioned tension in Asante between accumulation for oneself and for the community. As Skinner explains with regard to mass education in 1950s Asante, there was not necessarily a 'conflict between the material advancement of individuals and the collective improvement of their hometown' (2009: 487). In the same way, accumulation for oneself, as preached in charismatic churches, does not at the conceptual level imply neglect of the community. Many pastors talked about church members' responsibilities vis-à-vis their families and hometowns. One pastor explained how church members living abroad send money and commodities to the church and to their hometowns: 'They also help their communities and village they came from because God has blessed them, they put at least something in their community to show God's love for them and also to prove that I am a good citizen.'[17] It would be pushing the argument too far to suggest that the ideas around wealth as expressed in charismatic Christianity in Asante seek to overcome the tension between the self-interest and the community, as Skinner has argued with regard to mass education (2009: 492). The point is rather that this tension is reflected in the way pastors talk about and relate to wealth and is a prominent part of the public criticism of charismatic pastors.

Another aspect of refusing of poverty is the role of networks and social relations that Victor Osei alludes to when talking about 'being with the right people.' A pastor in Kumasi talked about the value of relationships in this way: 'I always try to keep relationships because money is a weapon, so is also a relationship, a godly relationship is also a weapon. God can reveal it to one person, who will stand and pray for me.'[18] In this way, a relationship serves as a way to strengthen a pastor's position and build up wealth. Another point is that people not only engage in relationships and exchange within the church but, as Berry has argued in a different context, 'people join social clubs, churches or Muslim brotherhoods, cooperatives and political parties, *and* concurrently maintain ties to kin, affines or members of their ancestral communities' (Berry 1995: 309). People (members and pastors) are not only members of a charismatic church, but are involved in multiple networks at the same time, a discussion I will return to in subsequent chapters.

Success, richness, and avoiding poverty require spiritual development and maturity, which implies 'getting to know God better'. Many pastors put great emphasis on spiritual growth that, for instance, requires discipline and persistence when it comes to reading the Bible, praying and fasting, worshipping, and giving. Attaining spiritual growth is often talked about in a management-inspired language. One pastor, for instance, advised people to set goals and visions for their spiritual life and to have a set calendar for praying and reading the Bible in order to achieve the set goal. The 'refusal of poverty' is presented as a process that involves claiming richness on the one hand and as requiring knowledge and a change of mentality on the other.

Fake Pastors and Spiritual Swindlers

Fake pastors or spiritual swindlers are common figures in Ghanaian public debate as well as in Ghanaian popular culture.[19] Being fake is often mentioned in criticism of charismatic pastors, but it is also a category that is used when discussing traditional healers and prophets (Shipley 2009). The following headlines of newspaper articles are only a few among many: 'Eliminate false prophets in society—vice president' (*Ghana News Agency*, 30 January 2011), 'False pastors on the increase' (*Daily Guide*, 4 June 2011), 'Faith healers vow to confront fake pastors' (*Ghana News Agency*, 16 November 2009).[20]

The general points of criticism are that charismatic pastors lack the right Christian foundation that they are self-proclaimed, have no official biblical training, and are under no overall regulation. In a series of four newspaper articles entitled 'Beware of false prophets (I–IV)', Joyce Aryee[21] writes about how to identify these men: 'If their predictions come true or they revise them to fit what has already happened?', 'Do they teach a small section of the Bible and neglect the rest?', 'Does the teaching contradict what the Bible says about God?', 'Do their teachings and practices glorify themselves or God?' and 'Do the teachings promote hostility toward other Christians?'. She then explains that pastors who are more concerned with their predictions being realised than with 'what is in the heart' are false because they are mainly concerned with their own personal progress. Some false pastors might appear good on the outside, but 'on the inside they are greedy and self-indulgent.' Some false pastors might have begun 'their ministry in sincerity, truth and genuine faith in Christ', but again because of pride and greed, they become false pastors or 'instruments of Satan'. She gives a particular advice on how to test false pastors with regard to money: 'see whether they insist on large amounts for their personal use and whether they handle all finances with integrity and responsibility. Some pastors and leaders refuse to account for finances—running the church like a personal business entity' and refers to 1 Timothy 3:3 ('not a drunkard, not violent but gentle, not quarrelsome, not a lover of money') and 1 Peter 5:1–2 ('shepherd the flock of God that is among you, exercising oversight, not under compulsion, but willingly, as God would have you; not for shameful gain, but eagerly') among others. She refers extensively to the Bible while deciphering how to identify fake pastors, but there are also distinct references to the concepts of wealth and *nokware* as well as the individual-community tension. There is strong focus on both knowledge of the word of God and truthfulness with regard to how one accumulates wealth. In her presentation, Aryee associates fakery with certain personal traits such as greed and pride, as well as a lack of knowledge and sincerity.[22]

Common tropes in public accusations of being a false pastor are sexual abuse, misuse of money, and accumulation of fast money. The idea of fakery is also a recurrent theme in internal debates within charismatic churches and in the sector as such. As will be discussed below, proving to be a 'genuine' pastor is important in terms of distinguishing oneself from fake pastors, and it is moreover a way to authenticate one's access to spiritual power.

Internal Debates and Disputes

In a booklet entitled 'Genuine or Counterfeit—Pastor/prophet', two Kumasi-based charismatic pastors address the downfall of some charismatic pastors and relate this to the distinction between true and false pastors.[23]

They write:

> We are living in days when the church has experienced a rise in carnality and spiritual disease. There has been highly dramatic, highly publicized moral features among a number of very prominent leaders of churches. Their fall have been amplified by the mass media [...] This brings the work of God's Minister into disrepute. And many think all pastors are the same, they all fail and fall short of expectation and there is no need to waste time in Church and listen to these blind leaders. However, in reality, **all Pastors are not the same. Some are good and some are fake.** (Owusu-Ansah 1999: 2)

They draw on the same categorisation as used in the public debate and also refer to morality as a criterion for distinction. Interestingly, they too establish a link between being 'counterfeit' and focusing too much on achieving wealth:

> There are many reasons why people enter into the ministry. Some rush into it because of financial gains, they think the work is now very lucrative, so it is good to enter for you will get money quick ... [They] work to please themselves and move heaven and earth to achieve their **canal objectives, to get wealth fast. They are counterfeit ministers** ... (Owusu-Ansah 1999: 7)

At the same time, and following the doctrine on prosperity, they see riches as an award from God, achieved through prayers:

> Pray to have financial freedom by giving to God. Many men of God are poor because they don't give to God ... Financial freedom begins with scriptual giving. Luke 6:38 says, 'give', and if we increase our tithe, He will increase our financial reward, it shall be given unto you ... Don't rob God ... If you give, you allow God to create employment or secure your job. (Owusu-Ansah 1999: 32–33)

As discussed above, this is the essence of the prosperity gospel. Richness is a sign of God's blessing and one receives richness by giving abundantly. Moreover, in these pastors' understanding there is no contradiction between emphasising that one has to give to God to get wealth in return and being a 'true' pastor. The distinction between 'true' and 'false' pastors is connected to morality (whether pastors live up to Christian values themselves) and is related to one's attitude towards wealth (are they attracted by fast wealth). Whereas pastors' collections of tithes and offerings in churches are often what gives them the reputation of stealing people's money and being false, this is not where the distinction lies in their own perception.[24]

The distinction 'true/false' is central. The contraposition is defined in absolute terms and often with references to Biblical texts, but the social process of defining oneself as a 'true' pastor or defining others as 'false' is an ongoing open process. Being recognised as a 'true' pastor within the religious community is a way to legitimatise a position as a pastor and as a public figure. The categorisation of 'fake' and 'true' pastors is moreover linked to verifying the source of pastors' spiritual power. If they fail in their careers as pastors or act immorally, that is seen as a sign that they did not have access to spiritual power or that they have used evil power (see Chap. 5).

The focus on fake pastors in charismatic churches is not a new phenomenon. In internal church reports from the 1980s, the role of pastors is discussed and in particular their 'misbehaviour' with regard to administering funds and to sexual morality. On 21 January 1983, the National Council of Pentecostal Churches issued a letter to all government departments, religious organisations, and chiefs, among others, warning against false pastors.

The letter, entitled 'Pastoral clearance—Spiritual church leaders/impersonators', is a warning to the public about 'spiritual swindlers' that are said to be an increasing phenomenon as the number of 'Spiritual churches' had been growing. At the same time, the National Council of Pentecostal Churches requested anyone to contact the council to check out the background of a pastor.[25] 'Spiritual Swindlers' are thought of as cheating people in spiritual matters. They are people who disguise themselves, but do not live up to the 'standards' or who do not act as they speak.

Accusation of fakery has also been a recurrent theme when explaining internal church conflicts and disputes. In a circular from 1985 to branch churches (assemblies) the Church of Christ (Spiritual Movement)[26] accounts for the suspension of some of the church's pastors and elders. In the document, which is titled 'House cleaning and accountability in the Church of Christ (SM)'[27] it is explained how the conduct of certain pastors has discredited and brought trouble to the church. The measures taken to overcome these problems are also outlined. As the title indicates, these measures are seen as an attempt to 'clean' the church from 'diabolic and inconsiderate souls'. There is a clear link in the report between the spiritual position of pastors (as for instance 'bad elements in the robes of Pastors') and the kind of offences committed (misuse of church funds, adultery and the like). The pastors in question are characterised as being diabolic and evil, hence false pastors, and this is linked to their 'clandestine activities' and 'reckless misappropriations' of church funds. There is a spiritual explanation of the act of misusing funds or a relation between spiritual positions and how money is acquired and used.

The report on senior Pastor J. Owusu-Ansah in the same document is an example of this:

> In 1964 he conived with some Pastors of the church among them was his brother Pastor D. O. Agyeman and brought division in the Kumasi Fanti Newtown Assembly of the church whereby a lot of the church members left and have since joined other churches. Pastor Owusu-Ansah convinced some of the members and parted with them to form his own church for his selfish gains but flopped totally. He sued the Prophet of an amount of ₤4894 (Four thousand, eight hundred and ninety-four pounds) which he alleged was their allowance.
>
> In 1983 he was transferred to Asonomaso where he embezzled the proceeds of this annual District harvest and instigated the members of the District to help him to break away and form his own church by name of

Reformed Church of Christ (SM) which leaked out and therefore flopped. Letter heads were even printed to this effect.

In 1984 he was transferred to Kumasi Central to join other Pastors there as a check on his activities, but here again he conspired with other Pastors and misled the New Spiritual Council to dismiss two Pastors who did not conform to their mischievous acts. The Pastors are Pastor Forson and Pastor Kofi Methews.[28]

The report comments on this pastor's numerous attempts to create a church on his own and how this failed. The failure is explained by his wish for 'selfish gains', and this questions his genuineness as a pastor. Moreover, he is accused of attempting to steal money from the church. Other reasons for suspending pastors and elders mentioned in this particular report were 'corruption naked', 'sexual immorality', 'divorce', 'indiscipline', and 'disobedience'.

The document moreover contains a description of false pastors and how they use the position as a pastor as a kind of protection and false status:

It is our burden and conviction that it is and should not be compulsory for anyone to force himself to be a PASTOR. Nor should anyone be allowed to be sheltered merely by the wearing of the priestly gown or sacerdotal robes nor should we tolerate or encourage or make it easy for them to parade as such. It should not [be] easy or pardonable for crooks and criminals to be allowed to use the gown and [cloister] to ruin or discredit the high office or calling of the cross of Christ bought by or paid for in or with the precious BLOOD OF JESUS, the ETERNAL LAMB OF GOD.[29]

The above examples show that accusations of being a false pastor have been recurrent since the emergence and growth of charismatic churches. But there seems to be a change with regard to the content of the accusations. In the citations above, morality (around family life and sexuality, for instance) as well as the misuse of church funds were prominent. Today the accusations are largely centred on false pastors that steal church members' money, misguide people and take people's time so they cannot work and contribute to the growth of the country. A theme that runs through all is the distinction between fast money and legitimate wealth and the relation of this to spiritual power. Moreover, both types of accusations are not concerned with doctrinal issues, but about being a true pastor or a false pastor.

These distinctions are in some ways similar to the accusations of witchcraft that Austin discusses in relation to the increase in cocoa production in the early twentieth century; 'witch hunting was one of the ways in which chiefs and communities were able to check the power of wealthy people' (2003: 19). Increase in wealth of certain individuals also led to the rise in witchcraft accusations as well as anti-witchcraft cults. Some suspected those who acquired wealth from the expanding cocoa and timber industry to use witchcraft to acquire that wealth, and at the same time those who became wealthy used the anti-witchcraft shrines to protect their wealth from other people. In the same way, pastors who attain wealth can be accused of accumulating fast money and through this their access to spiritual power can be questioned, and they are associated with evil power rather than the power of the Holy Ghost.

Pastors, Wealth, and Truthfulness

Pastors and churches also attempt to promote community wellbeing. To show and express concern for the community (both the church and the larger community one operates in) is important in order to be seen as being legitimate. This argument was used in a petition letter in an attempt by the Bantama branch of The Christ Apostolic Church of Ghana (Ashanti region) to become an independent church. Their explanation for this was built up around an argument that they were mainly collecting money for the head branch in Accra and not getting any funds in return to use for the development of their own community. They wrote:

> 2. Power belongs to the people and we will not sit down for only Nine (9) people who call themselves Church Executives to spend all our money leaving the church poor and handicapped.
> 3. For 72 years now, all our local funds even including Sunday Collections are sent to Accra and never comes back to us for development. Most of our Churches in Ashanti are broken down, many are in classrooms and others under thatched roofed houses. No schools, hospitals or any development that would help improve the community.
> 4. Every year alone the Ashanti Region alone sends more than Five Million cedis (c5,000,000.00) to Accra. Last year, we sent Six Million— (c6,000,000.00) and above to Accra. Out of this, only c400,000.00 was given as impress for the smooth running of the 67 local assemblies scattered throughout Ashanti. Last year alone the Executives collected c37,000,000.00 and as at now, no one knows how the money was expended ...[30]

This letter was issued as part of a larger conflict between the church leadership and the Bantama branch of the church (Adomako-Mensah 2010; Larbi 2001). Without getting into the details of that conflict, the letter shows how money and the use of wealth are a means to delegitimise someone's authority over the church. Specific reference is made to social services that benefit church members and society more generally and this is opposed to church leaders collecting money for themselves without accounting for its use.

Although charismatic pastors have a more outspoken focus on wealth and prosperity, there are also explicit attempts to strike the balance between promoting the individual and contributing to the wellbeing of society. One example of this was a convention entitled 'Anti-armed robbery fasting and prayers' organised by Pastor Joshua Kas-Vorsah in Daban, Kumasi. The theme of the convention was to fight armed robbery, corruption and road accidents through prayer, issues that were perceived as being impediments to the wellbeing of society (see Fig. 3.1).

The theme of the prayer programme was different from other programmes that would (at least in their titles) focus more on individual suc-

Fig. 3.1 Banner announcing prayer meeting, Ahodwo roundabout, Kumasi

cess, as for instance the programme entitled 'Break in, Break free, Break through' referred to above. There are many more examples of pastors who present and promote themselves as helpers of the community, for instance, by setting up vocational schools, giving sponsorships for education, and the like. *The Ghanaian Chronicle*, for instance, reports on 22 November 2010 that one church (The Resurrection Power & Living Bread Ministries) in Kumasi gave food and second-hand clothes to the King Jesus Charity Home as 'part of annual policy to reach out to the poor and the destitute in society.' In the article, the pastor explains that the church was particularly concerned about children and that the donation was part of the church's social intervention activities.[31] Giving charity has historically been an important part of churches' role in society and seen in this perspective, it might not be surprising that charismatic churches are engaged in social programmes. It is nevertheless important to point out, because charismatic churches are known for their huge attention on prosperity gospel and individual accumulation, both in public debates and scholarship.

It is not only in relation to how pastors appear to the outside world that they are concerned with being truthful and caring for the wellbeing of their community. One pastor explained that while collecting money in his newly started church (for buying chairs) he hesitated to ask people to donate, because he knew some people would go and sell, for example, their cell phones to be able to contribute. But collecting for the community is legitimate. He explained that his own wife sold her phone and bought chairs for the church and later received a new cell phone as a gift. This was presented as an example of 'sowing and reaping'. Still, the pastor found it problematic to 'use the Bible to extract money from people' and made a distinction between making a voluntary contribution in church for a common purpose and then 'go about begging your church members, please give me money, anybody you pray for "pay money," anybody you interact with "pay money" ... ethically it is wrong'.[32]

Another pastor, referred to above, explained his church's practice with regard to collecting tithes:

> We record everything on cards, and then, into the computer. We also make accounts to the church and, sometimes, to the government to ensure transparency. This church does not belong to me even though I started it. It is for all of us. If you want to progress, you have to be accountable to the people. People would see through you that you are not transparent and after some

time, they will leave the church. People are still with us because they see genuineness.[33]

In the way this pastor outlines how they account for the money collected in church, he emphasises the need for transparency and seeing the church as a collective rather than a private enterprise. And being transparent with regard to how much money is collected and how it is used is linked to being genuine and the ability to keeping a stable and loyal flock.

Discussion

By bringing in broader concepts of wealth and truthfulness in the analysis of pastoral careers and relating these to the ideology of charismatic Christianity on prosperity as well as the schism between true and false, I have intended to broaden our understanding of these ideas (as well as the making and re-making of them) in African charismatic Christianity.

One argument has been that wealth is perceived and engaged with as more than money in the charismatic churches studied in this book. Wealth also lies in people, in social relations, in time, and not the least, wealth is about displaying it. Moreover, wealth and the way it is accumulated and redistributed enables pastors to prove truthfulness and hence gain legitimacy.

What is at stake is the legitimisation of pastors, and this is achieved in relation to how they talk about wealth and how they act and build it up. Moreover, wealth is strongly linked to the notion of poverty and how to avoid and refuse poverty. It is a question of morality but at the same time relates to how this morality is reflected in social practice.

The church and religious ideology can be understood as an arena for negotiating claims to wealth, where one's success is dependent on the ability to mobilise supporters. This is in line with former ways of claiming wealth (Berry 1995: 307). Berry argues that, historically, access to wealth or resources was linked to social identity and therefore 'the valuation of goods and services was inextricably bound up with the negotiation of social identities and allegiances' (Berry 1995: 308).

In order to become a truthful pastor, one needs to live up to a certain morality on the one hand and on the other hand prove to be a legitimate religious leader by being able to accumulate and display wealth publicly. This is the delicate balance between individual and community that charismatic, small 'big men' seek to establish, to borrow the words of Gyekye (1987).

Notes

1. Sections of this chapter have earlier been published in Lauterbach ([2009] 2006).
2. For a discussion of a similar concept see Lonsdale's (1992) discussion of the Kikuyu expression 'say and do' (*kuuga na gwika*) that implies that 'authority comes from preaching what he commendably practices' (1992: 337). Lonsdale moreover discusses changes in perceptions to wealth caused by monetisation of the economy.
3. Personal communication, Francis Afrifa, 12 March 2013.
4. Interview with Seth Osei-Kuffour, Kumasi, 18 August 2013 (conducted by James Boafo).
5. Interview Francis Afrifa, 13 September 2005, Kumasi.
6. Interview with Edward Otu, Kumasi, 22 February 2005.
7. See Ukah (2003, 2005) for a thorough analysis of how this ideological change has taken place within the Redeemed Christian Church of God in Nigeria.
8. The origins of the faith gospel are ascribed to American evangelists such as Kenneth Copeland, Oral Roberts and T. S. Osborn (Gifford 2001: 62–63).
9. On the theological background of this principle, see Asamoah-Gyadu (2005a). On giving see also Maxwell (2006a: 149).
10. Evening service, Harvest Chapel International, head branch, 7 December 2004.
11. Evening service, Harvest Chapel International, head branch, 7 December 2004.
12. Sermon at Family Chapel International, Atonsu/Gyinyase branch, 20 February 2005.
13. Making special programmes where external pastors are invited to preach is a very common practice in charismatic churches.
14. Family Chapel International, Sunday service, 21 August 2005. This is not unique to churches, but a common practice in Ghana and elsewhere in Africa.
15. Family Chapel International, Father's Cathedral, 21 February 2005.
16. Family Chapel International, Father's Cathedral, 21 August 2005.
17. Interview with Edward Otu, Kumasi, 22 February 2005.
18. Interview with Francis Afrifa, Kumasi, 13 September 2005.

19. The idea of false pastors and prophets is not unique to Ghana, but is widely found in African societies. Moreover, it is a well-known theme in the Bible.
20. See Shipley (2009) for an analysis of charismatic pastors and comedians in Ghana and the fear of fakery.
21. Joyce Aryee is a Ghanaian businesswoman, politician and former minister under Rawlings. She was Chief Executive Officer of The Ghana Chamber of Mines, received the African Female Business Leader of the Year Award for 2009, and is the founder and Executive Director of the para-church organisation Salt & Light Ministries based in Accra.
22. 'Beware of false prophets (1),' *Ghanaian Chronicle Online*, 9 September 2011, 'Beware of false prophets (II),' *Ghanaian Chronicle Online*, 16 September 2011, 'Beware of false prophets (III),' *Ghanaian Chronicle Online*, 23 September 2011, 'Salt & Light: Beware of false prophets (IV),' *Ghanaian Chronicle Online*, 30 September 2011.
23. The authors are the founders of a Kumasi-based church called 'Great Expectations Ministries International' that has branches in Ghana and Great Britain. The authors' merits as pastors are listed at the back of the book: 'They are seasoned international preachers. They have travelled extensively in the United States of America and have ministered in many cities there. They were used tremendously of God in Savannah Georgia to meet spiritual needs of both whites and blacks... They also preach in Conferences, Seminars, and Churches throughout Ghana, Nigeria, Great Britain and other places. They broadcast on two F.M. Stations Kapital Radio 97.1 and Garden City Radio 92.1 in Kumasi, Ghana.' The booklet deals with various aspects of pastorship.
24. Note also the reference to getting money quickly. Here this is a distinction between 'quick money' and 'slow money.' See also Lindhardt (2008).
25. ARG 2/30/2/1/1–2, 'Pastoral clearance-Spiritual church leaders/impersonators,' letter from Rev. Dr. J. K. Ohene, Secretary General of National Council of Pentecostal Churches, 21 January 1983.
26. The Church of Christ Spiritual Movement was established in 1958 by John Kojo Sarfo Mensah, http://cocsmyf.webs.com/ (accessed 28 March 2014).

27. ARG 2/30/2/1/2 (109), 'Circular to all assemblies' from The Church of Christ (Spiritual Movement) signed by the Secretary General, the National Chairman and the Life Trustee, 7 July 1985.
28. ARG 2/30/2/1/2 (109), 'Circular to all assemblies' from The Church of Christ (Spiritual Movement) signed by the Secretary General, the National Chairman and the Life Trustee, 7 July 1985.
29. ARG 2/30/2/1/2 (109), 'Circular to all assemblies' from The Church of Christ (Spiritual Movement) signed by the Secretary General, the National Chairman and the Life Trustee, 7 July 1985.
30. ARG 2/30/2/2 (169) 'Petition/Resolution', Christ Apostolic Church, Regional Office, Bantama, Kumasi, 2 June 1989. The Christ Apostolic Church of Ghana is a classical Pentecostal church founded in 1917 by Peter Anim.
31. http://www.modernghana.com/news/305230/1/resurrection-power-amp-living-bread-ministries-giv.html (accessed December 2011).
32. Interview with Francis Afrifa, Kumasi, 13 September 2005.
33. Interview with Victor Osei, Kumasi, 3 February 2005.

References

Adomako-Mensah, P. (2010). *The growth of the Christ apostolic church international (CACI), Ghana from 1980–2008.* BA thesis in theology, Kwame Nkrumah University of Science and Technology, Kumasi.

Arhin, K. (1976/77). The pressure of cash and its political consequences in Asante in the colonial period. *Journal of African Studies, 3*(4), 453–468.

Asamoah-Gyadu, J. K. (2005a). *African Charismatics. Current developments within independent indigenous pentecostalism in Ghana.* Leiden: Brill.

Austin, G. (2003, May 8). *Moneylending and witchcraft: The moral economy of accumulation in colonial Asante.* Paper presented for the Modern Economic History Seminar, LSE.

Berry, S. (1995). Stable prizes, unstables values: Some thoughts on monetization and the meaning of transactions in West African economies. In J. Guyer (Ed.), *Money matters. Instability, values and social payments in the modern history of West African communities.* Portsmouth: Heinemann.

Bonsu, S. K., & Belk, R. W. (2010). Marketing a new African God: Pentecostalism and material salvation in Ghana. *International Journal of Nonprofit and Voluntary Sector Marketing, 15,* 305–323.

Comaroff, J., & Comaroff, J. (2000). Millennial capitalism: First thoughts on a second coming. *Public Culture, 12*(2), 291–343.

Gerth, H. H., & Wright Mills, C. (Eds.) (1991). *From max weber. Essays in sociology*. London: Routledge.

Gifford, P. (1998). *African Christianity. Its public role*. London: Hurst & Company.

Gifford, P. (2001). The complex provenance of some elements of African Pentecostal theology. In A. Corton & R. Marshall-Fratani (Eds.), *Between babel and Pentecost. Transnational Pentecostalism in African and Latin America*. Bloomington and Indianapolis: Indiana University Press.

Gifford, P. (2004). *Ghana's new Christianity. Pentecostalism in a globalising African economy*. London: Hurst & Company.

Guyer, J. I. (1995). Wealth in people, wealth in things—Introduction. *Journal of African History*, 36(1), 83–90.

Gyekye, K. (1987). *An essay on African philosophical thought. The Akan conceptual scheme*. Cambridge: Cambridge University Press.

Haynes, N. (2012). Pentecostalism and the morality of money: Prosperity, inequality, and religious sociality on the Zambian Copperbelt. *Journal of the Royal Anthropological Institute*, 18(1), 123–139.

Lambek, M. (2002). General introduction. In M. Lambek (Ed.), *A reader in the anthropology of religion*. Malden, MA: Blackwell Publishing.

Larbi, E. K. (2001). *Pentecostalism. The eddies of Ghanaian Christianity*. Accra: Centre for Pentecostal and Charismatic Studies.

Lauterbach, K. (2006 [published 2009]). Wealth and worth: Pastorship and neo-Pentecostalism in Kumasi. *Ghana Studies*, 9, 91–121.

Lindhardt, M. (2008, February 27–29). *More than just money. The faith gospel and occult economies in contemporary Tanzania*. Paper presented at the Ph.D. workshop 'Religion and Public Moral Debate in Africa, Copenhagen.

Lonsdale, J. (1992). The moral economy of mau mau: Wealth, poverty and civic virtue in kikuyu political thought. In B. Berman & J. Lonsdale (Eds.), *Unhappy valley: Conflict in Kenya and Africa*. London: James Currey.

Maxwell, D. (2006a). *African gifts of the spirit. Pentecostalism & the rise of a Zimbabwean transnational religious movement*. Oxford: James Currey.

McCaskie, T. C. (1983). Accumulation, wealth and belief in Asante history. I. To the close of the nineteenth century. *Africa*, 53(1), 23–43. .

McCaskie, T. C. (1986a). Accumulation: Wealth and belief in Asante history: II the twentieth century. *Africa*, 56(1), 3–23.

McCaskie, T. C. (1986b). Komfo Anokye of Asante: Meaning, history and philosophy in an African society. *Journal of African History*, 27, 315–339.

McCaskie, T. C. (1995). *State and society in pre-colonial Asante*. Cambridge: Cambridge University Press.

McCaskie, T. C. (2000). *Asante identities: History and modernity in an African village 1850–1950*. International African Institute, London: Edinburgh University Press.

McCaskie, T. C. (2008a). *Akwantemfi*–'In mid-journey': An Asante shrine today and its clients. *Journal of Religion in Africa, 38*(1), 1–24.

McCaskie, T. C. (2008c). Gun culture in Kumasi. *Africa, 78*(3), 433–454.

Meyer, B. (1998a). 'Make a complete break with the past', memory and post-colonial modernity in Ghanaian Pentecostalist discourse. *Journal of Religion in Africa, 28*(3), 316–349.

Meyer, B. (1998b). The power of money: Politics, occult forces, and Pentecostalism in Ghana. *African Studies Review, 41*(3), 15–37.

Meyer, B. (1998c). Commodities and the power of prayer: Pentecostalist attitudes towards consumption in contemporary Ghana. *Development and Change, 29*(4), 751–776.

Owusu-Ansah, K. & B. (1999). *Genuine or counterfeit pastors/prophets*. Greatline Publications.

Shipley, J. W. (2009). Comedians, pastors, and the miraculous agency of charisma in Ghana. *Cultural Anthropology, 24*(3), 523–552.

Skinner, K. (2009). 'It brought some kind of neatness to mankind': Mass literacy, community development and democracy in 1950s Asante. *Africa, 79*(4), 479–499.

Soothill, J. E. (2007). *Gender, social change and spiritual power. Charismatic Christianity in Ghana*. Brill: Leiden.

Ukah, A. (2003). *The Redeemed Christian Church of God (RCCG), Nigeria. Local Identities and Global Processes in African Pentecostalism*. Doctoral thesis, University of Bayreuth, Bayreuth.

Ukah, A.F.K. (2005). "Those who trade with god never lose": The economics of Pentecostal activism in Nigeria. In T. Falola (Ed.), *Christianity and social change in Africa. Essays in honor of J.D.Y. peel*. Durham, NC: Caroliba Academic Press.

van Dijk, R. (1999). The Pentecostal gift: Ghanaian charismatic churches and the moral innocence of the global economy. In R. Fardon, W. van Binsbergen, & R. van Dijk (Eds.), *Modernity on a shoestring. Dimensions of modernization, consumption and development in Africa and beyond*. Leiden and London: EIDOS.

Weber, M. ([1930] 2001). *The protestant ethic and the spirit of capitalism*. London and New York: Routledge.

Wiredu, K. (1998). The concept of truth in the Akan language. In P. H. Coetzee & A. P. J. Roux (Eds.), *The African philosophy reader*. London and New York: Routledge.

CHAPTER 4

The Craft of Pastorship

This chapter is about the craft of pastorship. It analyses the internal dynamics of pastorship and discusses how one becomes a pastor and how such a position is authorised, legitimised, and stabilised. More concretely, it looks at the pastoral calling and its social approval, the training of young pastors, the work that pastors are doing, as well as the relationship between pastor and congregation. In this analysis, I approach pastorship both as profession and as destiny. This implies that pastorship is a career trajectory that requires training and certain skills and at the same time a trajectory one engages in because of a calling from God. This duality involves formal church leadership as well as the personification of spiritual power. This and the following chapter unfold the argument that pastors build up authority and stabilise their positions by engaging both in processes of formalisation and the performance of spiritual power. Moreover, a successful pastor is perceived as a complete pastor in the sense that completeness invokes an idea of performing in different spheres at the same time.

Before turning to the closer description and analysis of the internal dynamics of pastorship, I will briefly reiterate the point that religious experts have historically held a specific position in Asante society and that charismatic pastors in many ways draw on this history when building up and legitimising their positions as pastors. In this, they have to show access to the spiritual realm and thereby spiritual power. One way of showing this is through the display of wealth and the performance of knowledge and also by showing the ability to perform miracles. This is discussed further in Chap. 5.

Pastoral Calling

A divine calling (God's calling—*onyame frɛ*) is a central element in how pastors narrate their pastoral careers. Many had received a calling through either a vision or a dream, through which God talked to them and called them to work for him. In his study of the careers of pastors and prophets in Winneba, Wyllie finds that pastors in classical Pentecostal churches entered pastoral careers mostly after having been actively involved in church affairs for some time. Leaders of the AICs, on the other hand, entered into ministry after having received a calling through a dream or a vision (Wyllie 1974: 191). Similar to the prophets and leaders of the AICs, the charismatic pastors dealt with in this book narrated their engagement in a pastoral trajectory as a divine calling that manifested through prophecies, visions, and dreams. For some it required being in close connection with God and being open, and for others it was something they tried to ignore or postpone. One young man, who was not yet a pastor, said: 'I am still hoping and praying that one day I will hear the call. I would only know if I got into a close relationship with God and humble myself so that he talks to me.'[1] By putting emphasis on becoming a pastor as something that was chosen by God, the young pastors added an element of predetermination and perceived their pastoral careers as a destiny. Another young man, who had received a calling but not yet become a pastor, explained:

> Becoming a man of God is not for me to decide. I have been seeing myself in dreams. I have those dreams almost every night. I sometimes dream of healing people, ministering to people ... I tell pastor about it and he tells me God has purposed it for my life, but I should not rush into it. I have to wait for God.[2]

Understanding a religious career as destiny is not unique to Christian pastors. In his analysis of the career of a shrine priest in present-day Kumasi, McCaskie (2008a) shows how becoming a priest (*ɔkɔmfoɔ*) is understood as part of one's destiny and entails engaging on a 'path' or a 'journey'. This is, moreover, strongly linked to the Asante '[o]ntological idea of shaped destiny or individual fate (*nkrabea*)' (McCaskie 1992: 230). According to Gyekey, the Akan concept of destiny (*nkrabea*[3]) is experiential in the sense that destiny can be seen 'in life itself' (Gyekye 1987: 106). Also, Wiredu argues that what is particular about the Akan idea of fate is not only the notion of predestination but also 'the personal directness and individual immediacy of the doctrine of fate and, further, in the sincerity and practical seriousness with which it is entertained in the day-to-day life of our people' (Wiredu 1980: 18). In the Akan understanding, destiny is not only an abstract idea, but also something that God communicates to each person individually.

These ideas of destiny and a path in life are reflected in pastors' experiences and narrations of their pastoral callings. They oftentimes referred to concrete events like specific occasions and physical places where God spoke to them and they received their pastoral calling. The parallels and resonance in ideas of pastoral calling, destiny, and fate between prophets and traditional priests on the one hand and charismatic pastors on the other suggest that the charismatic pastors build on concepts that are locally and historically embedded at the same time as they refer to a Christian God as the source of their callings.

Typologies of Pastoral Calling

Some visions and dreams did not only include a calling to become a pastor, but also indicated to the aspiring person what direction his or her career would take. Based on the young pastors' narrations it is possible to distinguish between different types of calling.[4] One such type is defined as a '*global calling*'. As one pastor explained, 'I think part of my calling is a global. It's something that I think that God has given me that in my little way that I can also contribute to the Christian world.'[5] Others explained that they have a calling to evangelise among the citizens of a particular nation. Many of these pastors travelled a lot, had many contacts with charismatic churches in other parts of the world (mainly the USA and Europe), and were invited to preach in these places. A variation of this type of calling is the '*diaspora calling*'. One example of this is a pastor in Copenhagen who explained that his calling from God was a calling to gather Ghanaians in Denmark and bring them back to 'the gospel'. This type of calling is both linked to a sense of belonging to a global Christian community as well as to pastors' work among Ghanaians living abroad.

To define a calling as a '*teaching calling*' (to teach the words of the Bible) is a way for pastors to differentiate themselves from pastors who mostly emphasise prosperity. The calling is concerned with getting knowledge about the Bible and thereby to 'grow and mature spiritually'. This calling was often described as a difficult one, as church members were thought of as being more interested in getting concrete results than in reading the Bible. Knowledge of the Bible, in this case, does not seem to have the same status. Bishop Addae of the Shiloh United Church explained how focusing on teaching was seen as a barrier when he first started his church:

> But you know people like to see miracles and those things, so if you take on Bible teaching lines, it doesn't go fast. But I wasn't bothered. I wasn't worried at all. So by and by people were joining, but not as fast as others.[6]

This comment on the calling to teach reflects the idea and expectation that pastors should deliver concrete results to church members and this expectation is seen as an impediment to get church members into studying the Bible. Pastors with a 'teaching calling' implicitly present themselves as pastors not focusing on prosperity in their preaching and in this way distance themselves from pastors who put emphasis on wealth and the public critique of these pastors. Moreover, pastors with a 'teaching calling' tap into ideas around knowledge and literacy that are important both in an Asante setting and within Christianity. Possessing knowledge of the Bible and being able to perform that knowledge, for instance when pursuing a calling to teach the word of God, is essential in terms of being a 'big man of God'. Being able to teach the Bible is a way to show that one possesses knowledge, which in the Asante context is a means through which to access power (Akyeampong and Obeng 1995). The point is that pursuing a calling to teach is a difficult path, but overcoming this path is at the same time central for growing as a pastor.

Those who identify their pastoral careers with the '*prayer calling*' put emphasis on praying as the most important aspect of Christian life. It implies persistence and the devotion of time to pray in order to get close to God. Pastors see it as their main task to get people to pray for issues such as themselves, the church, the nation, health, security, and Ghanaians living overseas. For example, Pastor Joshua Kas-Vorsah defined his ministry as 'more into prayer and spiritual warfare',[7] and he used prayer as a way to show participation in society and contribute to resolving problems such as crime and road accidents. Such pastors also claim that the pastors and churches that are involved in all sorts of activities and programmes refrain from complying with the need to pray extensively.

This calling is in some ways similar to the 'teaching calling' as it is understood as different from those who pursue quick fame by focusing on prosperity and healing. This is also an expression of critique of pastors who are too glamorous and who focus excessively on money and their public appearance. Among the pastors I interviewed, none identified their calling specifically as a 'prosperity calling' or a calling to perform miracles, which are features that, in the literature, are highlighted as central to the success of charismatic pastors. However, some would preach on gaining success, for example, through starting a business.

It is noteworthy that one of the ways in which these pastors seek distinction is in the field of knowledge. As mentioned above, in Asante, knowledge was linked to power located in the spiritual realm (Akyeampong and Obeng 1995; McCaskie 1995). The call to teach the word of God builds on the idea that possessing knowledge of God is a way to legitimise one's position as pastor. At the same time, by pointing out that one has a 'teacher calling', pastors identify with the virtues of being a teacher that were promoted during colonial times, such as being literate and being educated (Miescher 2005). They distinguish themselves from other pastors that focus more on wealth by relating to a different register of legitimacy.[8]

Resistance

Resistance to a calling was a common element in pastors' narrations of their callings. One pastor was at university in Winneba when he had a calling to go into full-time ministry. This eventually resulted in him giving up his studies at university. He recounted:

> I had been praying and fasting for about a week and all of a sudden as I lay in my bed at about 7pm, I was in a flat at the time. Someone sat on my bed, and as he began to speak, and it was a clear voice, "if I ask you not to go to school any more what would you say?" Now, what made that encounter so unique and powerful was the fact that I was answering a person whom I believe was Jesus in my mind but was communicating with me in a clear voice within my thought. So I said to him, "well we were over 200 people who took the examination and only 31 of us passed. And I believe God you helped me and I passed and now I am in the university". So he outlined to me a number of things which would happen to me if I went and I would never feel happy, because the calling upon my life was so heavy. But I would be running to and fro trying to preach and school at the same time. That was what happened to me. After lectures I quickly went to Kumasi to do preaching and try to get back in the evening. And it went on and on I could not take it anymore. Now when that voice came I said to God, "Jesus if this is real: Come back again." He told me "I would be back at 11 pm," and when that happened I continued to lie on my bed, I slept some. I got up and

I was praying. I heard the clock strike from my hall at 11 pm. He was sitting by and he said "I told you that I would come back", and that blew my mind. I believed in God at that time. I knew God was there. I was a Christian but this encounter really affected my life. Even though I disobeyed and went but I never had my peace. Eventually after the first semester I could not go back [to university] any longer.[9]

In the above quote, being a university student is seen as a hindrance to fulfilling God's calling. Although this pastor had succeeded in passing a difficult exam, being a university student (that would eventually qualify him to becoming a teacher by profession) was a path that would be incompatible with being pastor. Resisting the calling impeded the pastor's happiness and peace, which also implies that not following God's calling leads to failure in life at a more general level. The calling is moreover understood as a 'heavy calling' and hence as even more difficult to resist and disobey.

Some pastors said that initially they did not want to become pastors, either because they had other career plans or because they did not like pastors. However, they also explained, like in the above case, that they could not defy the will of God and that they eventually had to comply. If someone resisted or did not take up the 'work of God', it would lead to failure in life.[10] In many narratives, there was a time lag between the actual calling and the moment the person took the step to become a pastor. This time lag is explained as a time of preparation, or that the person was not ready to do the 'work of God'. Both resistance and struggle are part of the path to become a pastor. The path is not straightforward; it is full of obstacles and requires persistence. The perception is that the journey has to be troublesome and hard and that is part of the formation of a religious expert.

One pastor had trained as an accountant and attended polytechnic school. After graduating, he did his national service in the finance department of Techiman District Assembly for a couple of years and then worked with the Internal Revenue Service for another year. After that, he worked as an accountant with the Ghana Broadcasting Cooperation. At the same time, he started a fellowship[11] in Techiman, but he realised that he could not do both at the same time and eventually left his job as an accountant. He explained:

I realised that I couldn't combine them so I had to abandon one. Becoming a pastor was a call from God and I had no option than to honour it. People saw it as an unwise decision on my part and my mother was even one of them, but now she understands me.[12]

This account points to the understanding of a pastoral calling as unavoidable and incompatible with other types of profession due to its divine source. As this example also shows, embarking on a pastoral career is not only related to younger people having difficulties finding employment after graduating. This pastor left his job as an accountant first to start a fellowship and later to become a pastor in church. He supplemented his work as a pastor with income generated from having a printing shop and a poultry farm.

Many also associated the acceptance of the calling with an internal struggle. Pastor Francis explained how he at first tried to resist the calling as he had aspirations other than becoming a pastor:

> But initially I wasn't opening up to God in order to take the task, because I heard many pastors complaining that it is difficult, it is not easy, the problems you face, so I had not wanted to engage myself in anything that has got to do with God. I just decided to go to church and be a normal Christian, an ordinary church member and also go about my normal lifestyle with my business. And yet as God will have it, God just called me, he also confirmed it through many pastors that God has spoken to me, that he wants to use you, that he wants you to be his servant.[13]

In this account, the fact that other pastors approved the calling served as a way to tackle the internal struggle and accept the calling. Other pastors explained that they were confused about their pastoral callings, and did not know how to react, as they had not wanted to become pastors. They referred to the difficulties associated with pastoral work, such as the difficult living and working conditions of pastors. Francis also mentioned that he had other career plans and dreamt of becoming a pilot or a businessman.

For the young pastors, becoming a pastor is not a choice of their own, or a choice of a profession like becoming a teacher or an accountant. It is a fulfilment of one's destiny. Pastors thought about becoming a pastor as a journey in life, which they engaged in upon a divine calling. This calling could not be refused and the journey not avoided. Historically, the idea of resisting a calling or one's destiny was also an element in the trajectories of traditional priests (*akɔmfoɔ*). The destiny of traditional priests was often revealed to them or other family members in their childhood and part of the process of becoming a priest was a 'struggle to come to terms with and accept a vocation first revealed, and often frighteningly, in childhood' (McCaskie 2008a: 61). In this way, charismatic pastors in present-day Asante draw on similar ideas of destiny and resistance as did traditional priests, and thereby some of the same fundamental ideas around sources of authority and legitimacy. This, in many ways, is different from how pastors and priests in the mainline churches understand their trajectories, which are more related to formal training and seen as a choice of career.

Social Approval

An important aspect of a pastoral calling is the approval by others. A pastoral calling is not only something that the individual experiences. The calling is also seen or received by others, such as pastors, church leaders, and family members, through dreams and visions. Referring to others having received one's calling is a way to confirm and legitimise it. The confirmation of a calling by social surroundings functions as testimony and proof of its sincerity. At a prayer meeting in Kumasi, a young man's pastoral calling was announced by the head pastor. The young man was asked to stand in front of the congregation and everyone prayed for him, and the head pastor and a visiting guest preacher laid hands on him while praying for his success as a pastor.[14] This young man had taken his first step to becoming a pastor, which was demonstrated in public, approved, and supported by the leader of the church (Lauterbach 2010).

Another example of how a calling was confirmed by others is that of Pastor Gloria. She explained how her calling was foreseen by someone in her social network:

> The wife of my head pastor had a vision in 1996 about me. I owned a provision shop with things like soap … People were coming in their numbers. This means I had something good to offer people. After I was told the vision, my husband encouraged me to go to the Bible school to know more about God and how to deal with people.[15]

In this case, there is a link between being able to perform materially and being able to perform spiritually, and these two forms of performances are seen as mutually profitable. Gloria's calling to serve God manifested materially and the fact that she was successful in her business was, at the same time, a sign that she would be able to succeed as a pastor. It is also significant that the person who received this vision was the wife of her senior pastor and thus a person in a high position in the social and religious hierarchy.

Young pastors depend on the approval and legitimisation of the social surroundings and need the acceptance of a calling by established church people. This approval is at the same time an approval of the young persons' credibility. Confirming a calling does not necessitate an official or formalised approval, but is done informally when young pastors refer to senior people who have seen their calling in a vision. Being able to refer to a senior person that has confirmed a religious calling is also a way to establish a spiritual genealogy from which the young pastor descends.

Young pastors depend on their social networks to show that their calling is divine or true. They build up their credibility by referring to senior religious people. There is some ambiguity as to whether pastors claim charisma and spiritual power from other senior pastors. Most pastors would clearly state that spiritual power derives from God and not from other people. At the same time, many pastors explain their spiritual power and heritage by referring to their spiritual fathers, and they thereby draw on the merits and names of these people. This also relates to the statement or analysis that the Pentecostal and charismatic movement in Ghana has brought with it 'a democratisation of charisma' in which access to God is more direct than in the mission churches (Asamoah-Gyadu 2005a). As mentioned above, there is ambiguity in the explanation of pastors' access to spiritual power and their dependency on senior pastors and social hierarchies.

Pastors' families also play a role in approving their calling. In many of the small and newly established churches in Kumasi that I visited, the church membership was constituted of a combination of family members, friends, neighbours, and people who the pastors had invited to come. Although family members were not members of the church or denomination, there was among some a sense of familial responsibility to support a newly established church or pastor. By attending church as a sign of loyalty and support, these family members were also acknowledging the social position of the pastor.

The social approval of a pastoral calling reflects Weber's point about the establishment of charismatic authority as a dialectical process between a religious leader and the followers (Weber 1978, see also Kirsch 2014 on the co-production of charisma and authority). In this case though, recognition and social approval is not only established in the relationship between a pastor and his followers, but is moreover co-produced by senior religious leaders and family members and through this within existing social hierarchies. The following section on spiritual genealogies is also an expression of this.

Charisma and Spiritual Genealogy

One way of building up a position as pastor is by establishing a spiritual genealogy and thereby getting access to the charisma of other pastors. They explicitly refer to who they descend from spiritually, for instance who they trained under, who ordained them and so on. Joshua Kas-Vorsah, founder of the Resurrection Faith in Christ Ministries in Kumasi, claimed Benson Idahosa from Nigeria as his spiritual mentor. This is common. Many of Ghana's top charismatic pastors, such as Duncan-Williams and Charles Agyin Asare, have attended Idahosa's Bible school in Nigeria and therefore consider him their mentor. However, Joshua Kas-Vorsah had not attended Idahosa's Bible school, but had a dream where Idahosa laid his hands on him and blessed him. This is his account[16]:

> So when the Archbishop Benson Idahosa died we organized a very big memorial programme for him. I gathered people in the radio and they converged at the place and we did a memorial service for him. So somebody called on the radio and wept and said that he was brought up by Archbishop Idahosa. Actually I never saw Benson Idahosa with my eyes. But after that programme the person said [that] God is going to bless me, and the spirit of Benson Idahosa is going to bless me … I had a dream and in the dream I saw Benson Idahosa, he came in his ceremonial dress … and there were some ladies there, so they said to me, if you want to go abroad, we can take you abroad and I said, no, no, no, I don't want to go abroad. I want the grace of that man. So Benson Idahosa said 'call me that boy. Kneel down'. So he laid hands on me in the dream and he prayed. After that he said follow me. And I followed him. And then Benson Idahosa said 'you, whenever you get a platform, don't promote yourself, if you promote yourself you will go up but you will not last and your enemies will fight you and bring you down because God will not save you because you promoted yourself. But if you get a platform, promote Christ and whosoever Christ exalts nobody can bring down. Go.' Then I remembered in the dream that this man is dead, then I woke up.

After this dream, Joshua talked to a friend who was an adopted daughter of Idahosa. This woman said that Reverend Mark Adu Gyamfi from

London had heard of Joshua and wanted to speak to him. They met in Accra and:

> when we went he said the last time Archbishop Idahosa came to London to hold the largest crusade ever was in 1987. And when he finished preaching, the dress he was wearing, this African boubou, he removed it and gave it to him [Mark Adu Gyamfi], that, with the sweat in it, gave it to him that he should keep it and then he [Mark Adu Gyamfi] said 'Papa', everybody call him papa, 'what should I use it for?' He said 'you keep it, at the right time the owner will come for it'. So he sensed in his spirit that this is the time he wants to give me the dress of the Archbishop. So I remembered the dream and I remembered how he prayed for me. And he brought the dress. As soon as I saw the dress, goose pimples covered my body. So I kept the dress, wore the dress and I prayed 'God if it is really from you, let your will be done, let the grace come upon my life' and since then, my life has never been the same.

Later on, another senior religious person, closely related to Idahosa, confirmed the blessing Joshua received through the dress:

> So a personal assistant of the Archbishop called Dr. Lawrence Obada, came to Ghana, I talked to him and I hosted him in my programme. I invited him for dinner, I and my wife and I told him about what I've just told you. Why I like mentioning Archbishop's name so much. So he said, he want to look at the dress and said he remembers this dress, that day at the crusade he was there when Archbishop professed over the dress. And he said I and Archbishop has a lot of things in common. Archbishop was a very bold person. He was somebody who understands the language of prayer. I wasn't that bold. But since I put on that dress my boldness was increased; now I have confidence and God has increased my faith so much. I've not put my trust in that dress, but I'm looking beyond the dress.

This case is an example of how a relationship to a big 'man of God' (here established in a dream) is seen as a blessing, and constitutes a way in which younger pastors can get access and draw on the spiritual power and charisma of more senior pastors. By establishing a relationship with Idahosa, one that importantly also includes Idahosa selecting him, the young pastor enables himself to draw on and claim the spiritual power of Idahosa; something that is widely recognised in an African Pentecostal and charismatic context (Kalu 2007). Likewise, Soothill states that 'Many key charismatic figures position themselves within the Idahosa "lineage" in order to give weight to their claims of divine favour' (2007: 176). Establishing a spiritual genealogy and through this invoking the spiritual power of Idahosa is a way for younger pastors to build up their charismatic authority. What is particularly interesting about this case is the way in which he uses the dress as a token of transference of charisma. By wearing the dress of Idahosa (with his sweat), Joshua becomes him. He described how he resembled Idahosa more after he received and wore the dress.

The account moreover shows that Idahosa recognised the spiritual relationship, which is of importance when thinking about authority-making and charisma as a two-way process. As mentioned above, pastors build up charisma, not only through their congregations recognising it, but also by drawing on the charisma and legitimacy of other big 'men of God'. The religious leader claims and proves his access to spiritual power and charisma by relating to more senior people in a spiritual hierarchy. At the same time, this has to be recognised and legitimised by a following or congregation. As Barker has pointed out, charisma is not an attribute, but something one builds up through social relationships (Barker 1993: 182).

Soothill also mentions the particular role of Benson Idahosa as someone who charismatic pastors draw charisma and legitimacy from and describes it as a '"grandfather-father-grandchildren" hierarchy ... in which children and grandchildren share in the spiritual or "genetic" heritage of the late Archbishop Idahosa' (Soothill 2007: 176). Joshua Kas-Vorsah, for instance, was ordained by Bishop Charles Agyin Asare of the World Miracle Church International in Accra on 26 March 2003. Charles Agyin Asare also trained under Idahosa. However, Joshua said that 'if the Archbishop Idahosa were to be alive, he would have ordained me', and he therefore considered himself to be the son rather than the grandson of Idahosa and thereby established a closer link to the source of spiritual power. He also told how he had hosted Matthew Ashimolowo from London on his radio programme and emphasised his 'bigness' as a means to render legitimate the approval (in the form of a prophecy) this pastor gave Joshua:

> Before the commencement of this ministry I hosted one preacher from London called Matthew Ashimolowo. He has the largest church in Europe[17] and I hosted him ... So he prophesised over me and said God is going to use me, God is going to restore things in my life.

By establishing links to these powerful 'men of God', Joshua draws on their credibility as well as on their spiritual power, and this is done through dreams, visions, and as with pastoral callings, by others approving and confirming these dreams and visions. Moreover, this way of mapping out one's spiritual genealogy allows for innovation and flexibility in who one can establish links to, as there are no formal rules to follow and these relationships do not need to follow institutional boundaries. Claiming spiritual heritage is a way to build up a position as a pastor, and one sign of this heritage is that there are resemblances between those who are linked. Pastors explained how they became like or resembled their spiritual fathers, how they acted and preached like them, and how other people recognised this.

Training and Bible Schools

After having received a pastoral calling, young pastors start a process of training and apprenticeship. Most pastors learn how to become a pastor primarily from working under a senior pastor and secondarily from attending Bible school. Attending Bible school is not a prerequisite for becoming a pastor or for starting a church and there are no formal requirements for entering into ministry. Most often pastors embark on their careers and attend Bible school at a later stage. This is evidently a major difference as compared to the mainline churches, in which one needs to go through seminary training to become a pastor (for instance at the Trinity Theological Seminary, which is affiliated with the University of Ghana).

Young pastors perceive the training they get from senior pastors as different from the teaching they receive when attending Bible school. Working with a senior pastor is understood as a form of apprenticeship, where young pastors learn from being with someone who is spiritually mature. This relationship includes both learning the craft of pastorship, as well as getting access to a senior pastor's spiritual power and legitimacy. Going to Bible school, on the other hand, is seen as a way to refine one's pastoral practices and ethics as well as knowledge of the Bible, but is not considered as important in terms of acquiring charismatic power. Still, attending Bible school, graduating and getting a diploma is important as a means to achieve recognition and social status, but within a different realm. Being educated is valued as a way to obtain knowledge and is a supplement to getting access to spiritual and charismatic sources of power.

Informal Training and Apprenticeship

The informal training of pastors is a form of apprenticeship where young men and women learn under a senior pastor. It consists of practical elements, such as conducting church services, leading prayer sessions, and evangelising, and at the same time represents an opportunity to draw on a senior pastor's spiritual power and legitimacy when building up their careers. This form of apprenticeship is, moreover, a process in which young pastors create social bonds to more senior pastors, and one that enables senior pastors to test and select among the young pastors as I have also described elsewhere (Lauterbach 2010).

A pastor explained that when you come to a church as a young pastor and present yourself by saying that you have received the calling of God, you will first go through a period of training:

> you go about visiting people … and also coming to lead prayers in the church and also you will be sent around on errands, go and do this, go and do that … that is the kind of training you go through … whenever he [the senior pastor] is praying for people you have to stand at their back, when they are falling you hold them.[18]

As the quote indicates, this training is both about learning from a senior pastor and about engaging in a junior-senior relationship that entails subordination and protection. Another pastor from a small church in Kumasi described his training as a pastor in this way:

> Most of the training was practical. I was always following him [the pastor] for his evangelism in the villages. He used to take along television which we used for our movie shows to win souls … We had never met before, but he was able to tell me who I was and what was on my mind, so it was some kind of prophecy. So when he told me the purpose of God for my life, I decided to join hands with him to learn from him. Apart from me there were other 20 guys who he was training.[19]

Apprenticeship is a combination of practical training with more spiritual elements in which a pastor can discern the purpose and genuineness of a pastor's calling.

Entering apprenticeship with a senior pastor is a way to create social bonds and pastors refer to the pastor they trained under as their 'spiritual father'. When entering a relation of apprenticeship, young pastors not only learn about the Bible and how to conduct a church service, but they also learn how to perform pastorship and behave as pastors, which includes showing spiritual authority. The crucial element when being an apprentice is that the senior pastor has a certain legitimacy that can be drawn upon. One pastor, who headed a sub-branch of a large charismatic church in Kumasi, explained how he had wanted to work under the head pastor. The pastor endeavoured to resemble the head pastor, who became his spiritual father, because of his ability to heal people and thus manifest the power of God in him. He referred to how affiliation with the head pastor made his pastoral work easier, because he could draw on his credibility:

> Certain things are above your knowledge, experience and age and you need someone who is well vested in there whereby you relate with him. And also he has made a name for himself, though in the Lord, but that credibility alone makes it easy for you to make inroads into the ministry than to be alone; nobody knows you, nobody knows your root, credibility and your background and so people cannot entrust their lives to you. Because of that we are sort of bonded in the form of a fatherly relationship sort of.[20]

Another pastor, who had trained under the same head pastor, also explained how people thought he resembled his spiritual father as he talked and preached like him. These are ways in which being in a relationship of apprenticeship allows younger pastors to draw on the charismatic authority of senior pastors. It has been recognised in other types of apprenticeship relationships that these are not only about learning a craft or a particular skill. As Miescher notes in his book on the life histories of eight Kwaku men, entering apprenticeship is also an exposure to the ideals and values of the mentor or senior person (2005: 82), and in the case of the charismatic pastors, it is about getting access to a senior person's charismatic power as well as his or her credibility.

Likewise, Wilks (1993) describes how, in an Asante historical context, being trained by a mentor for a particular profession was both a form of training and a socialising process. To obtain a position in the administrative class in nineteenth-century Asante, one went through training (Wilks 1993: 303). This served both as a means to transfer skills and as a selection of young professionals by their seniors. Being under a senior pastor in a charismatic church in present-day Ghana also involves a process of selection and of testing, where senior pastors assess and observe the younger pastors. It is their spiritual skills that are observed, as well as their faithfulness to God and the senior pastor. The progress of their careers, how fast they grow, and in particular their ability to perform spiritually is observed because the master-apprenticeship relationship can become one of challenge and restraint if the younger pastors feel that they can no longer grow in that relationships and therefore seek to escape the subordination that is also part of the relationship.

From the perspective of the young pastors, however, there are not many possibilities for advancement within the well-established charismatic churches. The strong focus on the head pastor is a barrier for younger pastors when they seek to advance and grow. Some young pastors complain because they are not allowed to preach on Sundays or when the head pastor is present. This is a reflection of the control of younger pastors and the attempt to keep them distanced from the platform from which leading pastors perform spiritual power. This reflects an aspect of hierarchy building within the charismatic churches. The low degree of formal procedures with regard to how young pastors rise in the church hierarchy is limiting for some younger pastors, and they therefore create their own churches in order to attain more status and grow faster. This strong focus on the pastor, the founder and the leader make these churches hierarchical, although in a way that is different from the mission churches, and also leads to the so-called mushrooming of small new churches.[21]

Inherent in pastors' informal training is both a process of undergoing training and at the same time being in a relationship where older pastors recognise their spiritual gifts and talents and through this also see what way they should go as pastors. This means that at the same time as receiving training, they engage in a relationship that is about recognition. It is moreover a form of selection mechanism, in which older pastors decide who is spiritually mature and can go on and establish their own churches. The relationship between older pastors and younger pastors is also about younger pastors submitting themselves to the older pastors; they go through a testing period in which they have to fulfil various tasks, and assist and be behind the older pastor. It is a relationship of recognition through submission, but one in which younger pastors are also able to draw on the legitimacy of older pastors.

Bible Schools

Attending a Bible school is another important step when building up a career as a pastor; it provides a certificate, a title, and an occasion to gather friends, family, and colleagues at the graduation ceremony that makes one's new status public and opens up for financial support. Bible schools are most often privately owned institutions that provide training for young pastors in the charismatic sector. Some are very small and have established classrooms in pastors' houses, whereas others have a more established infrastructure. Besides providing theological training, Bible schools permit young pastors to make social bonds with the head of the Bible school and other students. Some students develop a relationship or an attachment to the leader of the school and continue to refer to him and participate in seminars after graduation (Lauterbach 2010).

Most of the pastors I interviewed had been to Bible school for one to three years, but this was not necessarily at the beginning of the careers. Often, they needed to have their pastoral calling accepted by a pastor and by a church to get their school fees funded. One pastor from Kumasi enrolled in Christian Service College[22] for a diploma in Theology. He explained this with a need to refine his teachings, and that the education he received changed what he said in church. He does not think that it will make his preaching more powerful: 'It's better, I won't say more powerful. It's God who gives the power, Bible school doesn't give you power. But it is more refined, some words I used to say, I say them no more.'[23] In this way, he distinguishes between spiritual power that derives from God and theological knowledge that can be obtained through training.

Only a few pastors had no Bible school or theological training. One of these pastors, who is now a well-established pastor in Kumasi, explained that he had not attended any Bible school because he was an educated man who did a lot of reading, and therefore did not feel there was a need for him to attend a Bible school. It is widely believed that reading books written by other charismatic and Pentecostal pastors (American, Nigerian and others) is a way to ameliorate one's theological knowledge. Many pastors refer to their reading of particular authors when explaining how they were trained. In a similar way, Asamoah-Gyadu (2005b: 99) writes about a Ghanaian charismatic evangelist based in London who describes himself in this way: '"I have no seminary training" … "Anytime I visited a seminary, it means I am the one going to do the teaching."' The two pastors mentioned here had reached a certain level of advancement that did not require them to attend school, because this would call into question their status as big 'men of God'. The pastors at this level are self-made in the sense that their training mainly consists of having worked under an older and more senior pastor, from which they draw their credibility.

The Bible schools which the pastors had attended were mostly schools set up by Pentecostal and charismatic pastors, such as Oasis of Love Bible College at Ahodwo, Kumasi, that was founded by Christiana and Kwabena Darko (Kwabena Darko is also the head of one of Ghana's largest companies, Darko Farms & Co. Ltd, was board member of the Bank of Ghana, and candidate for the 1992 presidential elections), Shiloh Bible Training Centre for Pastors (headed by Bishop Addae), School of the Word (founded by the church House of Faith), and Charisma Bible College, Tafo-Nhyieaso, Kumasi, led by Bishop Nicholas Asare.

Of the pastors I met, some had been to Bible schools in Kumasi, but others had attended schools in, for instance, Denmark, New Zealand, Australia, and Singapore. Those who attended Bible school abroad had either been sent by their churches or had gone independently with financial assistance from, for instance, family members. Pastors in Calvary Charismatic Centre (CCC) could go to Singapore for six months, because CCC was related to a church there (Victory Family Centre, formerly also called Calvary Charismatic Centre). Two pastors had been to the Copenhagen Bible Training Centre for a two year-course. This school was founded by Jens Garnfeldt in 1989. He himself was trained at Livets Ord Bible school in Uppsala, Sweden. The cost of attending Bible school ranged between 1,000,000 and 3,000,000 cedis[24] (approximately 110 USD–330 USD).

It is moreover common practice to organise seminars and programmes that gather pastors from different denominations. In August 2005, such a pastoral seminar was organised by Bishop Addae of the Shiloh Bible Training Centre for Pastors at Ohwim, Kumasi. Around 600 pastors, mainly younger pastors or pastors who had recently established churches, attended the seminar. Many had attended Bishop Addae's Bible school. The overall theme of the seminar was 'Ministerial Excellence' and the programme consisted of various teachings on how to succeed as a pastor, such as: 'How to keep your gifts of grace', 'The moral and spiritual life of a pastor', 'Knowing the gifts of your wife', 'Pastors and finances of church', 'Pastors, church and hypocrisy', and 'Accomplishing God's Given Task'. The teachings covered administrative and organisational aspects, for instance, how to keep church members, the pastor as a public figure, as well as topics such as the legitimacy of the pastor, the pastor as God's messenger, and the spiritual aspects of pastoral work. The classes were given by a number of senior pastors from different denominations (including a Methodist minister).

The content of the teachings, and the advice pastors were given, centred on criteria for success. Social relationships were mentioned as particularly important for success, alongside spiritual power. This was based on the understanding that one cannot succeed alone, but needs good relationships with other people. Being accountable was also emphasised as essential when establishing oneself as a pastor, which relates to the discussion in Chap. 3 on pastorship, wealth and truthfulness. It was also mentioned that pastors should be generous and not expect money too fast ('Anointing without enough finances is annoying, but God opens doors', and 'Generosity is a life style. Giving, the battle is in your mind').

Graduation

Graduating from a Bible school is an important event for young pastors. It is an occasion during which one can display a new status and formalise it by receiving certificates and titles. At the Charisma Bible College they operate with three different certificates; (1) Apprentice in ministry, (2) Fully ordained minister, and (3) Senior minister. The new status acquired is moreover recognised by others such as pastors, church members, family and friends who participate in the event. One pastor described the graduation ceremony thus:

> During the graduation a little insight was given about the existence of the school and the status of the graduates. It was made known that we were part of the 8th graduation ceremony. Prizes were subsequently given to members who were always consistent for the entire programme and out of the four presented with the award, I was one of them. The ceremony was interesting. We started in the morning dressed up. We started with prayer. We were later advised to be cautious with what we had learnt, we should not be self centred and focus on how the training was going to help you achieve your individual motive, but rather count it as the grace of God that has brought to this far … After which we took a lot of photographs with graduates and staff and also with our families. Those whose family members came to support them went to their homes and where celebrations and encouragements were required it was given by family and friends. The certificates were also given to graduates.[25]

There was also the expectation that people should give money to a newly graduated pastor. Before the ceremony, the pastor distributed envelopes to friends, family, church members, and other pastors. These served both as an invitation to the ceremony and as a request to assist the pastor financially. The pastor quoted above was not supported by his church, but by family and friends. As mentioned in Chap. 2, this expectation and practice of giving pastors who graduate from Bible school money entails a relation of reciprocity. It is a way to acknowledge a newly acquired status, but it is also a form of giving from which family and other relations expect to get a return either from the pastor (in the form of religious services) or directly from God.

Some schools gave the students who graduated a licence, which they paid for and had to renew every year. This was the case with the Shiloh Bible Training Centre for Pastors. A renewal of a licence cost around 20 pounds. This was both a way for the Bible school leaders to keep the graduated students attached to them and a means to formalise the graduates' status as pastors. Some also founded pastoral associations and networks, and in this way tried to influence and guide their students after they had left Bible school. Some explicitly said that there was a need to frame and guide young pastors. One pastor, who founded a Bible school in 1994, explained:

> but when I came [to Kumasi] I observed something, that there were a lot of youngsters who were very eager to do the Lord's work. And they were also saying that they had got the call of God. And some were preaching on the streets and at some places, public places.[26]

This reflects the somewhat informal and non-hierarchical set-up of charismatic churches, as well as the non-institutionalised way in which the charismatic sector has grown. The founding of Bible schools and creation of relations between a school leader and a student can also be interpreted as a way to establish and formalise social networks and relations of dependency. In this way, junior pastors relate not only to their senior pastor and spiritual father, but also to the leader of the Bible school they attended. The fact that these also issue licences adds an aspect of authority building to the relationship between the pastor and his mentor. The leader of the Bible school makes the pastors' status official by issuing licences and certificates, and the graduates confer authority on the leader of the Bible school (who most often is also the founder/leader of a church) by referring to him as a religious leader and by continuing 'to be under his name'.

Having founded a Bible school also increases one's status as a pastor in the sense that it adds an imprimatur of academia and literacy to pastors. This is linked to the earlier discussion of values associated with the calling to teach, and also to the status attached to being a teacher in both colonial and post-independent times. As Miescher (2005: 105) notes, becoming a teacher was something that shaped people's identities, which again implied inhabiting a specific social position. Although the status of being a civil servant, and employed as a teacher, has declined in present-day Ghana, the value and status of being a literate person as well as the symbolic value of being a teacher is carried over in these Bible schools. Being a pastor and a teacher allows people to combine two social positions that, in colonial times, were connected and part of the same social category. Being a pastor and teacher also entails engaging in senior-junior relationships, implying that there is a 'fathering' dimension to the teacher/pastor role which adds to the completeness of being a big pastor.

TITLES

Charismatic pastors work within what they define as the 'five-fold ministry'; that is, as pastor, evangelist, prophet, apostle, and teacher.[27] This five-fold ministry derives from Ephesians 4:11 ('And he gave some, apostles; and some prophets; and some, evangelist; and some pastors and teachers') and it emphasises, in particular, the charismatic gifts. According to Adubofour, the concept was introduced by the Morris Cerullo 'School of Ministry'[28] and 'gained currency among evangelical Pentecostals in Ghana' (1994: 341). This idea of the fivefold ministry is reflected in the typologies of callings discussed above.

The title of pastors partly depends on the type of calling the person has received and partly on the title given by the church leadership. If someone, for instance, has had a calling as a prophet, the person would call himself pastor and prophet. Others would refer to themselves as pastor and evangelist and so on.

Another title commonly used is 'Reverend Doctor'. The title is used when pastors have received Honorary Doctoral Degrees, most often from a religious university in the USA, with which they have connections. There is great awareness of the corruption of the system by, for example, position-conscious ministers, who want to rise quickly. Some told stories of pastors who went to London to buy their titles. Again, the tension between being genuine and false is reflected in the practices and ideas around the use of these kinds of titles.

Bishop and archbishop are also used as titles. Some leaders of charismatic churches refuse to entertain such titles and contest their use. They think it takes the focus away from the work of the pastor and puts more attention on the man as such. One pastor did not like the inflation in titles and thought that 'your work should prove your office'.[29] This criticism reflects both the tension between being a genuine or a false pastor as well as the different sources of power and authority pastors draw on as discussed above in the section on typologies of pastoral calling.

Others employ the titles and become consecrated as bishops and archbishops, as a way of recognising and increasing their position and credentials. It was claimed by several that the use of such titles was inspired partly by the Nigerian Benson Idahosa and partly by the Catholic Church. This suggests a desire to introduce more symbols of hierarchy into the charismatic churches as expressions of distinction. The use of an Episcopal hat and stick also indicates the influence of the Catholic Church. This practice is, however, criticised both from within the charismatic churches themselves and from outside. One church leader in Kumasi said, 'If you don't have the power, you don't need the form'. He furthermore compared religious leaders who are attracted by titles and symbols of power with Asante traditional leaders. He explained: 'In the family I don't need to say who I am, they know I am the father, if I did they would wonder, so if you are sure you don't need to say who you are.'[30] In a discussion of the role of charismatic pastors in contemporary Ghana, Adubofour also touches on the issue of titles and relates it to the role of traditional priests:

> if you are a pastor everybody would call you by your title. They are very generous in their dealings with you. Whether you are properly ordained or not, there is that respectability because it is tradition. Within our traditional society the traditional priest serves in the royal courts. Life revolves around the priest. The chief most depend on the chief priest for guidance in life. Many people these days consult them. They have become more or less a spiritual consultant.[31]

Titles are, in Adubofour's understanding, a way for adherents and others to acknowledge the position of pastors. Some pastors were, however, inclined to downplay the importance of their formal titles and would rather draw attention to other ways in which they were recognised. This position and title as pastor is combined with a range of other leadership positions such as chairman, secretary, and treasurer, which all allude to a more formalised and hierarchical institutional set-up. One pastor explained how he assumed a leadership position in a Christian youth fellowship he and some friends had established in Sunyani in the mid-1980s. When explaining his position he said:

> So it got to a point where all the leaders left, so I became a leader, but it was like I was the patron, so I appointed the president and the other executives … When I became the patron that is where I brought in the ranks and positions. So we had the financial secretary, secretary, organising secretary, treasurer and the president.[32]

I then asked what his title was and he replied, 'I had no title. I was seen as the patron and they were calling me daddy.'[33] His response illustrates the multiple positions pastors have and which their congregations recognise. The question of titles and positions also touches upon the broader point of what sources of power and legitimacy pastors and others in similar positions draw on and what kind of social relationships this entails. Being a pastor or a prophet involves access to spiritual power as well as the knowledge of how to use and mediate this power. While also acting and being approached as patron or father, pastors are more complete figures, in the sense that they are not only mediators of spiritual power, but are also providers and protectors in a more physical and materialistic sense.

Pastor-Congregation

The relationship between pastors and their congregations is an important part of how pastors build up status and power. In Chap. 3, I argued that one way in which pastors build up wealth is by having a congregation that gives time and presence. At the same time, the relationship between pastors and congregation is a mutual relationship that is beneficial to both. Pastors provide religious services and access to spiritual power, while church members recognise pastors as leaders and this constitutes their authority as leaders.

The hierarchy among pastors, and a pastor's status, influences the way members relate to different pastors. Senior pastors are generally seen as having more spiritual power than younger pastors and their presence and services are more valued. When, for instance, church members fall into a trance during prayer, they often lie on the ground until they have been prayed for and touched by a leading pastor. Lack of attention from a senior pastor was also mentioned as a reason for leaving church. One pastor explained that a member of his church had left because he did not visit her personally while she was sick:

> but because I did not come in person, she was disappointed … I called her on the phone and asked the junior pastors to go and visit her. I therefore did not understand why she still wanted me to come … Maybe they take pride in the fact that their pastors come and visit them. I believe so because they admire you and they see you as their all apart from God, so when you are not there, it's like they are down a bit when they do not see you.[34]

In this example, the visit of the junior pastors was not recognised by the sick woman as sufficiently beneficial, and she was disappointed. Her response was to stop coming to church. This indicates that pastors and some churches members have a close and sometimes personal relationship, or that church members have an expectation of a personal relationship with their pastor. This is a way for church members to see God and to get access to God. The above-mentioned pastor further explained: 'It is normal because the pastor is the one they know, because they might have seen what God has been using you to do. So they might come to church mainly to see the pastor.' By this, he refers to the direct link between God, a specific pastor and a church member. This link is not a mere theoretical or imagined link; it is also assessed by church members who observe how God manifests himself in a particular pastor.

There is a tension, however, between the crucial role of the pastor and the idea within Pentecostal and charismatic Christianity that everyone has direct access to God and the power of the Holy Spirit and that this form of Christianity represents a so-called democratisation of faith. Pastors themselves seek to balance this tension by, on the one hand, insisting on the accessibility to God, and on the other hand, having to perform the manifestation of spiritual power in order to become recognised. In relation to this, the same pastor said: 'When they come, you let them know that you are not God and that it is decentralised so they can go to any of the pastors.' This tension is productive in the sense that the huge attention given to pastors is constitutive of pastors' authority and status, and at the same time, charismatic Christianity allows and encourages adherents and lay preachers to have access to God through personal prayers and in this way experience the manifestation of spiritual power at an individual level. This last aspect creates an idea of openness to individual agency and represents opportunity for the individual that lies only within the relationship between him or her and God, and is not as such guided by social control. For analytical purposes though, it is important to pay attention to how this tension is expressed in the social relations between pastors and church members.

Besides spiritual services and guidance, pastors also provide other forms of support and advice to their members, for instance with regard to business and investment. One church member of a large charismatic church in Kumasi had received support from her pastor both in relation to an earlier marriage and when she started her own business (three restaurants in Kumasi). She explained: 'He has helped me a lot. I had problems from my first marriage but he came in to help me. Even if I had no money, he will give me some. Currently, my children always go to his house after school because of my work, where they are fed and catered for. He has been so nice.'[35] The woman had been a member of the church since it began and used to be a lead singer in the choir. She is therefore considered a core member of the church.

Assistance is not available for any church member: You need to be someone in the church. The church members' level of attachment to their church influences the kind of assistance they receive, for instance, when travelling abroad. If the person travelling is a member of the church's core group that consists of pastors, deacons, or members of various ministries (for instance, a choir or a youth group), the person is often allowed to use the name of the church or of the head pastor, but only with the approval of the head pastor. This means that the church will provide supportive letters; for instance, to obtain a visa or provide contact to churches abroad.[36] Moreover, regular contact will be maintained and the person travelling can seek advice from the pastor when he or she wants to invest at home, or when certain family problems occur and decisions have to be taken. If someone, on the other hand, is a more recent church member or someone who has not shown 'full commitment', the support would be limited to advice on how to prepare oneself culturally, on how to behave, and on how to remain strong in faith. The pastor would also pray for the person travelling. According to my information, the church members travelling would only in rare instances receive financial support from the church. This could happen if the church offered scholarships or access to scholarships in educational institutions abroad. As expressed by a head pastor from Kumasi, one has to be careful when selecting whom to help:

It all depends on who you are, and if I can trust you, because I have a name to protect. I must know that you meet the requirements because at the end of the day my name will be in the system. For some few people I will recommend.[37]

The focus on mobility, expressed as a dream of travelling that is often conveyed in sermons, is not necessarily linked to church members getting access to funds for travelling from their churches, or that church members become part of a transnational religious network. It seems important again to underline the difference when speaking of religious discourse and when speaking of the everyday lives of churchgoers. This is not to ignore the fact that the insistence on success in Pentecostal discourse is attractive, especially to the urban educated youth, but to point out that it is (in many cases) more a reflection of people's hopes and dreams than a reflection of the reality of their everyday lives. When it comes to church leaders, the picture is somewhat different. Pastors travel in order to visit church branches abroad and visit affiliated churches and other pastors. The pastors from the more established churches travel extensively, and some spend as much time outside Ghana as inside. They would either use their own money, get money from the church, or from the churches they are to visit abroad (Lauterbach 2016).

The pastor-congregation relationship takes a particular form when church members are living abroad. Pastors maintain close contact with some of their members living abroad, and these members contact their pastors in specific situations. Pastors can serve as a link between Ghanaian migrants and their homes. In some social situations such as funerals, the pastors attend the ceremony to represent the member who is living abroad and not able to be present physically. In this way, Ghanaian migrants use the pastors to represent them at these important events often also joined by other members of the church community. This often also involves a financial contribution from the church as a sign of commitment vis-à-vis the church member they are representing. This is exemplified by the story of a young Ghanaian woman who lived in Norway as a student. Her mother died in February 2005. She then contacted her pastor in Kumasi to inform him and to seek his advice. The pastor prayed with her over the phone and got the necessary information to represent her at the funeral ceremonies. He went to the funeral with several other members of the church and made a small financial contribution on her behalf. After the funeral, the church member got in touch with the pastor again to find out how the funeral went. The woman was also in touch with her family in order to contribute to the funeral arrangements and to know whether the pastor had been there and how much he had contributed.[38] Church members living abroad are still seen as part of the church, and therefore it is the task of the pastor to prepare a wedding, participate in a funeral or settle family disputes on their behalf. As one pastor said '[s]he belongs to us, but she is no longer here.'[39] This suggests that pastors occupy a position as mediators and linkage between migrants and their families in Ghana, as the case above illustrates. Pastors seek to maintain close ties with the members who have left, but not necessarily as a replacement of the migrants' link to their families.

Making Institutions: Formalisation

Within the charismatic sector, there are two processes of institution building taking place simultaneously: one of fragmentation and diffusion, and one of regulation and formalisation. The charismatic churches are not as institutionalised and formalised as the mission churches and are, as mentioned earlier, typically organised around one pastor (one-man-churches). Although the churches are mostly known to be rapidly changing, anti-hierarchical and network-like, there are clear tendencies that the more well-established churches have a certain and often very visible order and regulation of both hierarchy and church activities. Regulation is, for instance, installed by establishing criteria for membership, by routinising the collection of tithes, having a constitution, and having regular church programmes and activities. Pastors also set up broader institutional structures in the form of Bible schools and pastoral associations in which they coordinate activities and seek to continue the guidance of young pastors. One pastor, however, explained that he had been a member of a pastoral association but had left because 'there is too much competition and a deviation from the preaching of the gospel. There is so much emphasis on seniority based on the size of one church and how powerful the pastor is'.[40] This remark alludes to the tension in charismatic Christianity between personalised charisma on the one hand and formalisation on the other. In order to survive, the churches need regulation and regulation at the same time serves as a foundation for creating pastoral authority.

The rules on how to become a church member vary according to church and the size and level of institutionalisation of the church. In many of the bigger charismatic churches, there are clear procedures to follow. First, someone invites you to attend a church service. After having attended the church for a while, you can decide to become a member. In one particular church, new members had to take two courses. First, a course called discipleship class (or 'Foundation for Christian living') and then a course on the history and aims of the church. After that, they receive a membership card and are summoned to an interview to find out whether they are committed. Church members get an individual code number, which they use as identification and when they pay tithes.[41] Some people are actively involved in church groups and activities, whereas others are less active but still consider themselves as members. Some deliberately try to stay at the margin of the church and not get too involved because they find it too time-consuming. Members are closely monitored and the leaders seek to keep members engaged in the church. Every church member has a registration number and at each church service, one has to fill out a card with name and number.

An example of how smaller churches are formalising is the practice of collecting tithes. In one small and new church in Kumasi, the pastors wanted to install tithing.[42] The pastors explained the principles of tithing during the service. They told the attendants that paying tithes is paying one tenth of what we earn, and it is a way to be accountable to God. They explained that the money goes to the pastors, the orphans, the widows, and the needy and poor. One pastor explained: 'tithe is giving back ten percent of what God has given to you as a steward. It is re-giving.' After this explanation, there was a long sequence with questions from church members and replies from the pastors. Some members were confused about when to pay tithe:

Question:	Should we pay tithe in case we don't work but your mother caters for you?
Reply:	Whatever you are given, you should pay ten percent.
Question:	What does tithe mean? If you don't work you don't have to pay tithe?
Reply:	If someone gives you money because you did something good, you have to pay tithe, not only of work.
Question:	Should you pay ten percent of full salary or after you have paid your bills?
Reply:	We pay tithe according to gross income, not net. If you earn 600,000 [cedis], and owe someone 100,000, you should still pay according to the 600,000. We don't pay

	on money we borrow. If you use it to work and make profit, then you pay.
Question:	Should you pay at the end of the month or when you get money? Because if you wait then you might have spent the money on food.
Reply:	Some churches ask for tithes every Sunday. You have to put something aside every day, otherwise it's too difficult.

The conclusion of the discussion was that 'if you pay tithe, God will be faithful and help you and heal your sicknesses'. The majority of the questions were related to the technicalities of how to pay and about how much money to pay. The discussion is an example of how pastors introduce a regulating mechanism in church. But such regulations also give rise to questions and uncertainties. The process of regulation and formalisation is a two-way process between pastors and congregation that, as it appears from the above exchange, also touches upon issues around different understanding of money (such as debt, gifts, and salary).

Discussion

Throughout this chapter, I have described and discussed different stages of pastoral careers: callings, establishing spiritual genealogies, informal training, attending Bible schools, and processes of formalisation. The perspective has been on how a position as pastor and pastorship is stabilised and authorised. One aim of the chapter has been to highlight how various elements in the process of becoming a pastor, such as the narration of a pastoral calling, draw on and reflect historical understandings of the role of destiny in Asante as well as how a calling contains aspects of both resistance and social approval. Social approval and recognition is in many ways a recurrent theme in the making of pastoral careers; in the relationship between junior and senior pastors, in the relationship between pastors and congregations, but also in the relationship between pastors and their families. It is in these relationships that pastors stabilise their positions and build up authority. This double relationship of recognition and provision of religious services is a well-known principle in the construction of authority among religious leaders. As Kirsch notes 'the centrality of religious leaders can be said, to represent a "chronically unstable *co*-production" between leaders and followers' (Kirsch 2014: 48). In the writings of Weber, this process of ascribing authority and recognition is centred on the notion of charisma (Weber 1978). I will return to a discussion of spiritual power and charisma in the next chapter, but for now I will take up the dialectical relationship that produces religious authority.

As we have seen in the various stages of the making of pastoral careers, the process of being recognised as a pastor contains more relations than what can be captured in the pastor-follower relationship. First, narration of a pastoral calling often contains an element of social performance and social approval, as does the establishing of spiritual genealogies. In this, young pastors prove the sincerity of their calling and their claimed destiny as a religious leader by the active contribution of senior religious leaders or family members (for instance, a mother confirming a religious calling through a dream). The same mechanism takes place in the training of young pastors, whether as informal training or in Bible schools. In their relationship with senior pastors, young ones draw on their legitimacy as well as on their spiritual power. In these early stages of becoming a pastor, building up authority and stabilising one's position as pastor is very much about inserting oneself in a hierarchy of religious leaders. This involves both social relationships of recognition between junior and senior pastors as well as making reference to the spiritual sphere and a divine calling. By having a particular focus on the early stages of young pastors' careers, we are able to get insight into the processes by which young pastors obtain success and advance. As has been demonstrated in this chapter, young pastors construct their careers by entering into relationships with more senior pastors and by being recognised by these, and at the same time also recognising the older pastor by subduing and accepting the hierarchical nature of the relationship. This focus draws away and nuances the usual attention on the pastor-follower relationship.

The process of establishing oneself as a pastor also involves elements of formalisation. But formalising for instance church regulations on tithing is not only an issue of bureaucratisation. It is also a way for pastors to show their knowledge of God's word when they explain the Biblical background for tithing. Likewise, when pastors write and publish books it is also both a formalisation and stabilisation of their positions as pastors and a way to expose knowledge and appear as a wise person. When young pastors attend Bible school and get a certificate it is a formal recognition of their positions as pastors and at the same time a way to engage in social relationships with more powerful pastors from whom they can draw spiritual power and legitimacy. The argument is that pastors seek to stabilise their positions both through formalisation and through the performance of wisdom and charisma that proves access to spiritual power; it is part of the same process of becoming a small 'big man' of God, which will be discussed in the following chapter.

Finally, pastors draw upon a variety of social roles: as pastor, father, patron, and teacher. Therefore, our understanding of their role in society and how their positions are legitimised is richer when employing an analytical lens that includes the cultural values and histories of these different figures. If thinking in Weberian terms, my argument is that pastors draw on and combine charismatic, bureaucratic and traditional forms of authority by being church leaders, patrons, and fathers at the same time. They become 'complete' pastors.

Notes

1. Interview with Francis Awuah, Kumasi, 14 December 2014.
2. Interview with Eric Opoku Danso, Kumasi, 11 December 2014.
3. *Nkrabea* meaning 'the message given by the Supreme Being to the individual soul, which (message) was to determine the manner in which the individual was to live in the world' (Gyekye 1987: 108).
4. The typology presented here is not exhaustive and more types could be defined on the basis of other pastors' trajectories and the type of their pastoral work.
5. Interview with Emmanuel Amoah, Kumasi, 23 August 2005.
6. Interview with Samuel Richard Addae, Kumasi, 6 September 2005.
7. Interview with Joshua Kas-Vorsah, Kumasi, 16 September 2005.
8. As also mentioned briefly in Chap. 3, there is a relation between accumulating wealth and being truthful that also includes being knowledgeable, and in this sense a focus on wealth and an identity as a pastor that teaches the word of God does not necessarily exclude one another.
9. Interview with Victor Osei, Kumasi, 3 February 2005.
10. Compare with Wiredu's writing on the Akan concept of destiny: 'everyone has his appointed destiny which nothing can change. As the traditional saying goes, there is no avoiding the destiny appointed to man by God' (*Onyame nkrabea nni kwatibea*) (1980: 19–20).
11. A fellowship is a group of people that meet for things such as praying and healing sessions. They could all be members of other churches (including mainline churches) and members of a fellow-

ship at the same time. Normally, people would pay tithes to their church and not to a fellowship. This was a widespread phenomenon in the 1980s and was how the charismatic movement started to become popular and spread. It is a more informal kind of organisation, where lay people can take up leadership positions.
12. Interview with Emmanuel Appiah, Techiman, 30 August 2005.
13. Interview with Francis Afrifa, Kumasi, 17 February 2005.
14. Resurrected Faith in Christ Ministries in Daban, Kumasi, 16 September 2005.
15. Interview with Gloria Mensah Afriyie, Kumasi, 1 September 2005.
16. The following is based on an interview with Joshua Kas-Vorsah, Daban, Kumasi, 16 September 2005.
17. The Kingsway International Christian Church (KICC) in the UK.
18. Interview with Francis Afrifa, Kumasi, 5 September 2005.
19. Interview with Daniel Darko Kabea, Kumasi, 12 September 2005.
20. Interview with Edward Otu, Kumasi, 22 February 2005.
21. For a critical discussion of the potential for democratisation and empowerment in charismatic churches, see Soothill (2007: 137 ff.).
22. Now Christian Service University College. This institution offered (in 2005) diplomas and BA degrees in theology and business administration. The college is affiliated to the University of Ghana and is an accredited teaching institution.
23. Interview with Joshua Kas-Vorsah, Kumasi, 16 September 2005.
24. In new cedi (1967–2007), and 2005 exchange rate.
25. Interview with James Abu, Kumasi, 13 February 2005.
26. Interview with Samuel Richard Addae, Kumasi, 6 September 2005.
27. Personal communication, Sylvia Owusu-Ansah, 5 August 2005.
28. The Morris Cerullo 'School of Ministry' was introduced in Ghana in 1978. See more in Adubofour (1994). Morris Cerullo visited the Calvary Charismatic Church in Kumasi as late as in October 2013 (http://cccghana.com/pages/gallery.php?siteid=ccc&id=59, accessed 31 October 2013).
29. Interview with Nicholas Asare, Kumasi, 5 September 2005.
30. Interview with Ransford Obeng, Kumasi, 11 September 2005.
31. Interview with Samuel Brefo Adubofour, Kumasi, 7 September 2005.
32. Interview with Emmanuel Owusu-Ansah, Sunyani/Kumasi, 15 August 2005.

33. Interview with Emmanuel Owusu-Ansah, Sunyani/Kumasi, 15 August 2005.
34. Interview with Seth Osei-Kuffuor, Kumasi, 8 December 2014.
35. Interview with Rosemary Ababio, Kumasi, 7 February 2005.
36. The majority of the churches I studied have branches abroad. One church was the daughter-church of a church in Copenhagen. In many cases, churches have been founded on request by Ghanaian migrants or Ghanaian churches sending out missionaries to plant churches.
37. Interview with Victor Osei, Kumasi, 3 February 2005.
38. Interview with Simon Ampofo and K's sister, Kumasi, 15 and 24 February 2005.
39. Interview with Simon Ampofo, Kumasi, 13 December 2004.
40. Interview with Seth Osei-Kuffour, Kumasi, 18 August 2013 (conducted by James Boafo).
41. Interview with Elizabeth Lawson, secretary, CCC, Kumasi, 26 August 2005.
42. Church service, Alive Bible Congregation, Kwadaso, Kumasi, 11 September 2005.

References

Adubofour, S. B. (1994). *Evangelic Parachurch movements in Ghanaian Christianity: c. 1950—Early 1990s.* Unpublished Ph.D. thesis, University of Edinburgh, Edinburgh.

Akyeampong, E., & Obeng, P. (1995). Spirituality, gender, and power in Asante history. *International Journal of African Historical Studies, 28*(3), 481–508.

Asamoah-Gyadu, J. K. (2005a). *African Charismatics. Current developments within independent indigenous pentecostalism in Ghana.* Leiden: Brill.

Asamoah-Gyadu, J. K. (2005b). "Christ is the answer": What is the question? A Ghana airways prayer vigil and its implications for religion, evil and public space. *Journal of Religion in Africa, 35*(1), 93–117.

Barker, E. (1993). Charismatization: The social production of 'an ethos propitious to the mobilisation of sentiments'. In E. Barker, J. A. Beckford, & K. Dobbelaere (Eds.), *Secularization, rationalism and sectarianism.* Oxford: Clarendon Press.

Gyekye, K. (1987). *An essay on African philosophical thought. The Akan conceptual scheme.* Cambridge: Cambridge University Press.

Kalu, O. U. (2007). Pentecostalism and Mission in Africa, 1970–2000. *Mission Studies, 24,* 9–45.

Kirsch, T. G. (2014). The precarious center: Religious leadership among African Christians. *Religion and Society, 5*(1), 47–64.

Lauterbach, K. (2010). Becoming a pastor: Youth and social aspirations in Ghana. *Young: Nordic Journal of Youth Research, 18*(3), 259–278.

Lauterbach, K. (2016). Religious entrepreneurs in Ghana. In U. Röschenthaler & D. Schulz (Eds.), *Cultural entrepreneurship in Africa*. London: Routledge.

McCaskie, T. C. (1992). People and animals: Constru(ct)ing the Asante experience. *Africa, 62*(2), 221–247.

McCaskie, T. C. (1995). *State and society in pre-colonial Asante*. Cambridge: Cambridge University Press.

McCaskie, T. C. (2008a). *Akwantemfi*–'In mid-journey': An Asante shrine today and its clients. *Journal of Religion in Africa, 38*(1), 1–24.

Miescher, S. (2005). *Making men in Ghana*. Bloomington & Indianapolis: Indiana University Press.

Soothill, J. E. (2007). *Gender, social change and spiritual power. Charismatic Christianity in Ghana*. Brill: Leiden.

Weber, M. (1978). In G. Roth & C. Wittich (Eds.), *Economy and society. An outline of interpretive sociology*. Berkeley: University of California Press.

Wilks, I. (1993). *Forest of gold: Essays on the Akan and the kingdom of Asante*. Athens, OH: Ohio University Press.

Wiredu, K. (1980). *Philosophy and an African culture*. Cambridge: Cambridge University Press.

Wyllie, R. W. (1974). Pastors and prophets in Winneba, Ghana: Their social background and career development. *Africa, 44*(2), 186–193.

CHAPTER 5

Performing Spiritual Power and Knowledge

I first came to think of pastorship as a way to be a 'big man' when attending a church service in one of Kumasi's bigger charismatic churches. I met the head pastor in the parking area outside the church. He had been travelling and had just returned. He stepped out of his car and from the passenger's seat came an assistant pastor, who had been accompanying him on the trip. The assistant pastor carried his Bible and walked behind the pastor as they entered church. Later that evening, we attended a church service, where the head pastor was sitting on stage in a large armchair with golden ornaments. Although other pastors were leading prayers and worship, the head pastor was in charge and orchestrated what happened. He did the preaching, and in this way performed knowledge of the word of God. He was also the one who mediated the power of the Holy Ghost. Through deliverance and divination, he performed access to and control of spiritual power.

This chapter delves into another aspect of the craft of pastorship, namely the performance and manifestation of spiritual power and knowledge of the word of God. Within the local Asante religious understanding, it is within these two domains that pastors need to perform well in order to prove that they have mastered the craft of pastorship. Church members highlight how pastors mediate the word of God and pastors' ability to show spiritual power, when they account for their attachment to a particular church and pastor. Pastors show and perform spiritual power in different ways, most often at church services, through prayers and performance of miracles, deliverance and divination. It is also within this domain that

© The Author(s) 2017
K. Lauterbach, *Christianity, Wealth, and Spiritual Power in Ghana*,
DOI 10.1007/978-3-319-33494-3_5

some charismatic pastors compete with each other or with neo-traditional priests about who possesses most spiritual power. The performance of spiritual power is therefore also a contested field in which accusations of using evil power and magic are made. In addition, pastors show knowledge of the word of God through their preaching and Bible teaching, and also through the publication of books and the use of social media. Having and using spiritual power is not only a question of access to the spiritual realm, but also a question of knowledge.

There has recently been scholarly interest in aesthetic forms and performative practice when analysing religious authority and leadership (De Witte et al. 2015). The aim is to shift focus from analysing religious authority as mainly located in textual and discursive realms to include its aesthetic and performative aspects of religious leadership. Although, I am not interested in discussing performance as such, but rather the role of spiritual power and knowledge, I share the view that performance is an important aspect in the construction of authority. It is in showing and doing that the pastor convinces his audience, not only in church, but also among the wider community. By including textual production in the analysis of how pastors show knowledge of the Bible, I also understand text as something that has a performative aspect to it.

Spiritual Power

As mentioned in the introductory chapter of this book, the spiritual realm is a source of power in the Asante context, and *tumi* (the ability to bring about change) is a form of power that originates in the spiritual realm (Akyeampong and Obeng 1995). It is the ability to join this form of power that is the key to success and self-realisation (McCaskie 2007c). We also need to recall that this form of power, or this local understanding of power, means that power is something you draw upon, and not something (an attribute) that lies within the individual. One needs to get access to it and master it, and this is done by having the knowledge on how to get access to these sources of power (Akyeampong 1996; Akyeampong and Obeng 1995; McCaskie 1995).

A powerful pastor in a charismatic context is one who is able to perform miracles; 'the transcendent realm is a realm of active power, interventions and refuge' (Asamoah-Gyadu 2005b: 105). The type of pastoral work that is related to mundane things, such as problem solving, counselling, and giving advice, is also closely linked to the pastor's spiritual power. An example of this is how church attendants approach pastors after church services on different matters. They seek advice and prayers in relation to education, exams, marriage and family matters, before travelling, or opening a business. They need spiritual power for success and protection. It is also common in a Ghanaian context to rely on spiritual persons when having problems. As Asamoah-Gyadu writes:

> ... when difficulties in life acquire a set pattern, it is a sign of the influence of evil powers at work. In such cases, you need one who could truly be called a 'man of God', that is one who has the anointing to deal with such supernatural interventions. (Asamoah-Gyadu 2005b: 102)

The religious expert is a mediator between the spiritual world and the material world and holds specific gifts and powers, which give him an, a priori, privileged position. Being a mediator implies controlling access to spiritual power and having the ability and power to make things change (*tumi*). Claiming access to the spiritual world has a specific meaning, not only in the church and among church members, but also because of its historic resonance in Asante. The wider recognition of a pastor's status reflects this perception of religious experts as mediators between the material world and the spiritual world and the status and power attached to this position (Akyeampong and Obeng 1995; Asamoah-Gyadu 2005a, b).

But spiritual power is also ambivalent. It is common among charismatics to believe that there are two basic sources of power. As one pastor explained: 'There is power from God and power from the Devil. Those are the two basic sources of power.'[1] He further said that to take power (*gye tumi*) means taking it from the spiritual realm: 'They take it from fetish priests, marine spirits, goddesses, mallams etc. There is a fetish priest (Kwaku Bonsam) who claims he gives several pastors power to operate with.' The pastor refers to charismatic pastors being suspected and accused of drawing on power that they get through traditional priests, which is seen to be associated with evil (*bone*). This claim is also made by some traditional priests themselves. It is said that in particular one traditional priest (Nana Kwaku Bonsam) provides spiritual power to many pastors and he also claims that himself.[2]

Making accusations of a traditional priest providing spiritual power to pastors and suspecting pastors of relying on evil power creates a common religious space, or battleground, that involves both traditional religion, Christianity and Islam.[3] What is of importance in these religious controversies is not doctrinal differences, but who provides power to whom and what the source of that power is. It is in particular the use of spiritual power associated with evil that is contested. In her work on the Ewe on Ghana, Meyer (1992, 1999) has shown how ideas of the devil were introduced with missionary Christianity, translated and appropriated in the Ewe context and later re-appropriated by charismatic Christianity. These ideas continue to play a role in conversion to Christianity as well as in moral discussions of good and bad. Rather than categorising the devil or evil forces as 'heathendom' as did Christian missionaries, charismatic Christianity draws on and refers to ideas of evil as co-existing with the spiritual force associated with God and the Holy Spirit. In this way, charismatic pastors use a conceptual language and frame of reference that corresponds with that of other religious specialists; they are in the same playing field, so to speak. An illustration of this is when pastors throw a spiritual challenge which involves a traditional priest. In one case, Pastor Obinim (a controversial pastor from Kumasi) threw a public challenge of 'miracles, signs and wonders' to prove that he had a divine calling. It was reported that one of his associated pastors had begged the traditional priest Nana Kwaku Bonsam not to take up the challenge, as they would not be sure of the outcome of the contest.[4]

The source of power that charismatic pastors use is the Holy Spirit. There are differences between the two sources of power in the sense that power associated with the devil can be difficult to discern or know about, and consequently difficult to leave. In a conversation about how to distinguish between the different sources of power, a pastor recounted a story about how a pastor built a church unknowingly with the use of evil power and this resulted in him having to abandon being a pastor:

> I remember of story from one pastor who had a congregation of about 40–60. He was jealous of a certain pastor who had about 500 members. He therefore went to the senior pastor and sought for his help. The other pastor asked him to come to his house the following day so they could talk more. He went there on the Sunday and the other pastor just advised him to be patient. Afterwards, food was served for both of them, rice and stew, and they both ate together. From then, the church of the younger pastor started growing rapidly. However, he started having dreams of sleeping with a particular lady frequently. At a point, his congregation grew to about 800 people. He was having a counselling session one day and a lady came and asked him to give money to rent an apartment but he had never seen her

before. He asked her where she knew him from and she said that she was the one who has been appearing in his dreams. She explained to him how it happened and said that the meat he ate in his friend's house was what was used to initiate him and that she was surprised his friend did not tell him about it. So he had become part of the cult without his knowledge. She said that she was now pregnant so when he rents the apartment, she would go and stay there so that when she delivers, they would pound the baby and it would add 500 congregation to his church. So anytime she delivered and the baby was pounded, there would be additional 500 members. He was afraid so he run to a church and told them to deliver him and take over his congregation. He quit being a pastor. It happened in Kumasi. I don't know him but a friend told me about it. In this case, he was not aware of what he was doing. You would have to be careful and be strong in your spiritual life.[5]

The important point in this story is that a pastor would not necessarily be aware of using power associated with evil and that it is very hard to disassociate from this form of power once one has taken it. In the story, there is also an element of jealousy, greed, or impatience that leads the younger pastor to rely on evil power in order to grow, although this took place without him being aware of it. This reflects the earlier discussion in Chap. 3 around the accumulation of wealth and truthful pastors, but it also reflects Asante notions of evil as associated with something hidden, with excess and envy (Olsen 2015: 305). There is a moral aspect associated with pastors' actions and behaviour, whether it concerns the accumulation and use of wealth or whether it is about their eagerness to grow and their use of evil power. Their legitimacy and authority as pastors is closely connected to where they insert themselves in this moral landscape and how they are able to show it to others. It might sound as if I am indicating that this is a strategic endeavour. This is not the purpose. What I am trying to convey is that a moral space is not something that one masters or operates within, but rather something that is under the influence of outside forces. At the same time, being truthful or having access to spiritual power that stems from God is something that pastors need to show and perform to the surrounding world. It is in this moment, where performance is being read, translated and approved by other people, that a pastor's position and authority is precarious, to use the phrase of Kirsch (2014). This religious space is an open space, and a space of interpretation. As the source of spiritual power is not always revealed or even knowable to the one using it, it is an issue that can always be debated and interpreted. The source of spiritual power is never permanently defined, which means that a pastor's position is fragile and can be destabilised. This, moreover, means that pastors can be tested, controlled, and challenged by other pastors or people who wish to question their authority. As mentioned in Chap. 2, chiefs tried to control the priests (*akɔmfoɔ*) by testing their spiritual skills and their ability to make prophecies. Within the religious landscape today, it is also the ability to control and master spiritual power that defines a person who has religious authority. This is tested through a pastor's ability to pray, to fight evil forces, to prophesise, and to show knowledge of the word of God.

Genuine pastors take power from the Holy Spirit, but the power of the Holy Spirit can leave. Pastor Daniel explained: 'It is very easy for the Holy Spirit to leave you and it is very easy for it to come back.' By this, he means that it is a form of power that is never entirely in your own control or a power that you possess. To have it requires spiritual maturity and spiritual strength. This indicates that pastors have to work constantly on their spiritual maturity in order to retain the power of the Holy Spirit. He furthermore explained that although the power of the Holy Spirit can leave, one's spiritual gifts could remain.

It is through a pastor's performance of spiritual power that the source of this power is recognised. The way a pastor preaches, the way a pastor uses money, or the way a pastor relates to other people are read as signs of from whence they take power. Pastor Daniel exemplifies this with how pastors who are too self-focused talk about their work: 'Some of the ministers are easily identified because of the way they talk. Some of them are very ignorant and make certain proclamations like "*magye wo*" (I have saved you) … The pastors attribute their being able to heal or perform miracles to the power they have so instead of saying "God has saved you," they say "I have saved you"'.[6] In this way, they do not acknowledge the power of God, or the Godly intervention, but ascribe what has happened to themselves.

Pastors use and perform spiritual power in different ways. As mentioned above, they provide spiritual protection and spiritual interventions to adherents. They do this in a number of ways such as the performance of miracles, deliverance of evil spirits, prayers, and prophesising. Praying in particular is seen as an important way to protect against evil forces and consequently to attain success. Praying is an individual practice of church members and pastors, but it can also be a collective practice in which joint praying leads to a stronger spiritual intervention (see also Daswani 2015).

When Pastor Seth founded a church (Hope Palace Chapel), it was first located in a school. After seven years, the church bought a plot of land in

Kokode in the Kwadaso Agric area of Kumasi. Because the area is seen as being under strong influence from evil spirits, the pastors need to be very strong and consistent in praying; otherwise, the church would not grow. The pastor organised a prayer chain consisting of 15 people, who pray all days of the week: it 'starts from around 7 p.m. which is the first batch to 10 p.m. They break and another batch take over till 1 a.m. The last batch comes at 1 a.m. and close at 4 a.m. where we close for the day.'[7] The prayer chain is necessary to keep the evil forces at bay, which are particularly strong in this area. The area hosts the agricultural college of Kumasi with many students coming from the northern parts of the country. In addition to that, the area has a shrine (named Ku Dapaakuo, meaning God of Wednesday). The particular spot on which the church was built had many big trees and was a meeting place for evil forces. Therefore, it was difficult for the church to take off and it lost members in the beginning. The members observed the presence of evil forces in the mad men coming to church services. These mad men were disguised evil forces coming from a nearby river, who had transformed themselves into human beings and came to the church to prevent it from succeeding (Fig. 5.1).

Fig. 5.1 Hope Palace Chapel, Kwadaso Agric, Kumasi

The church was the only one in the area and therefore the pastor's battle against the evil forces had to be intense and strong. Pastor Seth saw it as part of his obligation to take this on:

> It is the duty of the pastor to do that, protect his members, bless them and open doors for the church to grow ... They [the evil spirits] oppose the welfare of the church members, their Christian lives etc. So as a pastor, I need to pray and defend my people against these.[8]

Through the prayer chain, in which all pastors of the church pray in turns all days of the week, Pastor Seth demonstrates his access to and ability to invoke spiritual power. In this case, it is about the success of the church as well as the good of his members, but it is at the same time a question about spiritual domination of a place. As the place has a history of strong spiritual presence, Pastor Seth's ability to dominate, fight, and control the evil forces is proof of his power as a pastor.

The analysis of pastors' performance and use of spiritual power, which also includes their relationship to and understanding of evil forces, necessitates a few reflections on how to approach the domain of spiritual agency analytically. By this I am not entering a discussion of the occult as such, but simply wish to recognise that a modern religious movement has to be understood in relation to traditional forms of belief and that these sets of beliefs are mutually constitutive (Bernault 2013: 53; Ranger 2007). Taking a broader and longer historical perspective on the spiritual domain also reminds us of the political connotations of having access to spiritual power. As mentioned earlier, the chief is, in the Akan worldview, seen as someone who mediates between the living and the dead (Busia 1951: 26), and he is a medium through which people can gain access to spiritual power. Therefore, an analysis of charismatic pastors' reference to and struggle against evil forces can also be approached as an analysis of local theories of power. As Bernault has shown from the context of Equatorial Africa, the use of the fetish is both a reproduction of colonial categories, but it is at the same time a way to 'rely on a long-standing theory of composing power indifferent to the modern prescription on the separation of the secular and the mystical' (Bernault 2013: 66). In much the same way, charismatic pastors performing their ability to dominate evil forces are also demonstrating their power or *tumi*.

Church Services: *mise-en-scène*

Another aspect of performing spiritual power and knowledge is the staging of pastors, in particular during church services. I analyse the role of pastors during, before and after church services; how they perform and how they relate to attendants/audience and junior pastors. Church services provide a space for pastors to perform and present themselves. A church service is also a moment in which members show dedication, legitimise or validate the authority of the pastor (see Kirsch 2002 for a similar discussion in a Zambian context). The functions and performance of pastors at church services highlight the crucial elements of pastorship such as guidance and advice giving, being a role model, providing spiritual services such as prayers, prophesising, and displaying wealth. Pastors show and perform power in two ways. First, as power over people (subjects as wealth) in the sense that the pastor attracts people and thereby resources and attention. The pastor can get people to do things, which means he has control over people. Second, as spiritual power: a church service is the ultimate moment to show spiritual power and links to God. Spiritual power is shown in the way the pastors pray, in how the congregants feel the presence of the Holy Spirit, and when the pastor lays his hands on people. In these ways, he demonstrates his direct link to God and, for instance, his ability to heal.

The Sunday service is the event that the largest number of people attend. It is an occasion to see the pastor perform and it is the opportunity par excellence for the pastor to be staged. Often, Sunday Services are recorded so people can buy them afterwards and, in some cases, the services are transmitted over the radio. There are variations in how church services are conducted having to do with the size of church, location, the reputation of the pastor and so on. However, there are common traits with regard to the structure of the service. Church services in charismatic churches are, most often, divided into four parts: praise and worship (singing), offerings, prayers and sermon. In his book on the Church of Pentecost in Ghana, Daswani describes how the opening prayers and worship serve as a way to invoke the Holy Spirit and make attendants ready and open to receive the power of the Holy Spirit (Daswani 2015: 80). In the churches I studied, it was often younger pastors who lead these sessions and who could thus show their ability to call on and activate spiritual power. Other activities such as Bible studies, testimonies, alter calls, and announcements take place to a varying degree. Although the pastor does not play a central role in all these activities, he is involved in one way or the other, as observer or as participant. During the first part of a church service (praise and worship), the head pastor is most often not present. This depends on the size of the church, though. It was common that the head pastor, who would normally preach unless there was a visiting pastor, would come into the church when the church service had already started. In the bigger churches in Kumasi, people danced during the praise and worship session. Sometimes the head pastor would also dance, throw money at the musicians, or acknowledge what they were doing in some other way. An associate pastor would lead a prayer session in which everyone participated, and then introduce the head pastor. The pastor would be welcomed or introduced with music and people shouting.[9]

The sermon is an important moment of the church service. As a social phenomenon, it serves as a way to acquire knowledge from the Bible, and as a means for the pastor to show that he or she possess that knowledge and is able to mediate it in a powerful and relevant message (to show wisdom and knowledge). It is also a moment for the pastor to show access to spiritual power through the performance of spiritual services such as prophesising and deliverance and this provides the audience with the opportunity to receive such services. Normally, sermons are delivered in a very energetic way. The pastor talks loudly; shouts, runs and moves a lot and seeks to interact with people in the form of asking questions to the audience and getting responses. The audience gives comments, laughs, and claps. Sometimes it takes the form of the pastor shouting 'Hello' and the audience replying 'Hi' or 'talk to us daddy' and this exchange could be repeated many times during a sermon.

During church services, pastors are often sitting at a central place in a chair that is bigger than the chairs junior pastors and prominent guests use. In the bigger churches, the chair could be placed on the stage where musicians are, and in smaller churches at the front of the church. The chairs are upholstered with golden armrests. The symbolism of these chairs and the pastor being centrally placed during church service is not unique to the Asante context. Still, it is worthwhile drawing attention to Asante chiefs and the historic role and symbolism of stools. In an article on the Ghanaian seat of state as a piece of political iconography, Lentz (2010) points to the royal connotations of the seat and its resemblance to stools of Asante chiefs. She explains, 'stools are regarded as central objects of power that connect the chief with the ancestral world and the power of his predecessors' (Lentz 2010: 50).[10] Although the large decorated armchairs that some charismatic pastors use do not physically resemble traditional stools, there is a symbolism of power and links to the metaphysical world that is invoked.

After church services, many church members seek a more personal encounter with the pastor. In some churches, members queue outside the office of the pastor. In the bigger churches, the pastors might not be available for such an encounter so one would have to book an appointment through a secretary. People come with personal problems, seek advice, and ask for letters of recommendation and for prayers and healing. Church members would for instance ask for prayers before an exam or for counselling in case of family problems. This shows that the pastor is not only a figure that plays a role in church, but that he also has a more personal function related to the individual needs of the church members.

But not all pastors preach. Head pastors preach at Sunday services, while junior pastors conduct prayer sessions, do Bible studies, lead music and worship, and translate sermons. In other words, the work of pastors depend on the status they have in church. Preaching is considered important because it serves as a platform on which one can prove and perform spiritual power and therefore access to such a platform becomes an issue of control and power. If pastors are not permitted to preach, it is oftentimes perceived as a hindrance to their possibilities of growing and performing 'bigness' and spiritual power. Some pastors find other platforms from which they can preach and hence prove their ability to mediate the word of God.

One example of pastors who most often do not preach are female pastors. Although female pastors are accepted in charismatic churches, they are often not able to rise as much in the church hierarchy as men (an exception being when women have established their own churches, as for instance Christie Doe-Tetteh of Solid Rock Chapel International).[11] A female pastor had attended Bible school, but was not recognised as a pastor in her church. Explaining her situation she said:

> The pastoral work is hard in Ghana, especially for the women. My church doesn't accept lady pastors so in my church they just put me in charge of the ladies in all the branches, other than that they don't give women a permanent place to operate as a pastor. For instance, when I travelled recently I had a convention with the ladies in the Brong Ahafo region. It was a three-day convention. So I'll say that in a way I'm a pastor because to be

able to take or lead that amount of women for three days is not easy. For my salary, because I am not stationed as a pastor I don't really earn any big salary, but God has said that he is our rewarder. I get some income from the programmes we organise ... and I'm alright with it.[12]

This woman did pastoral work outside the church in order for her to function and perform as a pastor. She preached once a week in the information room at the Kejetia market in Kumasi, and that meant that her message and preaching was transmitted on loudspeakers all over the market. In other churches, female pastors are more accepted, but still women complain that they are not given the same positions and space as their male counterparts.

Many younger pastors express dissatisfaction if they are not allowed to preach, as they are not able to prove their ability to communicate the 'word of God'. Junior pastors perform in different ways; they accompany and assist senior pastors, translate sermons (and when doing this they also imitate the bodily and vocal expressions of the pastor preaching), conduct prayers, provide technical assistance, but they are not often at centre stage. A young pastor in Kumasi is a lay preacher in the Christ Apostolic Church. He takes care of the English service, and the head pastor does the service in Twi. In this church, the pastors are not allowed to do prophecy and deliverance on Sundays; these activities are allocated to other days of the week. As there are many young pastors in the church, it is difficult to get the chance to do prophecy and deliverance. The pastor explained: 'I do not have the opportunity to do that [prophecy] because there are lots of people doing that there. So I am not given the opportunity to do that there. I operate those gifts outside the church, in other places.'[13] This pastor helps a friend in a Bible school, where he teaches and instructs young pastors. He has also started his own fellowship, where he conducts Bible studies and prayer meetings.

Being a good preacher not only requires invoking spiritual power, it also demands that the pastor is able to perform knowledge.

The Production of Text, the Performance of Knowledge

This section offers an analysis of how pastors produce and perform text and knowledge. Pastors attach great importance to writing texts in the form of advice-giving books, pamphlets, biographies and autobiographies, as well as writings on social media. It is a way to raise one's status as a pastor and gain public attention (Gifford 2004: 36). The role of media (film, music) in charismatic Christianity has been analysed in particular as a self-promoting process, and also as transmission of religious values (De Witte 2003, 2005; Meyer 2001; Shipley 2009). Preaching is also a text producing and performing practice. In the following I will, however, concentrate only on written text. The argument also furthermore builds on the understanding that literacy, knowledge, and status are interwoven and that the production of text is a constitutive part of social being and social relations (Barber 2007a). Consequently, text is a way of portraying oneself as an important and 'big' person.

Pastors use text in different forms and ways to construct themselves as figures of authority and appear as trustworthy people. This implies showing that they possess knowledge and that this knowledge is based on and stems from the word of God. It is important for how they establish themselves publicly alongside other performative practices such as healing, prophesising, and praying. Producing and performing text is distinct, because it is a way to show that one possesses knowledge and wisdom. One way of showing this is by quoting the Bible in written text (Newell 2005). When describing what a good pastor and preacher is, both pastors and church members emphasise the ability to mediate the word of God. In the words of one pastor:

> It entails the choice of words, how the message impacts the listeners; being able to direct the listeners to the thinking of God from the Scripture. Somebody might read but not understand what God is about. A leader is supposed to discern and know what the scripture means or what God wants to say; making people accept what you say, but not twisting the truth to suit the preacher.[14]

In the quote, the pastor refers both to the knowledge of the Bible, and also to how this knowledge influences and affects the pastor's audience. This indicates that knowledge is both something one possesses and something that needs to be activated and manifested in other people in order to serve as a sign of a pastor's authority. Church members can discern the genuineness of a pastor through his teachings. A church member explained how she could distinguish between fake and genuine pastors because of the teachings of her pastor: 'From the teachings that I have had from this church, it would be easy to detect the fake ones. Here, we are fed with the unadulterated word of God … I do not believe so much in the working of the miracles.'[15] This woman sees the pastor's ability to teach the words of the Bible as more important than spiritual performances such as miracles.

The following analysis of pastors using the production and performance of text as a platform to build up status has resonance with Ghanaian traditions of using literature as a way to expose knowledge and wisdom. In her study on Ghanaian popular fiction, Newell discusses the proverb as a way to make sense of how authors 'quote from "outside" texts in order to generate further text of their own' (Newell 2000: 11). She shows how this practice was used by 'youngmen' and was a way to create a proverbial space in which their texts were recognised and through which they gained a form of authority. She notes, 'At the time of writing, then, these men probably would have been excluded from the formal status-conferring discourses of their elders' (Newell 2000: 11). To speak publicly was linked to age and status, but the ability to create a space for speaking and writing that transgressed these social boundary markers was a way to gain status. Pastors draw on similar practices when they for instance quote the Bible and other religious authorities to express 'truths about life' (Newell 2000: 12). By doing this, they are trying to bypass status and authority ascribed to older generations, who were traditionally seen as wise and as possessing knowledge.

In the analysis of text, I follow Barber's point on the double existence of text. First, text is a social act, a form of social behaviour meant to do certain things, and second, it is a reflection and a commentary on society (either to approve social facts or a form of social critique), which implies that texts are also reflexive (Barber 2007a: 3–4). I am particularly interested in this duality of text when analysing the making of pastoral careers. Text is produced in order to enhance the social status of a pastor, but it also provides a certain reading of society that is expressed through the text (see also Newell[2000: 8]). I do not, however, account for how pastors' publications and texts are perceived and used by those who read them. I am interested in the messages conveyed in these different publications and in how being capable of producing and publishing such texts is part of becoming a 'big' pastor.

When visiting the bigger charismatic churches, it is common to find a stand outside the church that sells books, magazines, CDs, DVDs, and other religious material. These stands often sell a mix of religious self-help literature of Ghanaian, Nigerian or American origin, and CDs and books with the local pastor's sermons and writings. The texts often contain advice on how to succeed in a certain spectrum of life (marriage, business, education, for instance), and on how to become a good Christian. Of the pastors I talked to, the 'biggest' ones had published at least one book, and many of the pastors who were on the ascendant talked about their plans to publish books.[16] The books are often locally produced and are not necessarily widely distributed, but sold in churches, local supermarkets and book stores and given out personally by the pastors (see also Newell 2005: 300). Most books had a word of dedication inside and some of the books had a foreword written by the spiritual father or mentor of the author.

The book that I analyse in the following section combines quotations from the Bible with the author's advice and thinking about the relation between wisdom and being spiritually mature. What is particular about proving wisdom through written text is, as Newell asserts, that 'publishing activities may enhance the perception that seems to prevail among authors that essential truths are locked within the written word, accessible only through one's intense study of the printed page' and when messages are written down 'they are instilled with divine importance' (Newell 2005: 302). Following this, pastors mediate and provide access to the word of God through their writings. In the case of charismatic pastors, however, oral texts as performed during preaching are also attached with importance and are often a more direct way church members get access to the pastor's knowledge.

'Building Your Spirit Man': On Wisdom and Knowledge of God

Victor Osei is the founder and leader of Family Chapel International in Kumasi. When I first met him in 2005 he had published two books, among which one was entitled 'Building your spirit man'. The book consists of 56 pages and five chapters called (1) 'Importance of Building your spirit man', (2) 'Obtain', (3) 'Maintain', (4) 'Abstain', and (5) 'Sustaining the blessing'. The book is structured in the way that it contains quotes from the Bible combined with advice on how to become a strong and faithful Christian and hence successful in life.

Several themes run through the book, such as how to become successful, how to grow spiritually, how to develop a good character and the role of wisdom and knowledge in order to become spiritually mature. The importance and the nature of wisdom and knowledge are discussed extensively throughout the book. In the beginning of the book (in the chapter 'Importance of building your spirit man') the author discusses the relation between wisdom and age. He starts by quoting the Bible:

> I said, Days should speak, and multitude of years should teach wisdom. But there is a spirit in man: and the inspiration of the almighty giveth them understanding. Great men are not always wise: neither do the aged understand judgement. (Job 32: 7–9, in Osei 2005: 13)

As mentioned earlier, Biblical quotations are used as a means to give the text authority as it associates the author's written word closely with the word of God. The author then goes on to define what knowledge is by writing what it is not. This touches, in particular, on the relation between wisdom and age:

> Wisdom does not come with age. It comes by the knowledge of God. There are many who think they qualify to be called wise by virtue of their age or their status in society. I beg to differ. Wisdom is of the Lord and he gives it to those who serve and obey him. There are instances where children have proven wiser than their parents and there have been occasions where students have proven wiser than their teachers. Wisdom and age have nothing in common. The wisdom of the aged is experience. Remember God communicates with our spirit, imparting wisdom and understanding. (Osei 2005: 13)

In this quote, the author disconnects wisdom and age. This is a challenge to the understanding in Akan societies that old people possess wisdom and knowledge and that their role is to give advice to younger people, settle disputes and so on (Miescher 2005; van der Geest 2002). Victor Osei thereby puts forward a critique or commentary on the social structures of the society in which he lives. He touches on the actual meaning of wisdom and how it is acquired, and also challenges the understanding that wisdom is obtained by listening to older people and through experience as well as the understanding that 'the older you become, the more knowledge you collect' (van der Geest 2002: 440). Victor Osei, on the other hand, asserts that wisdom comes from God and by having knowledge about God.

He furthermore differentiates between wisdom (i.e. given by God) and experience (that comes with age). He transfers, although more indirectly, some of the virtues that are traditionally related to being an elderly person, to pastors (and himself). The pastor is the one who mediates the word of God, who knows the word of God, who has knowledge and thereby can give advice to other people. This understanding reflects the form of social critique that I mentioned earlier that challenges the prestige and power of elderly people. This understanding, however, not only contains a social critique or a discontinuity in ideas around wisdom, knowledge and belief. His formulations also draw on an Asante understanding of power as originating in the spiritual realm and where knowledge is acquired to get power (Akyeampong and Obeng 1995: 482).

In the book, Victor Osei also writes about the use of knowledge in terms of guidance on how to live your life. He writes:

> When a wise man that fears God speaks, it is as if you hear the voice of God. His words never fall to the ground. His words are held in high regard and anything he says is done. One vital trait of such a man is his good character … As we build our spirit man, we have to get wisdom in order to live the life God wants us to live. (Osei 2005: 14–15)

Here, Victor Osei establishes a link between being a wise person and being a mediator between the material and the spiritual world (a pastor), and that becoming such a person requires listening to the word of God. At the same time, in a more indirect manner, he reflects on the role of pastors in society; pastors both as people that are widely respected in society and as people that have good character, and these virtues depend upon their knowledge of the word of God. In this way, Victor Osei uses his writings to establish himself both through the production of text as well as via the messages of the text.

There are parallels between pastors' practices of producing text and the Ghanaian tradition of producing popular fiction and proverbs as mentioned above. To repeat Newell's point, it is a way for younger people to obtain status and gain access to a space where wisdom is performed. The writings of pastors and their use of various Biblical quotations can be seen, I argue, as analogous to former uses of the proverbial space.

Social Media and New Spaces of Textual Performance

A more recent way of producing and displaying text is pastors' writings on social media, where they post pictures of church events, provide thoughts and advice on life and religious matters and share ads on upcoming religious programmes.[17] They use these new platforms to expose themselves and their wisdom and knowledge. It is a way of displaying themselves publicly and at the same time a means to engage and interact with people directly through text. This is different both from writings published in books and from oral text performed for instance in church during preaching and prayers. Communication on social media allows pastors to communicate directly with their followers in a way that is exposed to other people, and this makes it a powerful tool in terms of portraying oneself as a 'big man of God'.

Many of the pastors I talked to during fieldwork have their own personal pages on Facebook. It is worth noting that these pages appear as their personal pages and not the pages of their respective churches. This underlines the point raised earlier that in the charismatic churches, the focus is much more on the pastor as a person than on the church as such; people attend a church to be under the name of a specific pastor. Some pastors posted updates, comments and pictures several times a week, whereas others did so more rarely. The pastors used the pages to make personal comments on various issues, to quote the Bible, to advertise activities in church, and to upload pictures of themselves or from church. People also write messages to pastors, for instance to show gratitude or to make contact. One pastor had more than 5000 friends, whereas others had between 400 and 800 friends.

In their writings, pastors reflect on life and offer 'truths about life', which people respond to or acknowledge through their replies or their likes. The writings could touch upon the following themes: 'gratefulness and how we depend on other people', 'disloyalty and betrayal', 'relationships', 'intimacy', 'personal growth', 'importance of praying and fasting' and in some rare occasions, political events like the petition on the Ghanaian presidential elections in 2012.

One example is Victor Osei, founder and leader of Family Chapel International in Kumasi, who has two Facebook pages. He is active in his use of Facebook and posts pictures from church events and videos from church services with his messages, as well as more personal pictures. At one point of time, he divided his comments into two overall categories: 'thots' (divided into sub categories such as 'mornin thots', 'noon thots', and 'nite thots') that contain his reflections on a number of issues and 'prayer train' where he writes and interprets quotes from the Bible.

In one update, he reflects on people's self-perception:

> Thots ... YOU THINK U ARE BUT U ARE NOT WHAT U THINK. YOU ARE ... # MR SOMEBODY NOBODY
> Comments:
> thi9s calls for deep wisdom to understand papa ... lol
> Sure papa, yet I will go for Nobody Somebody. For a nobody in the hands of God is Somebody. Humility must be the key then

> deep
> dis is wisdom! Deep thots[18]

Besides making a Biblical reference,[19] the post can be read as Victor Osei alluding to the issue of pastors' legitimacy in the sense that a pastor who promotes himself without having the merits to do so is a 'nobody' rather than the 'somebody' he pretends to be. This reflection touches upon the distinction between false and true pastor and the concept of truthfulness as discussed in Chap. 3.

Another of his Facebook postings resembled more of a prayer or a commandment under direct spiritual influence. It was liked by 88 people and 39 comments were made of which most were 'amen':

> Nite thots … I COMMAND HEALING INTO UR BODY NOW IN JESUS NAME … AMEN.[20]

Another pastor wrote the following message on his personal Facebook page:

> when yr mind is not develop you often despise important things

To which people responded and acknowledged the message as proof of the pastor's knowledge and wisdom:

> hmmmmmmmmmm true
> Deep!! Bless yu Man of God
> Thank you Rev., that is well said, GOD bless you[21]

In another update, the same pastor commented on the role of politicians as leaders and implicitly compared their role to the role pastors play as leaders. He referred to politicians as being more interested in their own future and success than in the good of society. This followed a common narrative of seeing politicians as self-promoting and afflicted by a culture of corruption. His reflection also touched upon being truthful as a leader by looking after the wellbeing of the community:

> Politicians are concerned about the next ELECTION, not about the wellbeing of the populace who voted them in power BUT real LEADERS are concern about the next GENERATION. How they can influence and impact the people they are and will be serving during their time on earth.[22]

In most of these writings, there are no direct Bible quotations, which is why they can be compared to the 'truths about life' mentioned above, rather than Bible teachings as such. Moreover, it is a pastor's 'friends' or 'followers' who, through their comments, place the virtue of wisdom on the pastors. There is an instant moment of recognition, which is expressed in the form of text and therefore is visible and displayed to other 'friends' and 'followers'.

Sometimes, but more rarely, pastors' writings touch more directly on current events and politics. At the end of August 2013, when the Ghanaian Supreme Court dismissed the petition of the New Patriotic Party (NPP) over alleged election fraud during the presidential elections in Ghana in December 2012 (which the NPP lost)[23], Victor Osei posted a number of comments to this political situation. He wrote:

> legal thots ... COURTS DO NOT DEAL WITH THE WISHES AND SENTIMENTS OF ORDINARY CITIZENS... THEY DEAL WITH LEGALITIES AND TECHNICALITIES...??? HMMMM

Some of the comments were:

> God bless u Papa
> true daddy
> Daddy infact this message sent me thinking the whole morning and now its very clear after the virdict was read. Ur truely a man of wisdom. Its like you had the vision already!!

> NOON THOTS ... GUILTINESS REST ON THEIR CONSCIENCE ... OH JEAH .. THEY LIVE A LIFE OF FALSE PRETENSE EVERY DAY THESE ARE THE BIG FISH WHO ALWAYS TRY TO EAT DOWN THE SMALL FISH ... THEY WILL DO ANYTHING TO MATERIALIZE THEIR EVERY WISH WOE TO THE DOWNPRESSOR ... THE EAT THE BREAD OF SORROWS ... THEY EAT THE BREAD OF SAD TOMORROW ... OH YEAH ... VERY PROPHETIC ... BOB MARLEY

Some of the comments were:

> hmmmm
> *Nsem pii* [many problems]
> All is well. Let all men be liars and God be true
> Daddy, well understood, God bless you
> Pastor, I am very proud you are my pastor. I think your next should be out now. Thanks
> iam waiting for tomorrow's sermon[24]

These last status updates are unusual in several ways. First, it is rare that charismatic pastors comment directly in favour of one political party (here the NPP). Although people know what party or politician a pastor might be linked to, it is rarely announced openly. And although Victor Osei's family background is well known in Kumasi, they would not be referred to explicitly. What is interesting is that in the above comments he reflects on the decision of the Supreme Court in a way that makes him appear 'above' politics in an ethical sense. He criticises the decision of the court by pointing to law and technicalities as their frame of reference and at the same time puts himself in a position, as a pastor, where he is closer to the wishes and feelings of the people. He is a man of the people. Second, when posing this criticism he refers to and quotes Bob Marley and by doing this, he draws on a different register of popular culture than what is normally done in charismatic churches.

In the above analysis of pastor's production and performance of texts, I have argued that both text as performance and text as commentary are important. By producing text, pastors show that they are knowledgeable, educated and literary, and at the same time by making reference to the Bible, they demonstrate their insight and knowledge about God. Pastors, moreover, produce text that consists of 'truths of life' that are more personalised messages and that convey pastors' knowledge as broad and touching upon different aspects of life, more ethical questions, and also questions of relevance in everyday life.

Discussion

Pastors build up authority and legitimise their positions by referring both to their access to spiritual power and to possessing knowledge. When analysing the public role of charismatic pastors, Asamoah-Gyadu (2005b) draws parallels to the roles played by prophets in the spiritual churches and traditional diviners. He argues that a common feature is the paramount importance of the access to the divine, which enables the religious expert to provide spiritual services. Similarly, Larbi (2001) and Adubofour (1994) interpret the independent charismatic movement in Ghana as a re-appropriation and reinvention of African prophetism, in particular with regard to the centrality of the person.[25] Asamoah-Gyadu (2005b) draws on the work of Baëta ([1962] 2004), who argues that the person or personality is 'the basic operative element' in the spiritual churches (Baëta [1962] 2004: 6). Baëta writes:

> Whether in relation to or independently of events or developments in society, the individual endowed with a striking personality and the ability to impose his own will on others, believing himself, and believed by others to be a special agent of some supernatural being or force, will emerge from time to time and secure a following. Powers traditionally credited to such persons, of healing, of revealing hidden things, predicting the future, cursing and blessing effectually, etc., will be attributed to him whether he claims them or not. (Baëta [1962] 2004: 6)

My argument throughout this book is that, in order to understand the role of charismatic pastors in Ghanaian society today, we need to expand the scope of analysis to include not only the religious domain, but also broader processes of how one achieves wealth and power and becomes 'big'. The argument can be pushed further by suggesting that a successful pastor is perceived of as a complete pastor. The idea of completeness implies that pastors perform and act in different spheres at the same time. Pastors act as spiritual performers, as teachers, as providers and protectors, as father figures, and as persons that build up institutions (cf. Chap. 4). Thereby, they exercise different forms of authority (such as charismatic and bureaucratic) at the same time. The point is that the making of pastorship contains several elements of authority building in an integrated manner, and that this line of thinking questions seeing charismatic and bureaucratic authority as distinct categories.

In his book on writing and charisma in Christian churches in Zambia, Kirsch (2008) questions and moves beyond the classical Weberian distinction between charismatic and bureaucratic authority. He challenges in particular the idea of routinisation of charisma and argues that the written documentation of pastors' sermons, for instance, is a way to authorise their charismatic authority rather than a process of routinisation. He thereby suspends the non-complementarity and separation of the two forms of authority. Instead, Kirsch approaches bureaucratisation as a social practice and argues that "the bureaucratic aspects of this Church are accommodated to local conceptions of religious power" (2008: 184).

Werbner touches upon a similar discussion in his study of young urban charismatics in Apostolic faith-healing churches in Botswana, whom he refers to as 'holy hustlers'. In these churches, there is a clear division and distinction between the young charismatics (prophets and healers) and the leaders of religious office (pastors, bishops and archbishops), which places the charismatic healers outside the official church hierarchy (see also Daswani 2015). This indicates that there is a division between charismatic work and more institutionalised tasks (Werbner 2011: 16, 43). As Werbner writes 'what the prophet has ... is not a definable office within the church hierarchy but a spiritual gift of charisma from God that is thus extrahierarchical' (Werbner 2011: 44). As opposed to the young charismatics in Werbner's work, the young pastors I studied combine both forms of work. They are healers, teachers of the Bible, evangelists, preachers, prophets, and church leaders in one person. The more attributes the more powerful, in the sense that the combination of types of authority and platforms of performance increases the 'bigness' of a pastor, in particular combining charismatic power, knowledge and strong leadership.

Notes

1. Interview with Daniel Darko, Kumasi, 5 December 2014.
2. In an interview on SaharaTV, Nana Kwaku Bonsam says that some pastors come to him to collect power, https://www.youtube.com/watch?v=USogrjgiAtI (accessed 12 April 2016). More recently, according to one source, Nana Kwaku Bonsam claims that he provides spiritual power to over 1700 pastors all over Africa including the renowned T.B. Joshua from Nigeria about who he says 'he is my boy,' BuzzGhana 27 January 2016, http://buzzghana.com/i-fortify-1700-prophets-including-tb-joshua-kwaku-bonsam/ (accessed 12 April 2016).
3. I do not deal with Islam as part of the religious landscape in this book, but it is clear that Muslim leaders are also part of a religious competitive marketplace in which one's spiritual capacities are advertised in public space.
4. GhanaWeb 28 August 2011, http://www.ghanaweb.com/GhanaHomePage/NewsArchive/artikel.php?ID=217328 (accessed 17 December 2014).
5. Interview with Daniel Darko, Kumasi, 5 December 2014.
6. Interview with Daniel Darko, Kumasi, 5 December 2014.
7. Interview with Seth Osei-Kuffour, Kumasi, 8 December 2014.
8. Interview with Seth Osei-Kuffour, Kumasi, 8 December 2014.
9. See also Maxwell (2006a: 141) on the staging of Ezekiel Guti. This pastor and founder of the ZAOGA in Zimbabwe was the last to enter and the first to leave a church service. He was followed by

pastors, and those who wanted to see him were waiting in the corridor outside his office.
10. See also McCaskie (1995: 127–128) on the importance of the belief in the Golden Stool's supernatural origin.
11. See Soothill (2007) for an analysis of the ministry of Christie Doe-Tetteh.
12. Interview with Gloria Mensah Afriyie, Kumasi, 1 September 2005.
13. Interview with Daniel Darko, Kumasi, 5 December 2014.
14. Interview with Seth Osei-Kuffour, Kumasi, 8 December 2014.
15. Interview with Abigail Osei Brefo, Kumasi, 11 December 2014.
16. The titles being for instance: 'Building your spirit man' by Victor Osei (this book will be analysed below), 'Stiring Up the Champion in you' by Solomon Kofi Marfo, 'My Journey with the Charismatics' by Emmanuel Kwabena Ansah, 'This is your breakthrough' by Paul Owusu Tabiri, 'The Singer's Vocal Manual' by Foster Odoi and 'Genuine or counterfeit pastor/prophet' by Kwame and Bea Owusu-Ansah.
17. The following is based on the writing on seven pastors (Daniel Darko Kobeah, Edward Otu, Emmanuel Kwabena Ansah, Francis Afrifa, Joshua Kas-Vorsh, Victor Osei, and Seth Osei-Kuffour) Facebook pages. I followed them mainly during 2013 and 2014. Since then some have stopped using their page and other update on a more irregular basis.
18. Victor Osei, Facebook page, 23 August 2013.
19. "Better to be a nobody and yet have a servant than pretend to be somebody and have no food" (Proverbs 12:9, New International Version).
20. Victor Osei, Facebook page, 31 January 2014.
21. Francis Afrifa, Facebook page, 25 June 2013.
22. Francis Afrifa, Facebook page, 24 January 2014.
23. GhanaWeb 29 August 2013, http://www.ghanaweb.com/GhanaHomePage/NewsArchive/artikel.php?ID=284111 (accessed 27 March 2014).
24. Victor Osei, Facebook page, 29 August 2013.
25. See also Gifford (2004) on the prophetic trend and personal status of pastors in charismatic Christianity in Ghana, and the work of Sundkler ([1948] 1961) on the Zionist movement in South Africa for similar trends in a different context.

References

Adubofour, S. B. (1994). *Evangelic Parachurch movements in Ghanaian Christianity: c. 1950—Early 1990s*. Unpublished Ph.D. thesis, University of Edinburgh, Edinburgh.

Akyeampong, E. (1996). *Drink, power, and cultural change. A social history of alcohol in Ghana, c. 1800 to recent times*. Portsmouth: Heinemann.

Akyeampong, E., & Obeng, P. (1995). Spirituality, gender, and power in Asante history. *International Journal of African Historical Studies, 28*(3), 481–508.

Asamoah-Gyadu, J. K. (2005a). *African Charismatics. Current developments within independent indigenous pentecostalism in Ghana*. Leiden: Brill.

Asamoah-Gyadu, J. K. (2005b). "Christ is the answer": What is the question? A Ghana airways prayer vigil and its implications for religion, evil and public space. *Journal of Religion in Africa, 35*(1), 93–117.

Baëta, C. G. ([1962] 2004). *Prophetism in Ghana. A study of some 'Spiritual' Churches*. Achimota: Africa Christian Press.

Barber, K. (2007a). *The anthropology of texts, persons and publics*. Cambridge: Cambridge University Press.

Bernault, F. (2013). Witchcraft and the colonial life of the fetish. In B. Meier & A. S. Steinforth (Eds.), *Spirits in politics: Uncertaincies of power and healing in African societies*. Frankfurt/New York: Campus Verlag.

Busia, K. A. (1951). *The position of the chief in the modern political system of Ashanti*. London: Oxford University Press.

Daswani, G. (2015). *Looking back, moving forward. Transformation and ethical practice in the Ghanaian Church of Pentecost*. Toronto, Buffalo, London: University of Toronto Press.

De Witte, M. (2003). Altar media's living word: Televised charismatic Christianity in Ghana. *Journal of Religion in Africa, 33*(2), 172–202.

De Witte, M. (2005). The spectacular and the spirits: Charismatics and neo-traditionalists on Ghanaian television. *Material Religion, 1*(3), 314–334.

De Witte, M., de Koning, M., & Sunier, T. (2015). Aesthetics of religious authority: Introdcution. *Culture and Religion: An Interdisciplinary Journal, 16*(2), 117–124.

Gifford, P. (2004). *Ghana's new Christianity. Pentecostalism in a globalising African economy*. London: Hurst & Company.

Kirsch, T. G. (2002). Performance and the negotiation of Charismatic authority in an African indigenous church in Zambia. *Paideuma, 48*, 57–76.

Kirsch, T. G. (2008). *Spirits and letters. Reading, writing and charisma in African Christianity*. New York and Oxford: Berghahn Books.

Kirsch, T. G. (2014). The precarious center: Religious leadership among African Christians. *Religion and Society, 5*(1), 47–64.

Larbi, E. K. (2001). *Pentecostalism. The eddies of Ghanaian Christianity*. Accra: Centre for Pentecostal and Charismatic Studies.
Lentz, C. (2010). Travelling emblems of power: The ghanaian seat of state. *Critical Interventions: Journal of African Art History and Visual Culture, 7*, 45–64.
Maxwell, D. (2006a). *African gifts of the spirit. Pentecostalism & the rise of a Zimbabwean transnational religious movement*. Oxford: James Currey.
McCaskie, T. C. (1995). *State and society in pre-colonial Asante*. Cambridge: Cambridge University Press.
McCaskie, T. C. (2007c). Asante history: A personal impression of forty years. *Ghana Studies, 10*, 145–161.
Meyer, B. (1992). 'If you are a devil, you are a witch and, if you are a witch, you are a devil'. The integration of 'pagan' ideas into the conceptual Universe of Ewe Christians in Southeastern Ghana. *Journal of Religion in Africa, 22*(2), 98–132.
Meyer, B. (1999). *Translating the devil: Religion and modernity among the ewe of Ghana*. Edinburgh: Edinburgh University Press.
Meyer, B. (2001). Prières, fusils et meutre rituel. Le cinéma populaire et ses nouvelles figures du pouvoir et du succès au Ghana. *Politique Africaine, 82*, 45–62.
Miescher, S. (2005). *Making men in Ghana*. Bloomington & Indianapolis: Indiana University Press.
Newell, S. (2000). *Ghanaian popular fiction*. Oxford: James Currey.
Newell, S. (2005). Devotion and domesticity: The reconfiguration of gender in popular Christian pamphlets from Ghana and Nigeria. *Journal of Religion in Africa, 35*(3), 296–323.
Olsen, W. C. (2015). Theft and evil in Asante. In W. C. Olsen & W. E. A. Van Beek (Eds.), *Evil in Africa. Encounters with the everyday*. Bloomington and Indianapolis: Indiana University Press.
Osei, V. (2005). *Building your spirit man*. London: Eagle Media House Ltd.
Ranger, T. (2007). Scotland yard in the bush: Medicine murders, child witches and the construction of the occult: A literature review. *Africa, 77*(2), 272–283.
Shipley, J. W. (2009). Comedians, pastors, and the miraculous agency of charisma in Ghana. *Cultural Anthropology, 24*(3), 523–552.
Soothill, J. E. (2007). *Gender, social change and spiritual power. Charismatic Christianity in Ghana*. Brill: Leiden.
Sundkler, B. G. M. ([1948] 1961). *Bantu prophets in South Africa*. London: Oxford University Press.
van der Geest, S. (2002). Respect and reciprocity: Care of elderly people in rural Ghana. *Journal of Cross-Cultural Gerontology, 17*(1), 3–31.
Werbner, R. (2011). *Holy hustlers, schism, and prophecy: Apostolic reformation in Botswana*. Berkeley: University of California Press.

CHAPTER 6

The Politics of Becoming a Small 'Big Man'

Through an exploration of pastoral trajectories, this chapter[1] unpacks the politics of becoming a small 'big man'. The discussion touches in particular upon two aspects of this. First, pastorship analysed as a way to join power, not only within the church but also in several spheres at the same time. And second, pastorship as involving processes of both apprenticeship and entrepreneurship and linked to this, generational dynamics of dependency and autonomy.

Following on from the idea of the complete pastor, outlined in the precedent chapter, I expand on the metaphor to include how pastors use their positions in the religious sphere to gain status and power in other social spheres, for instance within families and wider networks of kin. Becoming a successful pastor involves operating within and between various social spheres so that status achieved within one sphere is transferred to other platforms and thereby enhances the pastor's social position in more than one domain. In this way, the status that follows from being a pastor and leading a church also improves one's status and respectability within one's family, in other religious networks, or within the domains of politics and chieftaincy although in a more indirect and discrete way. This argument reflects the aforementioned work by Lentz (1998), in which she explores how three 'big men' from Northern Ghana draw on different types of power in order to become 'big'. She argues that 'the three "big men" … are the more powerful the better they are able to combine their stakes in different fields of action and to manoeuvre with different registers of legitimacy' (1998: 59). Likewise, I argue that pastors operate within and from different fields of action (such as family, politics, transnational connections) and by doing this they draw on various registers of power to build up 'bigness'. Viewing pastoral careers from this perspective allows for an approach that opens up the analysis of pastorship as a process of social mobility, and as ways to join power and escape subordination.

Many pastors not only perform pastoral work and provide spiritual services within the church, but also within the sphere of the extended family, the hometown, and other connections. Some for instance see their status within their families as having changed after they became pastors. Family members require spiritual services, and pastors are asked to perform certain tasks (mediators in conflicts, distribution of land, praying at certain social events). This illustrates how status within one sphere is transferable to another. Lentz's analysis focuses on the transferability and convertibility of status and power between traditional and modern political offices and between politics and business (Lentz 1998: 61), and hence not directly related to the religious sphere. I think, though, that it is fruitful to look at how status and power derived from the religious sphere also contain aspects that are convertible to political and economic power. As discussed later, there are examples of politicians and business people that engage in setting up churches and Bible schools and hence draw on the power and legitimacy that stems from the religious sphere. This is to be understood in relation to their specific role as mediators between the spiritual and the material worlds that religious experts have had and continue to have in Asante society. In this regard, it is worth mentioning that it is less frequent to see well-established successful pastors engage in political careers. This suggests that the power derived from the religious sphere is seen as different from political power, which in some religious circles (in particular the classical Pentecostal churches) is perceived as 'polluted' by mundane values such as greed and corruption.

The second point of this chapter is that pastoral careers contain relations of apprenticeship as well as elements of entrepreneurship, or moments of both dependency and autonomy-making. This is to be seen as part of how social relationships are used and shaped in the process of becoming a small 'big man'. Pastors engage in hierarchical relations with senior pastors. They subdue, serve, and learn under this person and draw on his legitimacy. However, at a certain stage in their careers, pastors have to become independent and escape restraining social bonds to senior pastors in order to grow sufficiently and eventually become 'big'. They draw on various social networks and are innovative in the sense that they set up new churches and establish themselves as leaders by bringing in whatever resources they have at their disposal. Some, for instance, talk about setting up a church as an investment (Lauterbach 2016). These aspects of pastorship reflect parallel trajectories of other types of 'big men' such as politicians, chiefs, and heads of families (Lentz 1998).

The careers that are analysed here include both successful and unsuccessful ones. It illustrates the choices pastors make in an early stage in their careers, the struggles and barriers they face, as well as some of the strategies that apparently did not work in the way intended. Consequently, my focus on pastors as entrepreneurs and innovators does not imply that all pastoral careers are successful or that anyone can become a pastor; many fail and give up, or supplement their pastoral work with other activities. The inclusion of unsuccessful pastors in the analysis sharpens our understanding of what it takes to become a successful pastor. What are the necessary resources and what is at stake? The unsuccessful careers demonstrate the efforts of those who failed or were likely to fail. The point is that they did try because they saw certain opportunities to fulfil their aspirations and 'if efforts to contest prevailing patterns are ignored or classified as insignificant merely because they may have been unsuccessful, then actual outcomes become endowed with a quality of *inevitability*, which removes from the historical process its precariousness and multistranded nature' as Lund (2008: 11) puts it.

All pastors operate in situations of uncertainty, in the sense that they do not know what the future will bring or what the outcome of their choices and actions will be. In the words of Bendix (1984: 48) the aim is 'to give back to men of the past the unpredictability of the future and the dignity of acting in the face of uncertainty'. Thus, my approach is that each pastor makes his actions based on choices that are sensible in that particular situation, at that particular moment, and from his particular horizon.

The first trajectory is about four young pastors who assisted a pastor living abroad with starting a church in his hometown, Kumasi. The story is about the young pastors' struggles to obtain leadership positions in the church and the obstacles they face when fulfilling their aspirations. It shows how young pastors attempt to utilise a fragile situation to ascend pastoral hierarchies. The second trajectory is that of Francis Afrifa, who heads a charismatic church (Fountain Life International Christian Centre) in Kumasi with a branch in Italy. He earlier worked for and trained under one of Kumasi's leading charismatic pastors. Francis' story illuminates how becoming a pastor involves both processes of entrepreneurship and apprenticeship. The general point that connects the stories, as well as other trajectories drawn upon in the chapter, is that pastorship is a life trajectory that demands skilful navigation between being protected and promoted by a senior pastor and at the same time making enough space to be able to grow and be an innovator. Not to forget that taking up a pastoral career involves struggle, deception, persistence, and hardship. In the subsequent analysis, I also include other people's trajectories as to broaden out the discussion.

BACKGROUND AND ASPIRATIONS

In order to contextualise and paint a broader picture of these pastors as a social group, I start by outlining their social and educational backgrounds. Obviously, this description is not representative of charismatic pastors in Ghana in general. Rather, the following depicts a certain type of pastor and I delve into the elements of their careers where they establish themselves and seek to achieve 'bigness'. The trajectories include mainly middle-level pastors who are established in and around Kumasi.

It is meaningful to talk about pastors as a social group in terms of their shared ideas on social aspiration and mobility, rather than as a group with a shared socio-economic background or as belonging to a distinct class. Throughout this book, I have drawn links to former Asante middle-level groups such as the *akonkofo* and the *nkwankwaa* (the 'youngmen'). In Miescher's work on the *akrakyefoɔ* (clerks, teachers, scholars) of the 1930s and 1940s, who were people in intermediary positions, he shows that they were people who 'experienced a double social exclusion. Most of them were neither part of the older and established chiefly elites who as "traditional rulers" were in charge of local administration under indirect rule nor did they belong to the highly educated and financially secure intelligentsia' (2005: 84). As the *akrakyefoɔ* in colonial Ghana, middle-level pastors strive to join power and to rise in social hierarchies, although many of them are not part of the established elite. The way to realise their aspirations is not through employment in the public sector or more traditional political careers. Engaging in a pastoral career is a way to join power that is accessible to middle-level people.

Miescher raises a point about the 'need to disaggregate the category of "youngmen"' (2005: 114), which is widely used in the literature on colonial Ghana. He draws attention to the importance of establishing a more specific and varied picture of who these people were by looking at their education and employment as well as links to their hometowns. Similarly, in her work on Asante nationalism, Allman notices the broadness with which the category of 'youngmen' has been defined (1993: 28–29). She argues for taking a longer historical perspective and highlights the aspect of being subordinate facing hindrances to economic and political advancement as characteristic for the group more than age itself.[2]

The group of middle-level pastors is constituted of people who took up pastoral careers straight after finishing school, people who had been employed prior to becoming a pastor, and people who were combining pastorship with other types of work. Most pastors had some formal education, both primary and post-primary. Most had finished secondary school (form V) and about half had been to a polytechnic, teacher training college, or university.[3] About a third had left school after the first level of secondary education and can therefore be characterised as school leavers. Within this group, unemployment is high, but school leavers still have aspirations for employment and the ensuing social recognition (Foster 1965: 201; Yamada 2005: 74, 84). It was moreover a common trait that the pastors I talked to had been involved in evangelism and prayer activities during their school years in, for instance, Scripture Union or other fellowships, and some had leading positions within these.

The educational background of the pastors could indicate that they were likely to aspire to a job in the public sector. In Ghana, there has been a general tendency to opt for academic schooling rather than vocational training (Palmer 2007: 20). Academic education was earlier perceived as the route to employment in the public sector, which was again seen as a way to achieve social status and economic mobility (King and Martin 2002: 9; Osei 2004: 431). Arhin also points out that social mobility in Ghana was achieved mainly through 'higher education, successful business activities or involvement in politics' (Arhin 1994: 317). However, about half of those leaving school after having completed JSS (junior secondary school) go into the informal economy (Palmer 2007: 26).

With regard to employment opportunities in the public sector there have been substantial reductions and decreasing salaries since the 1980s (King and Martin 2002: 6). This has among other things led to a change in terms of attitudes vis-à-vis jobs in the formal sector. King and Martin note that salaries from a public sector job were not sufficient to meet economic needs. This led many to take several jobs at the same time to supplement their income (Behrends and Lentz 2012; King and Martin 2002: 13).

About half of the pastors I interviewed had other professions before becoming a pastor, such as chartered accountant, teacher, mason, and shop owner. Some pastors had public sector jobs before entering into pastorship. They gave up their employment as civil servants in order to involve themselves in full-time ministry. This observation supports the argument that a pastoral career is more than a way of securing an income in a context with decreasing public sector jobs and a high level of unemployment. For some, pastoral work is attractive when one cannot live off a public service salary, as pastoral work permits both diversified sources of income and is associated with a different form of prestige linked to spiritual power.

One example is Pastor Emmanuel from Techiman, who was educated as an accountant and did his national service at the finance department of the Techiman District Assembly. He then worked with the Internal Revenue Service, and later became an accountant in the district office of the Ghana Broadcasting Cooperation. However, when he started a Christian fellowship, he left this job. At the same time, he started a printing shop with his wife and became self-employed. Later, he also invested in a poultry farm. During his career, he spent some years abroad in Germany and Denmark and upon his return he was waiting to be allocated to a position by his church, House of Faith. He had to wait a year for this and meanwhile worked for the church for free. During this time, he made his income from the poultry farm and the printing shop. He also envisaged to start a computer training school and an internet café and had brought old computers with him from Europe. Emmanuel became self-employed because it gave him the flexibility to work as a pastor and have another income at the same time, which he would not have had in a public service job where he could, for instance, be transferred to another town.[4]

Other pastors combined jobs at the university with being pastors (one was a full-time lecturer and at the same time general overseer of a church), and others, who were junior pastors, worked only part-time as pastors (mainly doing translation and prayer sessions) and combined this with other small jobs.

Another common feature is that many pastors had been abroad or had aspirations to go abroad. About half the pastors interviewed outside Ghana (most for a couple of years) and their travelling was primarily linked to their pastoral work and careers (attending Bible school, working as missionaries, or for other educational or work-related purposes). Although Pentecostalism and charismatic Christianity is known for its transnational form of organisation and many pastors travel due to their involvement in transnational religious networks and missionary work (Corten and Marshall-Fratani 2001), it is worth keeping in mind that migration and transnational forms of livelihoods are well-established features of Ghanaian society. The global outreach of Ghanaian charismatic churches is not a characteristic confined to these institutions. Rather it is a reflection of a much larger trend and history of migration in Ghana.

There is status attached to being a migrant and, as noted by Kabki et al migrants are respected by their families, especially if they are able to send back resources. Fulfilling such obligations and requests increases the migrant's status and 'gives a good name back home, which is culturally important for every Ghanaian' (Kabki et al. 2004: 90). Having a family member abroad is seen as a security as they will (ideally) be able to send money and assist family members at home (Arhinful 2001).

With regard to the pastors of this study, many only remitted smaller amounts of money, although some came back with goods such as computers and other technical equipment. Some of those who went abroad were dependent on resources from family members or church members in Ghana, as their primary occupation abroad was education and pastoral work, and not employment. Being abroad was, however, an investment in connection to other Ghanaians abroad (mainly family members or church members) that, in a longer time perspective, could be useful, for setting up churches abroad, for example. Among the middle-level pastors there was surprisingly little contact with colleagues or pastors they had been working with when being abroad, whereas the pastors that were leading the bigger churches were involved in more fully fledged transnational religious networks.

Trajectory I: The Establishment of a New Church[5]

Alive Bible Congregation (ABC)—a small church in Kwadaso, Kumasi that also appears in the beginning of this book—was established in September 2004 as a branch of a Ghanaian-founded church in Denmark. The head pastor had set up the branch in Kumasi to expand his church and for church members in Denmark to have 'their own' church to go to when they visited or returned to Ghana ('to remain within the family'). The establishment of the branch also reflected the ultimate goal of becoming an international church. The head pastor had given the responsibility of the church in Kumasi to a middle-aged pastor (Pastor Abu) who was attending Bible school. Meanwhile, a group of younger pastors were seeking to take over the leadership of the church. The trajectory of this church is interesting because it provides insights into the early phases of setting up a church, and the early stages of pastoral careers. It shows how pastors navigate in uncertain and fluid situations and seek to bypass norms of seniority.

The Church

ABC in Kumasi had a rather small and shifting membership. At the services I attended there were between 10 and 20 people, of which half were children. I got the impression that the church attendants were mainly friends and family of the church leadership, neighbours as well as a few outsiders. Sometimes members of ABC in Copenhagen visited the church. One of them was a Ghanaian woman, who was from Kumasi and had returned on a holiday. She attended the church once, which she explained was because she had to accompany me. She said that she would not have attended the service on her own, because her father was a pastor in another church, and therefore she would rather go there. Despite the ambition to create a church for members of the Danish branch, who either returned or visited their hometown, this was not what happened. The Ghanaian members in Denmark only rarely travelled to Ghana and those who did would rather go and worship in the churches they had belonged to before travelling, or the churches of their parents. A few other members of the church in Denmark had been visiting at a later stage. They were appointed as elders of the church and went there on a regular basis to oversee the church. One person was living in Accra, and came to Kumasi to visit the church once a month. This was at the initiative of the head pastor, who did not himself have the possibility of travelling to Ghana and wanted some more control over the church, and in particular over the guidance of the young pastors. The pastors did not receive a salary for their work, but the pastor in Denmark had sent 100 USD to Pastor Abu and also means for running the church. Later, the church in Denmark provided funding for buying electric instruments and for paying rent. As described in Chap. 4, the young pastors at one point tried to introduce tithing among the members in order to get some income, but in general the money collected in church was little (between 10,000 and 20,000 cedis).[6]

During the first year of the church's existence, it was located in three different places in the Kwadaso area of Kumasi. Kwadaso is located east of the town centre in the direction of Sunyani and the Brong-Ahafo region and is an area where migrants from the Brong-Ahafo region settle. In December 2004, the church was meeting and worshipping in a school classroom, as did many other small and new churches (See Fig 1.1). Pastor Abu was in charge along with Peter (the nephew of the head pastor in Denmark, though not the nephew in a biological sense; the two used to live in the same compound, *passenger house*, meaning different households living in the same house). Peter and his wife were in charge of church (including financial) affairs and were also the link between the pastor in Denmark and the church in Kumasi.

Early in January 2005 the church moved into a little store room with no windows. They moved because being at the school posed problems; they had difficulties getting access to the keys from the security man and often had to pay him extra money to enter the room. It was also a problem being next to other churches; sometimes church members got confused and ended up in a different church from the one they wanted to attend. Being in the store room was a temporary solution, as it was very small (Fig. 6.1).

Fig. 6.1 Church in store room, Kwadaso, Kumasi

The church was located there until they could afford to buy land. Five months later the church moved into a former restaurant, a place that was spacious and where the young pastors could lodge. The church in Copenhagen paid for the rent.[7] This building was very big compared to the other places. Only a quarter of it was used at church services. This permitted the pastors to organise special activities for children during the church service. The only decoration was a clock on the wall and a banner outside the church. Many of the members had joined the church recently and former members had left because the church had moved. People joined because of the evangelism the pastors did or during the all-night prayer they had every Friday (from 11 p.m. to 4 a.m.). A young woman who worshipped and sang had only joined the church three weeks before at an all-night prayer.

A year later one of the young pastors left the church to join Bible school and he lost track of the church. I was later told by the wife of Peter (who was in charge of the church) that due to financial constraints they had not been able to pay the pastors. She explained, 'The pastors were always on us concerning their salaries. We had to go look for money for them always. It came to a time we could not keep up with it.'[8] They had no contact with the head pastor in Denmark, so the church collapsed and the restaurant was taken over by another church. The fact that the church was unstable in terms of membership, leadership, and location shows some of the challenges that starting a church and establishing a pastoral career pose. In this case, being a transnational church was a hindrance to its success because there was a lack of strong senior members and resources, which destabilised the church.

Claiming Leadership

In 2004, when the church was newly established, it was led by Pastor Abu. He had been given this responsibility by the founding pastor who returned to Denmark shortly after having set up the church. Abu attended Bible school[9] and had been a member of Bethel Prayer Ministry International (BPMI),[10] where he also tried to become a pastor. He had left BPMI because he wanted to go to Bible school and the pastors did not support his decision. Abu explained that prior to that he had been moving between different churches because 'the head pastors in these churches did not treat me fairly.'[11] This indicates that he struggled to be accepted and recognised as a pastor. He also explained that to get an income besides his pastoral activities he decided to engage himself in cocoa farming and had been doing so for seven years by the time we first met in 2004. This income permitted him to attend Bible school, for which he also received financial support from friends and family, but not from the church.

Abu himself grew up in the Church of Pentecost, which both his parents also attended, although his father later became a Presbyterian. When Paul Owusu-Tabiri left the Church of Pentecost and founded BPMI, Abu joined and became a member of the new church. Abu's trajectory and choice to engage in setting up ABC indicates that being in a well-established church makes it more difficult to rise in the church hierarchy and to be recognised as a pastor. Being in a new and small independent church permitted Abu to become the head of a church and to work as a pastor and in this way to rise in status. What is important to note is that he left a well-established institution, where he did not have many possibilities of getting a position as a pastor, to follow an uncertain path that made him a church leader in a very small church and which ended up failing. In order to take this path, he depended on his work as a cocoa farmer. He is an example of an aspiring pastor in an insecure position that uses the open religious space to better his options for rising. But this was not without challenges. Due to his lack of connections to more powerful senior pastors, he did not have legitimacy and his position was fragile, which resulted in him being pushed out rather quickly by a group of younger pastors. Abu led the church for the first months, but soon the younger pastors claimed his position by questioning his legitimacy and loyalty.

The young pastors were introduced to the church by Peter and his wife. First they invited a friend (Edward), who was 20 years old and a young pastor. He was formerly part the Apostolic Church of Ghana and had also been in a prayer fellowship with Peter and his wife. When he came to the church there were about six members, and he saw it as his task to evangelise and make the church grow. He referred to himself as an 'associate pastor sort of' and a prophet of God and said that 'God speaks through me concerning the church and the members'.[12] Edward later invited more friends to join the church as pastors and in February 2005, there were three of them. They had, however, never met or spoken to the head pastor in Denmark, but they were backed up by Peter.

Despite their brief history in the church, the young pastors challenged the leadership position of the older pastor Abu. They accused him of keeping all the money sent from the mother church in Denmark and pocketing it, and they complained of not knowing what the money was used for.[13]

They moreover complained that Pastor Abu was only a part-time pastor in ABC, and that he did not behave as a leader. Abu had not been in the church for about a month and the young pastors thought this was because he was leading another church somewhere else. One of them said: 'We came to meet him here, but he has not even sat with us to preside over any meeting. He has not taken any leadership role,' and another supplemented: 'he couldn't remain faithful to this church, because of his own church that he was handling, and didn't have enough time for this church … So we were the boss and we are still the boss.'[14] The young pastors discredited Pastor Abu because of his lack of loyalty and commitment, his failure in taking on the leadership and handling the financial resources, and hence his performance as a pastor.

Three months after the young pastors joined the church, the older pastor Abu left and, according the young pastors, went back to his old church. He felt that the young pastors did not respect his position as a senior pastor and also that the head pastor in Denmark did not support him. He said:

> What worry me are the young men who … I know I have a lot of experience which they don't have. Their behaviour baffled me a bit and for this reason I wanted to talk to pastor [in Denmark] to know what he told them that warranted the actions they put up. But my phone was out of order as I said earlier. I wanted to quit but my wife advised that I had to listen to my master and for this reason I started coming over last week to assume some responsibilities.[15]

In the beginning, the pastor in Denmark did not acknowledge that status of the young pastors and accused them of lacking ethics. He did not see them as having any authority, and accused them of disrespect when they tried to push away Pastor Abu. He later accepted them but also managed to get an elder from the church in Copenhagen to act as a general overseer of the branch in Kumasi. On my last visit to the church in September 2005, there were (at least) four young pastors, of whom Edward took the leading role. He explained that they all assisted in setting up the church and they also went out to talk to people and to get more people coming to the church. As one of them said, 'We are all senior pastors'.

The struggle around claiming leadership positions in the church reflect criteria of success that are discussed earlier in this book, and relate to how one proves legitimacy as a pastor through truthfulness, knowledge of God and performance as a pastor, for instance when being a leader. Abu was pushed out of the church not only because he did not perform well as a pastor, but also because he was not sufficiently backed up by the head pastor in Denmark or someone else with seniority. The opportunities for building up status in this church were more apparent for the group of young pastors (at least in the first phase of setting up the church). As leading pastors of the church they were respected and listened to in a different way than they were in their former churches. At one church service, two elders from the church in Denmark visited. On this occasion the young pastors were at centre stage, leading the service, and because they were occupying positions in which they had access to spiritual power, they appeared as the ones in control and had gained some kind of momentum.

The Young Pastors

But who were these young pastors and why were they so eager to overtake this small church? The young pastors themselves did not have much money, nor did they have mobile phones, which meant, for instance, that they could not get in touch with the pastor in Copenhagen. They barely had a congregation other than a few friends, some family members of the pastor in Copenhagen and some outsiders. What they did have, however, was eight blue plastic chairs, a wooden pulpit, a few instruments, a banner and, not the least, contact with a church in Denmark (Fig. 6.2).

The leading young pastor (Edward) presented himself as a prophet and expressed that his aspiration was to one day lead a big church and move abroad. He was 20 years of age when he joined ABC. He was born in Wenchi in the Brong-Ahafo region, but grew up in Kumasi. He had completed secondary school and had also attended Bible school. Edward had a call from God when he was 12 years old and said 'God is still preparing me and the preparation has not ended. There are more things God wants to do in my life … Yes, God even told me that he would use me to save many people, even the dead'. He referred to an incident that occurred during the registration process for the elections in December 2004:

> I met one guy who was almost dead. I had even preached to him before. I was with my aunt and when I saw that guy lying there almost dead I approached there with my aunt. We prayed for about 5 minutes and the guy was revived. People around were shocked and surprised at what had happened. But I told them that God wanted to touch their hearts.[16]

Fig. 6.2 Young pastors in church, Kwadaso, Kumasi

By narrating this incidence Edward referred to his access to spiritual power and thereby also to his abilities and legitimacy as a pastor despite his young age. By identifying as a prophet, he accentuated his abilities of performing spiritual power. Edward lived with his parents, as he had no financial income. He did not receive any financial support from his parents as 'they want me to go and work. You see when I finished the secondary school, one company invited me to be accounts clerk and my parents supported that. But God wants me to do his work and that is that'.[17] He declined to work as an accounts clerk and instead supplemented his work as a pastor with small jobs that enabled him to eat.

Another one of the young pastors was Daniel. He said the following about how he became a pastor:

> It all started around 1999. It was then not [with] a church, it was a fellowship with a pastor called Agyemang Duah. The fellowship was called Jesus is the Lord. We started at Edwenase. We started going to the villages to evangelise in 1999 before I went to high school. In the school I teamed up with other boys and we applied for evangelism in Kumasi Chaplaincy

Board to be able to go to the registered schools and evangelise, so for the past 2–3 years we worked with the Board and even schools that were not under the board. I was doing this while I was in school. Besides I was the Scripture Union vice president from form 1 to 2. And then from form 2 to form 3 I became the president. It wasn't just secondary school; it was training colleges, vocational and technical schools. I was also organising the boys around for evangelism at the market place.[18]

He joined the church because he was a friend of Edward, and they went to school together. As the quote above shows, he had experience with Scripture Union before he became a pastor and therefore he got discouraged by his former church as they did not support and promote young pastors. The young pastors were friends and considered each other as brothers. They were young men with aspirations of becoming big 'men of God' and of leading a church. But they had hitherto not been able to function as fully acknowledged pastors. Daniel explained:

The issue is that I didn't like my church … My church did not encourage young pastors. They were old fashioned. They weren't active. At the fellowship I was a pastor, but in my church I was recognised as a member.[19]

Being connected to a church in Europe was attractive for the young pastors because among other things it linked them to returned migrants and hence people with potential resources and contacts. They could, moreover, operate rather independently without being under direct surveillance of a senior pastor. This meant that they at a very early stage in their careers called themselves senior pastors and had the responsibility of preaching and leading a church. It was, however, also a constraint in the sense that they lacked the means to communicate (no mobile phone and no money) with the head pastor in Denmark. This lack of a senior pastor turned out to be a limitation to the growth and success of the church. A year later in 2006, Daniel left the church to attend the Christian Service University College in Kumasi. After completing his studies and getting a degree in theology, he started his own fellowship of which he is still the leader.

What is worth pointing out in relation to the young pastors is that they had all been members and junior pastors in bigger and more well-established churches, which they left and broke away from. This is a common trajectory of breaking away in order to get the space to grow, but as the next trajectory will show growing as a pastor also requires links to more senior people and hence legitimacy. There needs to be a balance between autonomy and dependency (Le Meur 2008).

Hometown Church Building

The interest of the senior pastor in Copenhagen, on a long-term basis, might be to create a church in his hometown that he could one day return to. Building a church can be viewed as a hometown investment, though one that is not directed towards family and kin as would most often be the case (Manuh 2003). In this case the pastor/migrant has invested in a way that does not follow the more classical one of investing development projects in a hometown or the more individual-oriented investments in houses and businesses. Building a church can be seen as a new way of achieving status as a migrant.

The head pastor in Denmark complained that he did not have enough financial resources to construct a church building, not even to travel to Ghana a few times a year. Still, the symbolic value of having a project of building a church branch in Kumasi should not be neglected. Many of the Ghanaians in the Copenhagen branch were from Kumasi, and sympathised with the project. Moreover, if the pastor succeeded in building up the church he would enter a different league of international Ghanaian charismatic pastors, which would enable him not only to be a 'big man' among Ghanaians in Copenhagen, but also back home. One might add that it is more a personal project than a project of the whole church community.

The project of building a church at home can be seen as part of a larger trend where migrants from Kumasi make their hometown the 'center of their transnational activities' as Clark puts it (Clark 2003: 89). As she also points out the status migrants receive from their activities abroad need to be confirmed at home, for instance by investing in land, housings and funerals (Clark 2003: 94). The case in point shows that the arenas for achieving this recognition are expanding, and also include religious forms such as founding a small church. Building a church in Kumasi reflects the interest of migrants to increase or maintain their status at home and such 'conversions of transnational resources into locally significant arenas thus signalled the continuing primacy of Kumasi, both in symbolic and material terms' (Clark 2003: 94).

Therefore, this new form of hometown linkage can be compared with other types of migrant associations based on hometown, ethnicity, or profession that function as a way for migrants to keep ties to home and as forms of security and social network (Krause 2008: 238). Hometown associations are means to maintain links with an area of origin and to attract for instance development projects. They are often based on principles of reciprocity and obligation and have functioned as ways for urban elites to build up a clientele base (Woods 1994: 471–472). Along the same line, it might add to the status of the pastor that he is setting up a church in Kumasi, which is not only his hometown, but a place where many of the members in Copenhagen originate from. This suggests that although there might not be a direct involvement of the members abroad, the setting up of a hometown church can still enhance the position of the pastor. Moreover, it is a way for him to get leading members of the church attached to him in a more obligating way, as they also become leaders in the Ghanaian branch of the church. Building up a hometown church can thus be seen as an innovative way of maintaining ties to home; a way that differs from more traditional hometown associations as building a church means channelling resources to the church community and not necessarily to family or kin.[20] This does not, however, imply that church members and pastors from Denmark were not involved with their family and kin in terms of sending money and other goods. In one case a pastor returned to Ghana after some years in Denmark and chose to return to his former church and take up his family activities rather than being with the new church in Kumasi.

My contention is that this specific form of maintaining ties to home works along some of the same principles of other hometown associations (as ways to build up status and to create a 'flock' back home). It also represents a new platform from which pastors who are not from an elite background can operate, offering an opportunity for upward social mobility. The transnational character of the Pentecostal and charismatic movement makes it a significant platform that one can manoeuvre from abroad as well as at home. Coming home as a 'man of God' and a church founder is recognised in the same way as building a house or investing in a business.

Meanwhile, setting up a church and directing resources towards a church community rather than towards family and kin does not necessarily entail a disengagement from family relations as suggested by some (Krause 2008: 247; van Dijk 2001, 2002). As the trajectory of Francis Afrifa shows, transnational family relations can play a role when establishing oneself as a pastor.[21]

Unsuccessful Pastors

The career of Pastor Abu and his attempt to become a senior and head pastor of the small church ABC was a failure. First, he was not supported by his former church to attend Bible school and was not given the opportunity to act as a pastor. After joining the smaller church he was the senior pastor for a while but, as discussed above, was quickly overtaken by the group of younger pastors. They challenged him on not being loyal to the church. I have encountered a number of other pastors, who had either given up on their pastoral careers, or who had difficulties rising from the level of assistant pastor, where they were mainly translating sermons and responsible for prayer sessions. Some of these pastors had other employment besides and some were relying on assistance and gifts from church members and family on a more informal basis for making an income.

One example is Stephen Kwame Appea, who started doing pastoral work with Scripture Union while doing his undergraduate studies at KNUST (Kwame Nkrumah University of Science and Technology). He had an encounter with an angel who commanded him to dedicate his life to pastoral work. After he finished his undergraduate studies, he started a church with some friends. However, things did not go well and there were disputes with regard to the management of the church finances. He stopped being a pastor and now works as a planning officer at the Kumasi Metropolitan Assembly.[22]

Another unsuccessful pastoral career is that of Stephen Forkuo, who was a police sergeant in Kumasi and now on retirement. He grew up in the Seventh Day Adventist Church, where his mother was a member, but did not like the church. He shifted to the Catholic Church that his school friends were attending. He went to school and completed standard seven, which is the equivalent of JSS. After that, he learnt masonry and shoe-making and also worked at the National Archives with his brother. He joined the police service in 1978, because there were no other job opportunities, and spent the first eight years at the Suame police station in Kumasi. He was then transferred to another town and two years later to Techiman. He became interested in becoming a pastor in 1990 when he was 37 years old. This was in Techiman, where he met Pastor Emmanuel Appiah (see above), became part of his fellowship, and later joined Emmanuel's church (House of Faith). Stephen talks about Pastor Emmanuel as the one who introduced him to charismatic Christianity: 'I was changed by Emmanuel Appiah, so I named my child after him. He is my spiritual father.'[23] After five years in Techiman Stephen was transferred to a police station in Kumasi and at the same time went to Bible school for four years (School of the Word for the first two years and another school after that). After completing Bible school, he left House of Faith probably because he was not given a position as pastor. Instead, he joined another church (Miracle Gospel church). The pastor that Stephen worked under was, however, thrown out of the church by the head pastor, because their branch did not grow enough. They were then starting a new church, but Stephen gave up on being a pastor. He explains: 'I did not really become a full time pastor. I worked with a friend as an evangelist. I did this while still being a policeman … I took a three month leave from work and went to work with my friend to help him.' Still, he also argued that being a policeman and a preacher at the same time made people listen to him: 'They knew I was a policeman. In Ghana, policemen have a bad reputation, because most of them are corrupt, and they womanise and drink a lot. So when they realised that a policeman was preaching, they were amazed and so they listened.'[24] Although his career as a pastor did not succeed, he was an evangelist and went from house to house to preach and replaced the chaplain at the police station when he was absent. In this way, he was recognised by people as someone who knew the word of God, despite not being a pastor in a church.

These trajectories also point to the insecurity of being small churches, both in terms of problems related to keeping and using money and in terms of the difficulties related to establishing oneself as a pastor and starting new churches. It moreover relates to the issue of young pastors being impatient when embarking on their careers. When a pastoral career is not successful, it is often explained by others as a lack of knowledge. A young man, who was a church member and wanted to become a pastor, said:

> I can't just stand up and say I am a pastor. One problem we face in Ghana is that the moment someone sees a gift in him, he just stands out without waiting for God's directions. This is why most of them do not last because they do not have the skills and knowledge to go forward.[25]

Trajectory II: Francis Afrifa[26]

Francis was born and bred in Kumasi. When I first met him in 2005 he was 31 years old, married with three children. His wife ran a small shop. Francis lived with his family in the house of his aunt in the Bremang area of Kumasi. Francis was raised by his aunt, who now resided in Italy. He was from a Christian family, his grandmother was a Methodist and his parents were both pastors in a charismatic church in the Volta region of Ghana. Francis's hometown was Apenkra (16 miles from Kumasi), where his maternal grandfather, the late Joseph Kwasi Sarpong, came from. The grandfather was married to four women and had 28 children. His grandfather moved from Apenkra to Kumasi and had a family house in Oforikrom. Francis had a close relationship to the former chief of Apenkra (the *Apenkrahene*, Nana Dwamena Aktenten II), who considered Francis as his son and friend. Francis is the nephew of the *Akwamuhene* (a sub-chief and the linguist's deputy, who lived in Italy). Francis' grandmother lived in the family house in Oforikrom, where Francis was also born. Of his mother's siblings one was a professor at Legon, one a ship engineer, one was on the cocoa board, and one lived in Italy. Francis is the oldest of three siblings, of whom one lives in Italy and the other is a student in Accra.

The Calling

Francis became 'born-again' when he was in his early twenties and after that, he received his pastoral calling. In Francis' view, God knew that he would one day become a pastor, and so did many other people. In explaining this, Francis referred to the Bible (Jeremiah 1:5, King James version): 'Before I formed thee in the belly I knew thee; and before thou camest forth out of the womb I sanctified thee, and I ordained thee a prophet unto the nations.' Other people had dreams and visions that he would become a pastor. Especially Francis' mother, who had been insisting and praying to God for him to lead her son. She had taken Francis to a pastor that prayed for him, and even though Francis at that time wanted to become a pilot or a businessman and travel abroad, the pastor had seen (after three days of praying and fasting) that Francis would eventually become 'a servant of God'. This narration of his calling reflects the discussions in Chap. 4 on the calling as a destiny or path in life that cannot be refused as well as the importance of the acknowledgement and approval of this by the social surroundings.

At the time that Francis felt God's calling upon him, he was working as an accountant for his maternal grandfather, Joseph Kwasi Sarpong, who was a businessman in Kumasi. When Joseph K. Sarpong moved to Kumasi, he set up small businesses. He was, among other things, the first key distributor for Kumasi Brewery Ltd. Throughout his working life, he was able to make money and he built seven houses in Kumasi. Francis' grandfather was becoming a townsman. Having seven houses showed that he was a wealthy man and a successful businessman, someone for Francis to be subordinate to and to learn from (McCaskie 1986a: 7). At a certain stage in his career, however, Joseph K. Sarpong faced financial problems. He had problems with a business partner and this, according to Francis, was the beginning of the downfall of his grandfather. Eventually he had to sell five of the seven houses. At this time, Francis' grandfather asked him to come and work for him. According to Francis, they had a close and mutual relationship, because Francis' mother was the first-born child in the family and so was Francis. Francis stopped working for his grandfather, when he felt some of the family members were jealous. This was especially the case with the children of the grandfather's other wives, who thought that he 'was enjoying life over there, [and] was eating the money of their father'. Some of them joined the business and Francis thought it wise to leave.

As to his educational background, Francis finished form V (secondary school), but could not go to form VI (two-year university preparatory course), which puts him in the category of school leavers. One can see that Francis has had a long-term interest in establishing himself as someone through the fact that he started working for his grandfather. Becoming a businessman offered Francis the possibility of social mobility. Unfortunately, the business did not do well and there was the inevitable envy and jealousy in the family business. So this route to a career did not work out. While Francis worked for his grandfather he felt God's calling upon him and 'that was the time when I told him enough is enough ... So I just started'.

Being an Apprentice

At the beginning of his pastoral career, Francis spent time reading the Bible, other religious books and attending seminars:

> diligently I was studying the Bible, bla bla bla, flip flap, the whole book of the Bible, I have read it so many times ... I engaged myself in the things of God that way. I engaged myself in the things that will help *to establish me* in the things of God. (My emphasis)

Francis explained that in order to establish himself, he needed to find the right church, the right kind of people, and the right atmosphere. The way in which Francis speaks about 'establishing yourself in the things of God' indicates that he had to do this in a way that both gave him legitimacy to draw on and in a way that permitted him to grow.

Francis started his career as a pastor by working a few years in Accra with his father. He then went back to Kumasi: 'God also spoke to me that I wanted to be in Family Chapel under Victor Osei, because there are certain things in ministry that I wanted to understudy through Victor Osei.' Victor Osei is the founder and leader of Family Chapel International, one of Kumasi's biggest and earliest charismatic churches. Francis knew Victor Osei from Kumasi, not personally, but from radio programmes and banners around the city. Francis saw Victor Osei as someone who had made a name for himself; a man of influence, a 'big man'. By being under his tutelage, young pastors would get credibility, which they would not have had otherwise as young pastors.

Francis thought of himself as someone who would become an important pastor like Victor Osei and he therefore wanted to go and learn from him: 'if you want to go to a place, you must be able to find somebody and discuss with him, a person who has been there before. So that was the reason why God took me to Family Chapel.' The way in which Francis and other younger pastors describe the credibility of Victor Osei touches upon categories of age, experience and knowledge, and they explain that possessing this is what gives Victor Osei credibility, and for them to become pastors they need to learn from someone with those qualities. They refer to his credibility as stemming from his work of God, but they also make a connection between the credibility he has and his age, knowledge and experience, as well as his status in society. In this way they to some extent follow the rationale of linking age and wisdom that Victor Osei criticised in his book (as discussed in Chap. 5), where he on the contrary asserts that knowledge only stems from God and is not linked to age.

For Francis, Family Chapel International was the right church to 'be established in the things of God' and Victor Osei became his mentor and 'spiritual father'. Francis prayed and fasted for 21 days before he contacted Victor Osei. Seeking to be under Victor Osei was a big step to take and therefore he wanted to be sure that it was the direction of God and not 'my emotions trying to lead me astray". After the 21 days of praying and fasting, Francis had 'the green light' and went to see Victor Osei personally. Francis explained to Victor Osei that God had directed him to Family Chapel and asked Victor to pray for him and to confirm if it was really 'of God'. Victor Osei called a church council meeting and Francis was interviewed about his background and motivation for doing the 'work of God'. Francis was accepted and started working under Victor Osei. An important aspect of being a young pastor is entering into an apprentice-mentor relationship with a senior pastor (spiritual father). Training as a young pastor can be thought of as an informal apprenticeship, where good reputation and success influence a prospective pastor's choice of mentor (Miescher 2005; Peil 1970: 143–144). As argued earlier in the book, by claiming someone as a spiritual father, one also claims this person's access to divine power. The case of Francis shows that pastoral apprenticeship is both about training under someone and about being under someone's protection and credibility (see also Chap. 4).

Being an apprentice, however, also entails limits and restrictions to one's social and individual aspirations. In his first year in Family Chapel International, Francis worked as an usher. He felt degraded as he had already been doing pastoral work for some years, but also saw this experience as a natural step in his 'work for God' or on the way to becoming 'big': '... you know in God the way up is the higher way down, if you go down God will raise you up. So I started by being an usher.' By doing so, he had to submit himself to Victor Osei. He showed his loyalty and seriousness by subservience and by being humble. Within the first year, Francis was transferred to the teaching ministry (responsible for Sunday school) and later he was sent to Bible school in Kumasi. Even though both these steps were promotions, he explained that:

> It was difficult times, but God was faithful, because you know not many pastors take it upon themselves to go to school, all of them want just one day pew ... you are an icon of peoples' admiration. But for you to go and sit down for one good year, going through lectures and then no support, he, you have to believe God for your *penge* [money].[27]

Francis received an allowance from the church of 120,000 cedis[28] per month while in Bible school. During his stay at the Bible school, Francis was posted to one of the church branches in a village outside of Kumasi. Francis saw this as a promotion, but he also recognised that others might not perceive it that way:

> To the eyes of the onlookers, they saw it as a punishment to go to the village, but I saw it as a promotion, because there I was given the opportunity

to even stand and preach in the pulpit, so there I had my own church. Even now if you go there, my name is there.

Financially, it was difficult for him to go to school and to work in the church in the village at the same time. Family members in Italy, the USA, and Canada helped. However, working in a rural branch of the church was not the way for Francis to realise his aspirations. After working one and a half years in Mase, Francis got a scholarship and went to Bible school in Denmark. He stayed in Denmark for a year and a half and went to Italy afterwards. While in Denmark, he worked in a Ghanaian-founded church, International City Baptist Church (ICBC), went to language school, and had small jobs in addition to going to Bible school. He was acting like a pastor in ICBC, but also complained that he was never given the chance to do pastoral work: 'I was just there quietly.' He found it very difficult to work among Ghanaian pastors in Denmark, because he felt there was no room for 'outsiders'. Meanwhile, the pastor for whom Francis worked in Denmark described Francis as one of those 'young impatient pastors, who wants to get everything from the beginning, and who does not want to do the hard work [to serve under someone].'[29] After leaving Denmark, Francis stayed four months in Italy, working in the church of his aunt. Here he was able to make a little money, because he worked as a pastor and the congregation paid him.

As Francis was not able to work and establish himself as a pastor in Denmark, this step did not help him move forward in his career. It rather came to represent a number of constraints put on him by his surroundings. First, he was not able to work and to perform as a pastor, which also meant that he was not accepted and recognised as a pastor. His credibility as a pastor was not sufficient, and as a young pastor, he did not have an easy road into a well-established church. Second, a father–son relationship was not in place; he did not have a 'big man' behind him to provide sufficient support, and he did not get direct entrance to the pastoral networks of the Ghanaian churches abroad. His experience abroad did not consolidate his career, but did the very opposite. Francis did, however, make sense of his stay abroad as a learning experience and as a part of his pastoral career: 'You know if God has something big for you, he will cause you to go through all kinds of processes.' Even if going abroad in a Ghanaian context were to be seen as an advancement for his social status, Francis achieved his aspirations in Ghana to a much greater extent than in Denmark.

Breaking Bonds

Upon his return to Kumasi, Francis did not go back to Family Chapel International. Instead, he preached in various branches of the main charismatic churches in Kumasi, not wanting to belong to a specific church. He wanted to work as an evangelist, the American evangelist Benny Hinn being his role model. In a sermon at the Atonsu branch of Family Chapel International, Francis proclaimed that he did not believe in denominations, but only in relationships with God.[30] This statement is an indication of a break in the father–son relationship between Francis and Victor Osei. Francis had been reluctant to return because of finding the working conditions unsatisfactory, lack of recognition, as well as few possibilities to perform as a pastor. He lost Victor Osei's attention.

And Victor Osei lost control of Francis. He tried to get him back into the fold and informed Francis that if he would not work in the main church he should stop going to the branch churches. Francis decided not to go back and had a vision that he should start a church of his own. Even though Francis might not have been a very central figure among the junior pastors, he was not allowed to perform and preach in an uncontrolled manner elsewhere, as that could challenge the authority of Victor Osei. Victor managed to keep Francis, who became too independent, away from his territory. Francis, who no longer wanted to submit, found the constraints too many and left the protection of Victor Osei.

Francis presented the break in two different ways. First, he described the reason for the break with Victor Osei regarding him as a threat because people were reporting his good work to him. Being a threat to a senior pastor indicates maturity and suggests that you move away from your junior status. Second, Francis presented the break as something that took place by mutual consent and emphasised that there was no conflict involved in the break. It would be reasonable to suspect that there was more conflict involved in this schism than Francis explained. However, the relevant point for my argument is to stress the importance Francis attaches to representing the break as non-conflictual. Since the split with Victor Osei happened on a mutual basis, Francis was able to rest within the 'comfort zone' of Victor Osei. He still wishes to draw on the credibility of Victor Osei, by continuously claiming him as his spiritual father. Although Francis had officially left Family Chapel, he still had to go there for a last service so that the church could send him away in a proper manner. I suppose this step had a largely symbolic function, as it was important to show that the departure was not because of conflicts, did not create any splits, and that there still was a cordial relationship between Francis and Victor Osei. Francis still regarded Victor as his spiritual father, as he was trained under him. Francis recognised the merits of being under Victor Osei, not only in terms of training, but also as transference of access to spiritual power:

> I also learned his discipline, he is a disciplinary, and he is also a man of principles, and he is also very conscious of time, he doesn't waste time, he is a disciplinary and his moral character too … And there is also some kind of anointing upon me, the ability to teach from the Bible. God gave it to me from serving under him … at times I stand in a place preaching, somebody can come and ask me 'is your father Victor Osei?' and I will say 'Yes, he is my spiritual father.' Some people will say I preach like him, I do things like him.

Francis acknowledged Victor Osei as his spiritual father and saw himself in him. He understood the reason for his own success to be his resemblance to Victor Osei. Even when no longer under his direct protection, Francis still gained prestige from the relationship and from having trained under this 'big pastor'. Although a formal break had taken place, the father–son relationship was maintained in a new form with fewer protections and obligations. In the case of Francis, breaking bonds with Victor Osei did not entail limiting the social networks he engaged in. As discussed in the following section, Francis managed to become involved in other pastoral relationships, which enabled him to fulfil his aspirations of becoming a leader.

Becoming a 'Big Man' of a Small Church or Being an Innovator

On the 15 May 2005, Francis founded his own church called Fountain Life International Christian Centre in Suame, Kumasi. The first Sunday service took place in the house of his aunt, where he lived, and was attended by his wife and children. In September 2005, the church had about 50 members, some of them from Francis' family and others from the neighbourhood. The congregation worshipped in the garage of the house, but the plan was to construct a new church building: 'We wanted to build some kind of structure, big, huge structure that can contain about 500 people and we are praying and believing God for the funds.' The structure was to be built on the grounds of the house that belonged to Francis' aunt in Italy.

Francis saw the church he started as a response from God to his obedience: 'God honours obedience. If you obey his voice and follow, he will supply all the necessary things and he also brings the necessary people that we need in order to work effectively.' According to Francis, it is Jesus, not he, who brings people to the church. The church is not his, it belongs to Jesus, and he is the one who brings people in and out. None of the members were from his former church (Family Chapel International), as he wished to start afresh. He believed that 'whoever God calls, God also gives the person a proportion of land, and whoever God calls he also gives them a people to lead. Moses, the people of Israel were given to him to lead to the Promised Land, so I believe in that concept'. The role of the pastor is to lead a people.

In order to progress further in his pastoral career, it remained important for Francis to be 'fathered'. He was introduced by a friend to a Kumasi-based bishop, Nicholas Asare, who ordained Francis as a pastor in March 2005, and henceforth became a new father for him. Asare was the leader of a charismatic church and a Bible school in Kumasi. For Francis, becoming 'bigger' entailed maintaining and engaging in various relationships. Leaving Victor Osei and becoming involved with Asare did not mean replacing one father with another. Rather it meant drawing on a new set of relationships that provided a different set of opportunities. When explaining the importance of relationships and how to succeed as a pastor, Francis said (as also referred to in Chap. 3) that he tried to keep relationships 'because money is a weapon, so is also a relationship'. Although he was now an independent pastor he still needed to be guided 'because every pastor you must also get a superior'.

Francis and Asare worked closely together and Asare made Francis the president of a pastors' association (The Charisma Family Network) that he created. The idea of the association was to help and support young pastors, both in building up their character as pastors and by providing them with international links and affiliations. Asare made room for Francis to extend his leadership and his influence in a way that would not have been possible as a junior pastor under Victor Osei. By becoming the president of an association, Francis achieved a position where he would initiate and guide young pastors. Within his network and with the protection of Asare, Francis offered support and protection to these young pastors. He was himself becoming a mentor and a father. He saw his own role as someone who would build up the new pastors. He referred to pastoral work as a 'noble profession' in which it was necessary to build up the young pastors' character for them to be able to take on the profession. He said: 'moral wise we are building them up and character wise we are building them up, because character pieces the charisma, the anointing, it is got to do with the giftings … but if you don't have the character God can never anoint you.'

Francis' new mentor was less influential and less 'big' than the former. However, this relationship opened up new opportunities for Francis and permitted him to grow. By being attached to Asare, Francis extended his social world and, more importantly, he got a leadership position and an attachment to a Bible school. Later on, Francis left the association because of things he did not like: 'I was like an eagle in the midst of chicken, so I had to leave.'

I would suggest that in Kumasi, being a middle-level pastor is a plausible way to realise social aspirations by means of leading a Bible school and by getting younger pastors attached to you: by being a teacher or a mentor. These roles are important to take note of because they relate to earlier discussions of how to become 'big', namely, among other things, to possess and perform knowledge and display wealth. The discussion of Francis' trajectory (and the trajectories of the ABC pastors discussed previously) show that being in an apprentice-mentor relationship plays a role with regard to achieving 'bigness'. First, in the process of becoming 'big' young pastors depend on senior persons and second, 'big' pastors depend on having junior pastors under their protection and tutelage in order to confirm and confer their status and authority as 'big'. Building up large churches and congregations poses more of a challenge. Within the many small churches, the pastors are just as dependent on social relations to the family and other pastors as on the congregation as such.

Later on, Francis' church moved to a new premise, where they constructed a building for the church. He also became part of a new pastoral association, where he was ordained as apostle. This association is called Wesley Synod and is apparently associated with the Methodist church.[31]

Becoming a pastor was also important for the relationship Francis had to his hometown (Apenkra) and to his family. It changed his status in the family, and gave him a role whereby people would seek his advice. This renewed role also meant that Francis had more obligations towards the family and the hometown. Francis' aunt played a key role in establishing the church. She sent musical instruments from Italy and during a stay just after the church was founded she helped set up the church choir. Francis saw her as part of the church. Later on, Francis established a branch of his church in Italy and went there a couple of times every year. One could say that the church of Francis became a new form of family enterprise, which may prove to be more successful than the business of his grandfather.

The chief of the hometown (*Apenkrahene*) wanted Francis to become involved in youth projects in the town. Francis planned to do this, but he also felt pressured to bring money to the town. Before he founded a church he was preaching at the annual harvest festival in Apenkra and the *Apenkrahene* had 'chosen [him] as his mate'. During the annual harvest festival, a pastor is invited to preach for the town. Before Francis went to Denmark, he was the one they asked to preach and after his return he had taken up this responsibility again. During the praying ceremony he would pray for the hometown, the chiefs, the harvest and his services were to secure the wellbeing of the town. Francis' dilemma vis-à-vis his hometown resembles in many ways that of migrants or people who live in the cities. There is a certain status attached to coming back and being a pastor, and at the same time people are presented with obligations and expectations as to how they can contribute. It was important for how Francis built up his status that he was recognised as a pastor in his hometown. It gave him a broader respectability that was not limited to the sphere of the church. At the same time, the hometown drew on Francis' position as a pastor and as a townsman to further the interests of the community.

Francis also played a role as 'family pastor' in relation to the death of his grandfather, whom he 'liberated' before he died in June 2004, by making him accept 'Jesus as his Lord and personal saviour'. The grandfather was in a coma for 21 days, had an encounter with Jesus, and repented afterwards. To this Francis commented: 'By the grace of God I can do all things.' In this way, Francis also served as a pastor of the family and saw his own role as someone who brought success to the family. He also broke a spell that was put on the family by the ancestors and in this way liberated the family. As the first-born son of the family, as the son of pastors and as the grandson of a businessman, he lived up to the expectation of achieving a certain social standing and of becoming a 'big man'. The relationship with his aunt proved to be crucial for his careers in several aspects. First, she invested in the church he built in Kumasi and second, he later established a branch church in Italy, which in 2014 had around 100 members. Francis spends several months of the year in Italy looking after the church. The family invested in his career by providing financial support and the physical infrastructure for setting up a church. The family has permitted Francis to build a career and at the same time to grow within the family.

Francis has thus built his career by tapping into both pastoral and family networks.

Pastors and Family

In many cases, becoming a pastor entails an improvement of one's position within the family. Many say that they are more respected after they have become pastors than they were before. This is mainly explained by the access they claim to spiritual power. In the case of Francis, he had been invited to preach at his hometown's annual harvest festival, which is a recognition of his pastoral credentials and his status.

Another pastor in Kumasi explained how he had changed his status within his family and how he was responsible for the money of his sister who was living overseas: 'Because spiritually they see me on a higher higher plane.'[32] David Owusu Ameyaw, a pastor from Techiman, explained his family situation and his new position in it in this way:

> I belonged to a poverty stricken family and even ten years after becoming an evangelist I was still having financial problems. It was recently that we discovered and broke that covenant trough prayers ... According to a story told by our forefathers, this family was very rich, but was a very small family with few members and since in the olden days, human beings were preferred to riches, the members of the family consulted their gods and traded off their riches for human beings and ever since that time they begun to multiply whilst their financial position continued to deteriorate ... I met with some believers and we prayed fervently to God and fortunately for us the covenant was broken and our lives began to improve.[33]

In this account he portrays himself as contributing to the wellbeing of the family and as being the fixer of earlier spiritual imbalances and problems. Also, positions of trust can be conferred on pastors within families. David Owusu Ameyaw spoke about how he had received more respect in his family:

> When members of the family meet, they listen to our views. Moreover, the head of the family has entrusted the family's land to my care. Thus, I am now the custodian of the family's property even though I am not the eldest. If one wants to use the land he first has to see the head of the family and then directed to me for my approval. If I also agree we engage the service of surveyors and town and country planning officials to help demarcate the land. I issue receipts to the buyers, give the officials their share of the money

and give the rest to the head of the family ... They see me as someone who is trustworthy and this is as a result of my Christian background.[34]

Occupying various roles and playing on several registers of norms and power is a feature of the constitution of Asante families. It is possible within families to play on different registers at the same time and still be within the same 'playing field of kinship'. Clark writes:

> Asante social actors openly and consciously negotiate not only their own position and score within the playing field of kinship, but also the rules and even the name of the game. A person can concurrently invoke distinct and contradictory sets of kinship and marriage rules from Akan matriliny, fundamentalist Christianity and Western romantic secularism. Each is widely enough recognised to make an effective bargaining chip, without cancelling out the others. (Clark 1999: 70)

Hence, when becoming a 'man of God', neo-Pentecostal pastors can negotiate new positions within their families, positions that are not necessarily linked to the role of a pastor, but that add to the status and authority they seek to build up. Clark has furthermore pointed out that the Asante family system is characterised by flexibility and elasticity and that:

> Asante cultural norms allowed and actually required a high degree of individual autonomy to anchor the negotiating position of each social adult. (Clark 1999: 66)

This flexibility also applies to the religious affiliation of family members. The majority of Ghanaians I spoke to were from Christian families, in the sense that at least one of their parents was Christian. Parents had often converted to mainline churches during childhood or early in their adult life and some later became born-again, which means that family members were often affiliated to different churches.

As mentioned in the introductory chapter, rupture and individualisation[35] have been emphasised as prominent in discussions of the social importance of charismatic Christianity in Africa (Asamoah-Gyadu 2005a; Meyer 1998a; Van Dijk 2001, 2002; Laurent 2003). As argued by Van Dijk (2001: 226):

> Even confirmed Born Again believers may still feel haunted by ancestral curses and may therefore encounter the problems, afflictions and misfor-

tunes that result from their past and from the web of social relations and commitments that tie a person to the family ... Therefore, a complete break with the past usually implies a complete break with the family.

In Van Dijk's analysis there is no distinction between how spiritual conflicts and social conflicts are handled and therefore sorting out spiritual family problems through prayers, in a way that is understood to be through the intervention of God, cannot necessarily be interpreted as leading to a break with one's family. In my work, I encountered several examples of pastors who had spiritual problems in their families and saw it as their role to overcome them, and to enter a spiritual combat with elders in the family. But this did not lead to a break in family relations. On the contrary, performing this role led to a rise in esteem from some family members.

In above-mentioned literature, family relations are presented as static and fixed. This stands in contrast to the above-mentioned work of Clark (1999), and also the work of scholars like Berry (2001) and Lentz (1994), who emphasise kinship relations and family ties as changeable relations in the making. In his work among Pentecostals in Chinsapo, Malawi, Englund (2004: 307) discusses the links between Pentecostals and their non-Pentecostal kin. He argues that the township Pentecostals he studied rely on access to land and other resources to survive, and can therefore not afford to cut off the links that are supposed to provide this access. The point here is that family relations are flexible and although they in some aspects (access to positions of seniority) represent an obstacle to growth, family at the same time functions as a platform from which one can become recognised.

Relations to Stools

One area of kinship relations that is an object of contestation is inheritance of stools. Pastors in charismatic churches refuse to occupy stools because of the religious practices attached to such a position; for instance, pouring libation and worshipping ancestors. These practices are not seen as being in accordance with the Christian faith. When refusing a position as *ɔhene* or *ɔhemaa*, one also renounces the privileges attached to the positions, such as property, decision-making, and status. Or rather these positions are challenged and pastors seek to build up their status, wealth, and power in different ways that do not imply complete renunciation of these relations.

Pastor Emmanuel Appiah from Techiman comes from a royal family and his mother (Akosua Yeboah), who was a Methodist, was heir to become queen mother (*ɔhemaa*), but he advised her to renounce, because of the traditional religious practices that accompany such a position. According to Emmanuel, they negotiated with the family for six months, inter alia about the possibility of his mother being queen mother without carrying out the actual religious practices. This was not accepted and the position was transferred to her younger sister. Initially, the family was not happy with the situation, but according to Akosua Yeboah, they accepted and their relationship became normal. Akosua explained her refusal by referring to her status as a Christian. However, other Methodists like her would take the double role of chief/queen mother and Christian as, for instance, the queen mother of Techiman (Nana Afia Abrafie Koto), who was also a Methodist.[36] Instead of ascending the throne herself, Akosua's son became a pastor, the leader of a fellowship, one who travelled abroad and was the owner of a printing shop and chicken farm.[37] Moreover, Emmanuel relied on his relations to the stool (both in his ancestral town and in Techiman) when he established his chicken farm. He bought the land from the stool at a favourable price.

Another aspect of not accepting the occupation of a stool is the non-recognition of that authority. Pastor Gloria Mensah Afriyie is from a royal family in Adanse Fomena. Her grandmother was a queen mother and after her death, her great aunt took over the throne. Gloria's family is thus eligible to the stool. In 2004, Gloria's brother (who lived in Denmark) was supposed to be enstooled as chief in the town, but Gloria managed to get him to refuse this: 'I was able to talk him out of it. Even my mother as a Methodist wanted him to take the position, but through my advice he refused.' Other Christian family members were happy with the advice she had given to her brother. She said: 'they were happy that the pastor says it wasn't good, why do you think they didn't give you any problem? It is because they trust my judgment.' Instead of her brother, her cousin (who lived in Italy) became chief. Apparently, this was more acceptable to Gloria as he was not as closely related to her: 'he didn't need to take my advice, but I also believe that people are entitled to what they want to be, so I leave it to them after doing my best.' Her brother's refusal to accept the throne is also a way to mark distance from the authority of the elders in the hometown:

One of the reasons why my brother didn't accept to be enstooled was because he thought it would be waste of money sending money down here to the elders for everything that goes on ... Because the people (elders) cease this opportunity to ask for money for their personal use in the name of something relating to the stool.[38]

This can be seen as a way for pastors to seek influence in the family and at the same time to escape traditional power hierarchies. Pastors engage with holders of political office through advice giving, but at the same time encourage those in their families that are closest to them not to take up such positions. Having a close family member—such as wife, mother or brother—who holds political office calls into question the position of the pastor, as the two are seen as incompatible. My argument is that, rather than emphasising social breaks, pastors use family relations as a platform from which they can boost their status. This echoes Lentz's point referred to earlier, and which I will delve more into below, on straddling different registers of power.

BEING AN APPRENTICE, BEING AN INNOVATOR

The process of becoming a successful pastor requires involvement in two kinds of relations. First, becoming a pastor means entering an apprentice-mentor relationship with a senior pastor and, secondly, it means being involved in relations that permit and provide the possibilities of growing. The first relation is a vertical one between a junior person and a senior, well-established and recognised person. The second set of relations takes place on both a vertical and horizontal level between the young pastor and other pastors, friends, family and colleagues. The first junior–senior relation lies within the church, whereas the second most often transgresses the sphere of the church and involves relations with other senior pastors, colleagues, extended family, and other influential persons.[39]

In order to establish themselves, young pastors need to belong to someone. They build up careers through apprenticeship and by engaging in relations with more senior pastors. By being an apprentice, a young pastor draws on the credibility and power of a senior pastor. This gives a certain degree of legitimacy that is necessary when young pastors establish themselves. Writing on social stratification in pre-colonial Asante and Fante, Arhin (1983: 5) suggests, 'that there was a distinction of lineages due to the pre-eminence of certain individuals which was extended to their dependants.' In the same vein, I argue that a young pastor not only enters a relationship with a 'spiritual father' to learn, but also to draw on that person's eminence and in this way acquires prestige, respect and credibility. The relationship between a young pastor and a 'spiritual father' thus serves a double purpose. It is a way to achieve certain skills in relation to performing as a pastor, and it furthermore provides the aspirant with status and credibility.

The apprentice-mentor relation is moreover a two-way relationship. The 'spiritual father' conveys credibility and access to spiritual power. In return, the son (or junior pastor) provides services in the form of loyalty, presence and support (for instance by holding the Bible of the senior pastor when he moves from his car to the church or to a meeting). The authority of a head pastor serves as both protection and recognition, and the loyalty of junior pastors depends on the senior pastor's ability to build up their status. The authority of the senior pastor is not constant, but continuously constituted by the loyalty of the younger pastors (as well as congregations and other religious authorities).

The junior–senior pastoral relationship is in many ways a father–son relationship (senior pastors are referred to as 'spiritual fathers', and are called 'father', 'dadda', or 'papa'), which implies protection, guidance and provision of opportunities. It is a relation that implies positions of subordination and seniority. But in this context, outside of lineage or family, there are different opportunities for mobility between these positions of junior and senior status. As Le Meur has discussed in the context of migration of youth in Benin there is a 'productive tension between autonomy and dependency' (2008: 213). He argues that the emergence of new religious movements provided an 'opportunity to bypass seniority and escape the dilemma of dependency and autonomy' (Le Meur 2008: 213). This is a widespread argument within studies of Pentecostal and charismatic Christianity, but my analysis shows that belonging to a new religious movement of this kind does not necessarily imply the dissolution of relations of dependency, rather they are re-configured and adapted to the new social setting. From a Ghanaian context, Soothill (2007) discusses in particular the 'empowerment thesis' also prevalent in studies of Pentecostalism. She argues that new forms of gender authority emerge in this religious setting, but at the same time 're-legitimise established norms' (2007: ix).

The relation to a senior pastor is an ambivalent one. On the one hand, it serves as protection and legitimacy. But, on the other hand, it becomes an obstacle to the younger pastors' opportunities for advancement. The pastors eventually mature, and will be inclined to take over or start a church on their own.[40] However, as shown in the case of Francis, the need to be 'fathered' remains and pastors therefore have to navigate between seeking protection and being under someone and at the same time have enough room in order to manoeuvre to advance in their careers. Therefore the tension between apprenticeship and innovation (or dependency and autonomisation) is not in this case a straightforward process of moving from one category to the other, but rather to establish an equilibrium between the two sides, whilst at the same time securing that the process enables people to gain more status and 'bigness'.

It is striking that the trajectories depicted above which were less successful or those which failed were either related to issues of wealth (on the issues of wealth and *nokware*, see Chap. 3) or a lack of belonging to and being under the protection of a senior person. In the case of the young pastors in ABC, they tried to establish themselves as pastors in a new church, but also in a church where a senior figure was missing.

Concurrently, young and up-and-coming pastors are entrepreneurial and are involved in multiple networks (congregation, colleagues, and extended family) to realise their aspirations. In the case of Francis, he relied on family members both for material support, for church attendance and for building up his status by giving him special roles in the home community. He was innovative because he managed to escape a junior position within his extended family. He left the family business, travelled, returned, created a church, and came to occupy a new position of status and authority. In addition, joining a small church can be a way to start working as a pastor. The young pastors of ABC were not working as pastors in their former churches, but joining ABC gave them the opportunity to do so. One pastor had previously been a youth leader in the Baptist church and in ABC referred to himself as a senior pastor. The small churches provide opportunities to rise in the hierarchy relatively quickly, even if the positions they gain are fragile in the sense that they are not backed up by more senior people.

Van Dijk (1992) describes how young born-again preachers in Malawi act as 'religious entrepreneurs' in the sense that they combine pastoral work with their social careers (for instance doing business and evangelisation at the same time). He argues that they create a new urban space for social mobility and distance themselves from their seniors. I agree with van Dijk's point on pastorship as new routes for social climbing but, at the same time, I argue that this is a dual process. Pastors distance themselves from some relations with their seniors but, at the same time, engage in new relations that also contain new elements of seniority. Becoming a pastor does not mean becoming free of hierarchical relations.

If we think of apprenticeship and entrepreneurship as organising principles for social relations, we can see that, in the making of pastoral careers, the two principles are at work simultaneously. The two complement each other in the sense that the credibility and training one gets from being in an apprentice-mentor relationship is supplemented by the creation of some sort of independence from the 'spiritual father' (by creating an independent branch, church, or fellowship). This independence often appears as a split, ranging from an absolute split to a distancing from the attention of the 'spiritual father'. However, it is not suffice to become independent. A process of re-inventing and re-installing oneself in the position of pastor follows suit. In the case of Francis, he left Victor Osei in order to found a church on his own and, at the same time, he engaged in a bond with Nicholas Asare, who ordained him as a pastor and made him the president of a pastoral association. In this way, he re-entered a junior–senior relationship, but importantly one that allowed for more space to grow.

Discussion: Pastors, Power, and 'Bigness'

Pastoral careers constitute new modes of achieving social mobility and of ascending social hierarchies that include a spiritual dimension. As outlined in this chapter, a pastoral trajectory as a way to become a small 'big man' involves generational dynamics both with regard to church hierarchies, but also in relation to pastors' families. Some scholars have argued that becoming a pastor is a way to become a 'big man' in the sense that pastors replace earlier models of 'big men' such as the chief, but also reproduce clientilistic relationships (McCauley 2012). In the following discussion I argue that becoming a pastor and a small 'big man' is more about finding one's place in various social structures and relationships, and to do this in a way that permits one to join power and gain acknowledgement.

In the above analysis I have also discussed how status and power achieved in one sphere can be transferred to other spheres and how this can broaden the areas of influence of pastors and increase their 'bigness'. In this analysis, my understanding of 'bigness' and of the 'big man' figure relies more on the Asante understanding of the term *ɔbirɛmpɔn* and the related understandings of 'bigness', wealth, and knowledge rather than a more general understanding of the 'big man' as a political figure enmeshed in patron-client relations.

Being a pastor can, if successful, pave the way for entering into and gaining status in other social fields such as family and local politics, although pastorship does not entail taking formal positions within these fields (such as a lineage head or a political figure). What the above trajectories, or avenues to 'bigness', suggest is that 'different types of authority and legitimacy coexist and intersect' (Lentz 1998: 59). There are overlaps and shared criteria with regard to how power and status are legitimatised. One such criterion is the access to and mediation of spiritual power that is part of how chiefs, lineage heads and pastors legitimise their positions and define their roles.

That Francis had become a pastor with his own church in Kumasi and had travelled abroad made him look important. He was expected to join community projects in his ancestral village, and provide religious services, which then gave him social status. This indicates that the status he had achieved as a pastor was transferable to another social setting, that of his hometown, because the criteria according to which status as a pastor were evaluated were recognisable and had resonance in a different setting. This further indicates that his career was a dependent one, shaped by those around him and points to the limitations others could place on him in certain situations.

There are also examples of 'big people' that add on other leadership positions and in this way enter a higher level of 'bigness' or extend their 'bigness'. One such example is Kwabena Darko from Kumasi, who is a successful businessman (Ghana's largest producer of poultry and known as the 'poultry king'), the general overseer of The Oasis of Love International Church, and a former board member of Bank of Ghana and presidential candidate in the 1992 elections. It is noteworthy that the combination of positions lies within the economic, the political, and the religious spheres. Again, I follow Lentz who argues that '[t]here is a whole repertoire of techniques by which the "big men" stage their simultaneous involvement in different social and political fields and skilfully foreground the contextually most relevant element of legitimacy' (1998: 62).

Another example is the former Regional Minister of Ashanti, Sampson Kwaku Boafo, who is a lawyer by profession and had founded a church (City Temple International Church) with branches in London, Accra and Kumasi (*Ghanaian Chronicle*, 28 April 2005). He was formerly chairman of the NPP (New Patriotic Party) branch in London and founder of the

NPP branch in Toronto, Canada, and someone who was acknowledged for his 'meritorious services and contribution to the development of Ashanti' (*Ghanaian Chronicle*, 9 January 2006). In a weekly newspaper, he was called 'Lawyer-priest-MP, Minister Sampson Kweku Boafo' (*The Spectator*, 14 July 2007). These examples point to the status that being a religious expert can confer to other types of power positions or offices. But does this also imply that being a pastor is a new form of 'bigmanship' in the sense that it replaces other types of patron-client relationships?

McCauley discusses Pentecostal pastorship as a new type of 'big man' rule in Ghana. The premise of his analysis is 'the contemporary breakdown in the traditional system that has created space for the charismatic Pentecostal movement to emerge, for some, as an alternative to kinship ties' (2012: 3). Despite acknowledging the limitations in pursuing a line of analysis that closely follows classic neo-patrimonial thinking (distribution of resources in exchange for loyalty), McCauley argues that relations between pastors and congregants constitute a new form of patron-client relations and that these are particularly important to set in place as 'the charismatic Pentecostal movement encourages members to break completely with their past' (McCauley 2012: 11). However, by viewing the role of pastors in a narrow neo-patrimonial framework he misses out some of the nuances in the Asante understanding of achieving and legitimising 'bigness'. This is not an isolated political process (of redistribution and loyalty), but also one that involves ideas of the sources of power in the spiritual realm. Moreover, 'bigness' is not achieved solely in relation to congregants or in the field of the church, but, as I have shown in the above analysis, also by drawing on other social networks among kin and people in politics. My point is that we cannot transfer one model of understanding from one field to another, but instead must look for how various positions and offices draw on similar registers and understandings of power to become 'big'.

As I have shown, pastorship and the 'bigness' that comes with it can be seen as innovative ways of climbing social hierarchies, for instance through creating independent churches, creating pastoral associations, or conducting religious services in one's hometown. These creative organisational forms build on local values and practices, as for instance expressed in the influence pastors have in family matters (such as allocation of land, advice giving and as mediator in conflicts), as well as their influence on the local political scene. The chain of transactions (material, symbolic, and spiritual) involved in making pastoral careers go beyond the church as institution and includes other settings as well. This reflects the transferable and overlapping avenues of power that Lentz points to, rather than the more strict idea of pastor-congregant as a new version of the patron-client relation.

In his work, Gifford (2004) has also provided an understanding of the charismatic and new Pentecostal movement as a reproduction of a political culture based on neo-patrimonial and clientelistic relations. However, the conceptualisation can become deterministic and the mere idea of religious leadership as building on a neo-patrimonial political culture leaves out the nuances of the processes and social relations involved. In the case of Asante, becoming 'big' and being legitimate as a pastor, as with other types of leaders, is about finding a balance between individual accumulation and redistribution to the community and truthfulness (as discussed in Chap. 3), about claiming and performing wisdom and knowledge (as discussed in Chap. 5), and finally about the establishment of apprentice-mentor relations that allow for dependency and autonomy at the same time. I think therefore that analysing pastorship merely as providing resources in exchange for support and loyalty is too reductionist and does not take into consideration the local and historical understandings of 'bigness' and power. Pastors do engage in and draw on social networks and use these when building up their positions, but these have a more open-ended character. Pastors are able to move in and out of relationships so that they can continue to grow (as Francis leaving Victor Osei). Therefore, the social relations they take part in are more flexible and unbound than how the literature normally describes patron-client relations. It is noteworthy that there are several parallel ways to join power and that middle-level people piece together their routes of social ascension by operating in several fields at the same time. Pastors engage both in established relations of seniority on the one hand, and, on the other hand, are innovative and capable of moving beyond these relations when they become restrictive. It is by focussing on the social processes around pastorship that we learn how new forms of leadership and social ascension function and unfold.

Notes

1. Some passages of this chapter have also appeared in Lauterbach (2010).
2. See also Le Meur (2008) on a similar discussion of the category of youth in Benin 'as a moral and cognitive category' rather than a category linked narrowly to age.

3. The educational system in Ghana consists of six years primary school, three years junior secondary school, and three years of senior secondary school. After this there is the possibility of training in, for example, universities, polytechnics, and teacher training colleges. This system was put in place in 1987 and replaced a system of six years of primary school, four years of middle school, five years of secondary school (form I–V, O level), two years of secondary school advanced level (form VI, A level) (Foster 1965: 197; Kuyini 2013). A new reform of the educational system has been implemented in 2007 (Kuyini 2013).
4. Interview with Emmanuel Appiah, Techiman, 30 August 2005.
5. This section is based on interviews with James Abu (13 December 2004 and 13 February 2005), with Peter Duku (20 February 2005), with Rosemond Duku (9 December 2014), with Edward Owusu-Ansah (13 December 2004), with Edward Owusu-Ansah, Manfred Tawiah & Felix Addai (13 February 2005), Edward Owusu-Ansah, Daniel Darko Kobiah & Manfred Tawiah (12 September 2005), with Emmanuel Appiah (10 November 2004, 30 August 2005),, with Daniel Darko (5 December 2014) as well as various conversations with Chris Oduro in Copenhagen during 2004 and 2005, as well as shorter correspondences with Daniel Darko during 2013.
6. In new cedi (1967–2007), and 2005 exchange rate. The equivalent of 1–2 USD.
7. I was told that the house was rented for eight years at the price of 50,000,000 cedis (new cedi (1967–2007)) which is approximately 5500 USD.
8. Interview with Rosemond Duku, Kumasi, 9 December 2014.
9. Abu attended the Oasis Christian Academy in Ahodwo, Kumasi that was headed by Mrs. Christiana Darko, the late wife of Kwabena Darko (who was mostly known for being one of Ghana's most successful poultry farmers and a politician). Kwabena Darko is also the general overseer and the founder of Oasis of Love International Church based in Kumasi.
10. Bethel Prayer Ministry International is one of Ghana's largest Pentecostal churches. It was established by Paul Owusu-Tabiri after a division with The Church of Pentecost in Ghana.
11. Interview with James Abu, Kumasi, 13 February 2005.
12. Interview with Edward Owusu-Ansah, Kumasi, 13 December 2014.

13. Pastor Oduro had initially sent 200 USD of which 100 was for pastor Abu and the remaining for the church (administered by the nephew). The three young pastors had not received any money. During church offerings they would collect between 8000 and 25,000 cedis (new cedi (1967–2007)), which is the equivalent of between 1 and 3 USD. The money was given to the nephew.
14. Interview with the young ABC pastors, Kumasi, 13 February and 12 September 2005.
15. Interview with James Abu, Kumasi, 13 February 2005.
16. Interview with Edward Owusu-Ansah, Kumasi, 13 December 2004.
17. Interview with Edward Owusu-Ansah, Kumasi, 13 December 2004.
18. Interview with Daniel Darko Kobiah, Kumasi, 12 September 2005.
19. Interview with Daniel Darko Kobiah, Kumasi, 12 September 2005.
20. There were, however, unsuccessful attempts of the church becoming involved in development projects that were aimed at communities more widely.
21. It should be noted that the case discussed here is somewhat particular as it is a mother church abroad that planted a church in Ghana. Most often, it is the other way round. Churches in Ghana establish branches among Ghanaian migrants abroad.
22. Interview with Stephen Kwame Appea, Fumensua, Kumasi, 28 November 2013 (conducted by James Boafo).
23. Interview with Stephen Forkuo, Kumasi, 4 December 2014.
24. Interview with Stephen Forkuo, Kumasi, 4 December 2014.
25. Interview with Eric Opoku Danso, Kumasi, 11 December 2014.
26. The following is based on interviews with Francis Afrifa (17 February 2005, 5 and 13 September 2005, 11 December 2014), a visit to his hometown (Apenkra), interviews with the *Apenkrahene* and the *Bamuhene* of Apenkra (from Francis' family) (19 September 2005), as well as participation in church services and prayer meetings led by him. I have also interviewed two senior pastors, whom he worked under, and a colleague. However, the purpose of these interviews was to discuss the careers and work of these people

rather than the career of Francis. The interviews with Francis have been followed up by numerous phone conversations and e-mail correspondences.
27. *Penge* is the Danish word for money. By throwing in a foreign word, Francis refers to his knowledge of a foreign language and to his status as a pastor who has been abroad.
28. New cedi (1967–2007), and the equivalent of 13 USD.
29. Interview with Tony Acheampong, Copenhagen, 24 June 2005.
30. Sunday service, Family Chapel International, Atonsu branch, Kumasi, 20 February 2005.
31. I have unfortunately not had the opportunity to get further information on this, but it is interesting if Francis were involved in a pastoral association under the Methodist church. Francis talked about it as an association open to pastors from all denominations.
32. Interview with Sam Boateng-Sarpong, Kumasi, 26 August 2005.
33. Interview with David Owusu Ameyaw, Techiman, 9 September 2005.
34. Interview with David Owusu Ameyaw, Techiman, 9 September 2005.
35. Or the so-called complete break with the past that is widely and somewhat uncritically employed in the literature. See McCauley (2012) for an example of this.
36. Interview with Nana Afria Abrafie Koto (queen mother of Techiman), Techiman, 30 August 2005. See also Warren and Brempong (1971) on the history of Techiman and the stools.
37. Interviews with Emmanuel Appiah, Copenhagen, 10 November 2004, and Akosua Yeboah, Asueyi (Brong-Ahafo region), 11 February 2005, as well as numerous conversations with Emmanuel Appiah and his wife during my visit to Techiman in February 2005 and in September 2005.
38. Interview with Gloria Mensah Afriyie, Kumasi, 1 September 2005.
39. See also Peel (2000: 53–55) on sociality as both vertical and horizontal.
40. The ambivalence (or inherent opposition) of this relationship resembles other father-son relationships, for example, among the Mossi of Burkina Faso as described by Skinner (1961) and discussed by Balandier (1974).

References

Allman, J. (1993). *The quills of the porcupine: Asante nationalism in an emergent Ghana 1954–1957*. Madison: University of Wisconsin Press.

Arhin, K. (1983). Rank and class among the Asante and Fante in the nineteenth century. *Africa, 53*(1), 2–21.

Arhin, K. (1994). The economic implications of transformations in Akan funeral rites. *Africa, 64*(3), 307–322.

Arhinful, D. K. (2001). *"We think of them" How Ghanaian migrants in Amsterdam assist relatives at home. Research Report 62*. Leiden: African Studies Centre.

Asamoah-Gyadu, J. K. (2005a). *African Charismatics. Current developments within independent indigenous pentecostalism in Ghana*. Leiden: Brill.

Balandier, G. (1974). *Anthropo-logiques*. Paris: Presses Universitaires de France.

Behrends, A., & Lentz, C. (2012). Education, careers, and home ties: The ethnography of an emerging middle class from Northern Ghana. *Zeitschrift für Ethnologie, 137*, 139–164.

Bendix, R. (1984). *Force, fate, and freedom. On historical sociology*. Berkeley: University of California Press.

Berry, S. (2001). *Chiefs know their boundaries. Essays on property, power, and the past in Asante, 1896–1996*. Portsmouth: Heinemann.

Clark, G. (1999). Negotiating Asante family survival in Kumasi, Ghana. *Africa, 69*(1), 66–86.

Clark, G. (2003). Proto-metropolis meets post-metropolis in Kumasi, Ghana. *City & Society, 15*(1), 87–108.

Corten, A., & Marshall-Fratani, R. (2001). Introduction. In A. Corton & R. Marshall-Fratani (Eds.), *Between babel and Pentecost. Transnational Pentecostalism in African and Latin America*. Bloomington and Indianapolis: Indiana University Press.

Englund, H. (2004). Cosmopolitanism and the devil in Malawi. *Ethnos, 69*(3), 293–316.

Foster, P. J. (1965). *Education and social change in Ghana*. London: Routledge & Kegan Paul.

Gifford, P. (2004). *Ghana's new Christianity. Pentecostalism in a globalising African economy*. London: Hurst & Company.

Kabki, M., Mazzucato, V., & Appiah, E. (2004). 'Wo benane a eye bebree': The economic impact of remittances of Netherlands-based Ghanaian migrants on rural ashanti. *Population, Space and Place, 10*(2), 85–97.

King, K., & Martin, C. (2002). The vocational school fallacy revisited: Education, aspiration and work in Ghana 1959–2000. *Journal of Educational Development, 22*(1), 5–26.

Krause, K. (2008). Transnational therapy networks among Ghanaians in London. *Journal of Ethnic and Migration Studies, 34*(2), 235–251.

Kuyini, A. B. (2013). Ghana's education reform 2007: A realistic proposition or a crisis of vision? *International Review of Education, 59*, 157–176.

Laurent, P.-J. (2003). *Les pentecôtistes du Burkina Faso, Mariage, pouvoir et guérison*. Paris: IRD Éditions et Karthala.

Lauterbach, K. (2010). Becoming a pastor: Youth and social aspirations in Ghana. *Young: Nordic Journal of Youth Research, 18*(3), 259–278.

Lauterbach, K. (2016). Religious entrepreneurs in Ghana. In U. Röschenthaler & D. Schulz (Eds.), *Cultural entrepreneurship in Africa*. London: Routledge.

Le Meur, P.-Y. 2008. Between emancipation and patronage: Intergenerational relationships in Benin. In E. Alber, S. van der Geest, & S. R. Whyte (Eds.), *Generations in Africa. Connections and conflicts*. Berlin: LIT Verlag.

Lentz, C. (1994). Home, death and leadership: Discourses of an educated elite from north-western Ghana. *Social Anthropology, 2*(2), 149–169.

Lentz, C. (1998). The chief, the mine captain and the politician: Legitimating power in Northern Ghana. *Africa, 68*(1), 46–67.

Lund, C. (2008). *Local politics and the dynamics of property in Africa*. New York: Cambridge University Press.

Manuh, T. (2003). Ghanaian migrants in Toronto, Canada: Care of kin and gender relations. *Ghana Studies, 6*, 91–107.

McCaskie, T. C. (1986a). Accumulation: Wealth and belief in Asante history: II the twentieth century. *Africa, 56*(1), 3–23.

McCauley, J. F. (2012). Africa's new big man rule? Pentecostalism and patronage in Ghana. *African Affairs, 112*(446), 1–21.

Meyer, B. (1998a). 'Make a complete break with the past', memory and post-colonial modernity in Ghanaian Pentecostalist discourse. *Journal of Religion in Africa, 28*(3), 316–349.

Miescher, S. (2005). *Making men in Ghana*. Bloomington & Indianapolis: Indiana University Press.

Osei, G. M. (2004). The 1987 junior secondary-school reform in Ghana: Vocational or pre-vocational in nature? *International Review of Education, 50*(5–6), 425–446.

Palmer, R. (2007). Education, training and labour market outcomes in Ghana: A review of the evidence. In *RECOUP Working paper 9*. DFID & University of Cambridge.

Peel, J. D. Y. (2000). *Religious encounter and the making of the Yoruba*. Bloomington: Indiana University Press.

Peil, M. (1970). The apprenticeship system in Accra. *Africa, 40*(2), 137–150.

Skinner, E. P. (1961). Intergenerational conflict among the Mossi: Father and son. *The Journal of Conflict Resolution, 5*(5), 55–60.

Soothill, J. E. (2007). *Gender, social change and spiritual power. Charismatic Christianity in Ghana*. Brill: Leiden.

van Dijk, R. A. (1992). Young puritan preachers in post-independence Malawi. *Africa, 62*(2), 159–181.

van Dijk, R. (2001). Time and transcultural technologies of the self in the Ghanaian Pentecostal Diaspora. In A. Corten & R. Marshall-Fratani (Eds.), *Between babel and Pentecost. Transnational Pentecostalism in Africa and Latin America*. Bloomington: Indiana University Press.

van Dijk, R. (2002). Religion, reciprocity and restructuring family responsibility in the Ghanaian Pentecostal diaspora. In D. Bryceson & U. Vuorela (Eds.), *The transnational family*. Oxford: Berg.

Warren, D. M., & Brempong, K. O. (1971). *Techiman traditional state. Stool and town histories*. Institute of African Studies: Legon.

Woods, D. (1994). Elites, ethnicity, and 'home town' associations in the Côte d'Ivoire: An historical analysis of state-society links. *Africa, 64*(4), 465–483.

Yamada, S. (2005). Socio-moralist vocationalism and public aspirations: Secondary education policies in colonial and present-day Ghana. *Africa Today, 52*(1), 71–94.

CHAPTER 7

Conclusion

In a conversation, Pastor Joshua Kas-Vorsah stated that 'I'm not a presidential entity, I'm not a traditional ruler and I'm not a parliamentarian. I'm just a preacher of the gospel.'[1] By identifying himself as a preacher of the gospel and not as a politician or a chief, Joshua Kas-Vorsah talks about how he sees his role as a pastor in society. He acts as a public figure, holds prayer sessions for the wellbeing of the country, and organises prayers in Kumasi before the elections in December 2000. Although he does not define himself as someone with political power, he defines his role as a pastor in relation hereto. In this way, he sees a pastor as belonging to the same category of leaders as, for instance, a president, a chief, or a member of parliament. He put himself at the same level of the figures he refers to and, at the same time, he differentiates himself from these figures. He is different in the sense that being a preacher of the gospel implies being a mediator between God and the people, which additionally gives him the ability to intervene and to change things by divine force.

The main argument of this book is that becoming a successful pastor is about becoming 'big' and displaying 'bigness' in both a material and spiritual sense. Attaining these positions requires access to spiritual power, and also a formalisation of such a position. Moreover, pastors draw on a register of power that is linked to traditional forms of authority, for instance, the roles of chiefs and family heads, who are also thought of as being linked to the ancestors and the spiritual realm. In her article on power and legitimacy in Northern Ghana, Lentz (1998) questions the usefulness of the Weberian distinction between traditional, rational and charismatic authority and in particular the idea of a gradual movement from the traditional and the charismatic towards the bureaucratic. She argues that 'these different types of authority and legitimacy coexist and intersect' (1998: 59). As mentioned in the introductory chapter, she criticises some scholars' attempts to overcome this division by using the metaphor of straddling as it 'entails the danger of reifying different fields of action' (Lentz 1998: 61). She proposes 'to speak of the "combination" and "complementarity" of different registers of power than of the "straddling" of different spheres' (Lentz 1998: 61). Following this, I argue that pastors combine different registers of power when becoming 'big men of God' and they perform and function in terms of overlapping and multiple registers of power.

Lentz's argument also reflects the idea of the complete pastor in the sense that the complete pastor is one that plays several complementary roles and functions. The complete pastor echoes other types of 'big men', such as the chief, the fetish priest, the family head, and the political leader, as also alluded to in the abovementioned quote by Joshua Kas-Vorsah. Pastors have, in some ways, taken over some tasks of for instance family heads. Pastors are responsible for the wellbeing of both church and family members. They also act as mediators, go into family matters, settle disputes, and represent church members at social events such as funerals, if the members are not able to be present themselves. Pastors are new figures of success who build on existing forms of leadership (both religious and political) and introduce new elements into religious leadership, such as a focus on business, easier and different access to leadership positions and extending one's sphere of influence beyond the church. The point is that pastors are rounded people; they are part of the social, political, economic, and spiritual spheres.

The social mechanisms involved in the making of pastoral careers are not exclusive to leadership in charismatic churches, but are to be understood as part of more general patterns of how people build up positions of power. As Berry writes:

> Carefully cultivated, social relationships may enhance people's access to wealth and knowledge. Even if they fail—because conflict or a decline in other people's fortunes—the presumption of efficacy remains: if one relationship fails, people are more likely to seek new or alternative social ties than attempt to go alone. (Berry 2001: xxvi)

To build up a pastoral career one has to rely on social ties both to the congregation and to family and kin. A pastoral career is not merely about individual self-promotion, but it is also an investment in social relationships, which serve as the base from which to operate as a figure of authority in a given community. This is to say, becoming a pastor cannot be reduced to being a question of having a pastoral calling or studying the Bible. It is also a question of building and investing in the right social relationships, and of being able to impose oneself as a pastor, and perform the craft of pastorship.

The young men presented at the beginning of this book strive towards becoming small 'big men' and they do so by engaging in pastoral careers. They are middle-level young men who establish churches in classrooms, storerooms, garages, and former restaurants, places that are also symbolically small and middle-level. At the same time, these places are non-religious in the sense that they are used for mundane purposes. Occupying such places and taking such paths are ways to transgress traditional and religious hierarchies (both socially and symbolically), which permits them to carve out new places and positions for joining power. The image of a small church in a storeroom with few members present, and three young pastors praying (see Fig. 6.2) is thought-provoking. On the one hand, it signals smallness, emptiness, and powerlessness. On the other hand, it also represents an idea and a sentiment of possibility, creativity, and improvisation. To me this image captures the main argument of this book: that engaging in pastoral careers is a way for young men and women in Asante to become 'bigger', to take the possibility of acquiring wealth and joining power in a way that resonates with Asante ideas of 'bigness', wealth and power.

As such the young pastors represent a wider group of 'mobile, entrepreneurial, urban-oriented, aspiring strata' (Barber 2000: 2), groups of middle-level people for whom family networks, education, and diplomas do not provide what it takes to grow. Instead, they rely on religious and other informal social networks and also build on historic Asante aspiring groups such as the *akonkofoɔ*. Through their engagements in pastoral careers, they seek to escape insecure social positions of subordination and at the same time, they express a certain social critique of, for instance, political holders of power, traditional religious practices, and mainline churches.

Despite the smallness of both people and places, the engagement in pastoral careers and the taking on of their destiny and calling enabled these pastors to be in positions from which they could join power. By being a religious mediator, a young pastor can display that he possesses the knowledge that is required to join power; power in both its metaphysical and material sense. Becoming a charismatic pastor is a novel way in which young people in contemporary Asante realise their aspirations. It is new in the sense that it provides a platform from which one can grow, a platform that in some ways bypasses social hierarchies within families and more established religious institutions. Charismatic Christianity introduces new ideas and values about family life, traditional religion, accumulation of wealth, and politics. At the same time, these young charismatic pastors are recognised as religious experts not only in church, but also in their wider social networks. The positions they take and the institutions they build resonate with already existing ideas about access to spiritual power, 'bigness', and wealth and they are made sense of in relation to this.

The question of scale is important. Although the setting up of small churches and the pursuit of a pastoral career might end in failure (which some do), it is worthwhile because it provides a space and an opportunity to prove oneself as a truthful person (to realise *nokware*) and to become recognised as someone who has access to and can activate power. And these spaces and opportunities are accessible and can be seized by people from different social levels. Therefore becoming a small 'big man' is about taking the opportunities available at one's social scale.

Pastors are much more linked up to other social networks outside of the church than has hitherto been recognised in the literature on charismatic Christianity in Africa. As discussed in the book a large part of this literature has focused on and emphasised rupture, 'making a break with the past', and individualisation. This focus has to some degree prevented us from seeing the social and historic embeddedness of charismatic Christianity. The point is that our understanding of the significance of charismatic Christianity in Asante and elsewhere in Africa should be approached not solely as an analysis of church as an isolated unit, but should integrate the wider social setting and the historical context in relation to which pastors operate and navigate. The analysis of pastoral trajectories has shown that pastors are both dependent on their wider social networks when making their careers and it is at the same time these networks that provide recognition and confer status when a career is successful.

Being in possession of spiritual power and having access to the spiritual realm means being in a position to influence other peoples' lives. Berry, in her work on chiefs in Asante, touches upon these discussions and writes that '[p]eople act, with good or evil intent, but the social effectiveness of their actions depends not only on their own capacities but also on their access to sources of power that lie outside the individual and beyond his or her control' (Berry 2001: xxv). The point here is that in order to be successful one need not only rely on one's own capacities and abilities, but also rely largely on other people who have proven to have access to 'the power of God' (or other sources of power).

Approaching the making of pastoral careers as a process of becoming 'bigger' is a way to open up the study of charismatic Christianity in Africa. It offers a perspective that includes not only the religious sphere, but also takes into account the wider social surroundings of a pastor and views social relations as a means to access resources such as spiritual power, credibility, a congregation, and networks of pastors at a national and international level. To repeat my earlier point, pastoral careers, and through these charismatic Christianity, cannot be understood without understanding what they are surrounded by in time and space.

Focusing on processes of achieving 'bigness' also permits us to understand the social mechanisms at play when becoming a pastor, mechanisms that are relevant not only for this category of figures, but more broadly for understanding the relation between religion and social change in Africa. The book argues that the new pastors of charismatic churches in Asante are re-inventing the role of religious leaders as well as that of 'big men' or chiefs. On the one hand, pastors are performing as traditional religious leaders by providing access to spiritual power, prosperity, and protection against evil. On the other hand, they are also performing in ways that draw on a repertoire of political leadership: providing protection and recognition. One could say that pastorship in Asante is based on the model of an Asante chief in the sense that he is one who gives and one who takes and combines religious as well as political office. Pastors provide access to the spiritual world, and give protection and possibilities for gaining success, and at the same time they demand contributions in terms of time, money, and loyalty. Through the analysis of successful careers the book has also shown how 'big' pastors combine a number of figures: pastor, teacher, father, and businessman, for example.

Pastorship, Wealth, and Small 'Big Men'

In this book I have approached the engagement in pastorship as a process of becoming 'big' by drawing on the historical Asante figures of *ɔbirεmpɔn* and *ɔkɔmfɔ*, as well as later groups of rising young men (such as the *akonkofoɔ*). The book has highlighted the importance of history when understanding the significance of this current phenomenon and argues that charismatic pastors should be understood as part of a longer historical trajectory of changing significations of wealth and 'bigness'. Pastors represent a certain understanding of wealth that is part of a wider global religious movement (prosperity gospel), but they at the same time relate to existing conceptions of being a 'big man' and to the importance of striking a balance between accumulating for the self and for the wellbeing of the community.

Chapter 3 dealt in particular with the concept of wealth both in its historic Asante understanding and in relation to the discourse and practices of charismatic pastors. Approaching wealth in a way that takes into account its shifting meaning over time allows us to see that wealth in a charismatic setting is more than money. Building up a position as a pastor also requires wealth in terms of, for instance, control over people. Accumulating wealth and achieving power and status is not only a question of personal interests or rational calculation. It is a question of having the loyalty and attention of people. These relations of reciprocity are not rigid patron-client relations (as discussed in Chap. 6), but take place both horizontally and vertically. Pastors take part in several social networks and also replace apprentice-mentor relationships when they become restraining. Through taking a processual perspective, the analysis has highlighted both agency and the important role of social relations and networks.

Becoming a pastor is a career trajectory and a way to ascend social hierarchies. But it is more than that. Pastors also become leadership figures and become new versions of 'big men'. The spiritual dimension to this role is of paramount importance. Pastors act as mediators, brokers, gate-keepers, and add a spiritual dimension to that role. Their sphere of influence is enlarged because they provide access to divine powers and, through this, pastors provide both protection and are sources of success.

Pastors and Multiple Fields

Pastors operate in and between different social fields, and hence become 'big' in more than just the church. As they build up their positions as pastors they also obtain and build status, wealth, and power within other fields. At times, religious leadership translates into other types of leadership, and there is a fluidity and informality about these leadership positions that make them difficult to understand within a classical analytical perspective that distinguishes between, traditional, charismatic and bureaucratic forms of authority.

Charismatic churches overlap with and replace other kinds of social groups. This implies that pastors in some cases take on roles and tasks that are traditionally that of, for instance, a family head. Moreover, these religious institutions represent new circuits of accumulation and redistribution of wealth. Money and other forms of wealth are collected in church and redistributed either by the pastor or by church members receiving a blessing from God. Being part of such circuits permits aspiring pastors to build themselves up as 'big men'; they give and they take. Charismatic pastors challenge traditional power hierarchies, but do not question the fundamental idea of being an *ɔbirɛmpɔn*.

Religious office and the role of pastors have become less confined to dealing with religious matters such as praying, healing or providing access to the spiritual world (than for instance is the case with the mainline churches), and is more directly and indirectly involved in social and political issues. There has been an opening up of religious office, which constitutes a new platform from which politics engages with and power can be joined. In the Asante context, a pastoral career is attractive, because it is relatively more accessible than other career trajectories and the position as a religious mediator is recognised widely in society and not only within the boundaries of the church.

Religion and Social Change

This book is a commentary on trajectories of religious and social change in contemporary Asante, of new ways of building up wealth and status, and of joining power as exemplified by charismatic pastors. One of the opening remarks of the book was that new religious movements, such as the charismatic Christianity, are not necessarily responses to modernity or 'social malaise' or a specific period in time. That said, charismatic pastors not only reproduce the past, but reflect and engage in processes of social change. As has been discussed in the analysis of pastoral trajectories, becoming a pastor requires being innovative and entrepreneurial. Charismatic pastors, as a group, feed in and take part in debates and struggles over status, wealth, and power and the religious field is open and attractive, because it represents opportunities of social and economic ascension.

This book approaches social change through the lens of religion and on how religious institutions and ideas interact and overlap with other institutions and ideas. Continuity and change in ideas around status, wealth, and power are central, as are the ways in which religious ideas and doctrine are in affinity with people's interests and resonate with the past. By piecing together stories of pastoral careers from the perspective of middle-level pastors, religion is perceived of as a specific translation of the mundane (Fields 1985). In this way, religion is not defined within the dichotomy of 'substance' and 'function' or 'ideas' and 'institutions'. Trying to understand how religious careers unfold and are politicised by people adds to the understanding of how religion interacts with politics in the Asante context. It gives insight into the room for manoeuvre that charismatic Christianity provides and into how charismatic pastors advance by engaging in religious apprenticeship and entrepreneurship. This religious platform provides opportunities for re-inventing and occupying these social roles in ways that both build on historic figures and at the same time adapt these positions to the lives of men and women in contemporary Asante. Pastors also challenge existing power hierarchies by expressing social critique, as they establish new ways of social ascension. They thereby create order in the sense that the new forms of organisation and new ideas they introduce are adapted to and to some degree resonate with former ideas and practices. Pastors are embedded and enmeshed in both traditional structures and in broader processes of social change. They are not mere reflections hereof, but are constitutive for these processes.

The processes described and analysed here are not unique features of charismatic churches or religious institutions as such. They are variations of more general social processes involved when becoming 'big' and building up status, wealth, and power. Moreover, they reflect perceptions of the relation between access to spiritual power and authority that are rooted in Asante society (Akyeampong and Obeng 1995: 483). More broadly, one could say that the careers of pastors illuminate processes of wider social change: pastors are examples of new figures of success and power that transgress the classical division of religion, state and society.

Note

1. Interview with Joshua Kas-Vorsah, Daban, Kumasi, 16 September 2005.

References

Akyeampong, E., & Obeng, P. (1995). Spirituality, gender, and power in Asante history. *International Journal of African Historical Studies, 28*(3), 481–508.

Barber, K. (2000). *The generation of plays. Yorùbá popular life in theatre.* Bloomington and Indianapolis: Indiana University Press.

Berry, S. (2001). *Chiefs know their boundaries. Essays on property, power, and the past in Asante, 1896–1996.* Portsmouth: Heinemann.

Fields, K. E. (1985). *Revival and rebellion in colonial Central Africa.* Princeton: Princeton University Press.

Lentz, C. (1998). The chief, the mine captain and the politician: Legitimating power in Northern Ghana. *Africa, 68*(1), 46–67.

Appendix

List of Interviews

Below is a complete list of interviews that I conducted while doing fieldwork first for my PhD dissertation and later for a research project on wealth and power in Ghanaian Christianity. Not all interviews are drawn upon or quoted directly in the book, but they all serve as a basis on which the book was written. Interviews in Copenhagen, Accra, and London were conducted by Karen Lauterbach. Interviews in Kumasi and Techiman were conducted by Karen Lauterbach (except where marked otherwise) with the assistance of James Boafo, Michael Poku-Boansi, Munirat Tawiah, Naomi Adarkwa, and Phyllis Mensah, who also assisted with translation from Twi to English. Some interviews were recorded and others were written down either during or after the interview. The interviews lasted between 30 minutes and two hours. The introductory chapter of the book contains a fuller description of methodology including other material that I used when writing the book.

Copenhagen
1. Acheampong, Dora (wife of no. 2): 17 January 2005
2. Acheampong, Tony (pastor): 21 April 2005
3. Acheampong, Tony: 24 June 2005
4. Agyeman, Albert (chief of Akan association): 17 July 2005
5. Akoto-Banfo, Yaw (church member): 13 June 2005
6. Ansah, Francis (pastor): 1 August 2004

7. Appiah, Emmanuel Kwame (pastor): 10 November 2004
8. Ateko, Kofi Obam (chief of Ewe association): 28 June 2004
9. Bediako Bruun, Gladys (church member): 26 July 2005
10. Commey, Clara (pastor): 20 January 2005
11. Commey, James (pastor): 10 August 2004
12. Commey, James: 26 November 2004
13. Gyamfi, Ransford (church member): 1 July 2005
14. Odoom, Daniel (former chairman of Ghana Union in DK): 24 July 2004
15. Oduro, Chris Akwasi (pastor): 2 November 2004
16. Oduro, Chris Akwasi: 18 March 2005
17. Oduro, Chris Akwasi: 28 June 2005
18. Owusu-Ansah, Sylvia (pastor): 14 April 2005
19. Paa Kofi (church member and musician): 8 July 2004

London
20. Georgina Owusu-Tabiri & daughter (widow of bishop Owusu-Tabiri and apostle): 9 May 2006

Accra
21. Asamoah-Gyadu, J. Kwabena (scholar): 26 September 2005
22. Budu, Clifford (pastor): 5 December 2004
23. Dodoo, Daniel (church member in DK): 8 December 2004
24. Dordzie, Emmanuel K. (pastor & international missions director): 5 August 2005
25. Frimpong, Hansel (apostle): 7 August 2005
26. Gyamfi, Samuel, (church leader/general secretary): 26 September 2005
27. Jones, Amanor Darkwa (pastor & scholar): 8 December 2004
28. Jones, Amanor Darkwa: 5 August 2005
29. Larbi, Kingsley E. (Rev. Prof.): 9 August 2005
30. Laryea, Eleanor (sister to no. 5): 9 August 2005
31. Odonkor, Fitzgerald (church leader/general overseer): 9 December 2004
32. Omenyo, Ceraphim (scholar): 28 September 2005
33. Osei Owusu (pastor): 26 September 2005
34. Owusu, Sampson & Christiana (driver of bishop Owusu-Tabiri and driver's wife): 24 September 2005

Kumasi
35. Ababio, Rosemary (church member): 7 February 2005
36. Abu, James (pastor): 13 December 2004
37. Abu, James: 13 February 2005
38. Ackuaah, Mimi (church member): 6 September 2005
39. Addae, Samuel Richard (bishop): 6 September 2005
40. Adomako, Boadicea Nanaserwa (pastor): 23 August 2005
41. Adu-Gyamfi, Samuel (pastor and lecturer): December 2013 (conducted by Naomi Adarkwa)
42. Adu-Gyamfi, Samuel: 10 December 2014
43. Adubofour, Samuel Brefo (scholar): 7 September 2005
44. Adubofour, Samuel Brefo: 12 September 2005
45. Afrifa, Francis (pastor): 17 February 2005
46. Afrifa, Francis: 5 September 2005
47. Afrifa, Francis: 13 September 2005
48. Afrifa, Francis: 11 December 2014
49. Agamah, Seraphim (pastor/mission director): 8 September 2005
50. Agyekum, Martin Kwadwo (pastor): 16 December 2014
51. Amoah, Emmanuel (pastor): 23 August 2005
52. Amoako, Samuel (church member): 18 December 2005 (conducted by Munirat Tawiah)
53. Ampofo, Simon (pastor): 13 December 2004
54. Ampofo, Simon: 15 February 2005
55. Appea, Stephen Kwame (former pastor): 28 November 2013 (conducted by James Boafo)
56. Appiah, Maxwell (church member): 11 December 2014
57. Asamoah, Charles K. (pastor): 23 February 2005
58. Asare, Nicholas (bishop): 5 September 2005
59. Asenso, Michael (pastor): 23 August 2005
60. Bediako, Akwasi (parent to no. 9): 24 August 2005
61. Bediako, Akosua Saamaa (parent to no. 9): 24 August 2005
62. Boabye, Kingsley (church elder): 14 February 2005
63. Boateng-Sarpong, Sam (pastor): 26 August 2005
64. Darko Kabeah, Daniel (pastor): 12 September 2005
65. Darko Kabeah, Daniel: 5 December 2014
66. Duku, Peter (church elder): 20 February 2005
67. Duku, Rosemond (wife of no. 67): 9 December 2014
68. Forkuo, Steven (church member and friend to no. 7): 8 February 2005

69. Forkuo, Steven: 4 December 2014
70. Kas-Vorsah, Joshua (pastor, radio evangelist): 16 September 2005
71. Kensah, Afua (cousin to no. 5): 25 August 2005
72. Kwabena Nkrumah, Nana (church member): 14 December 2014
73. Lawson, Elizabeth (secretary of no. 79): 26 August 2005
74. Mensa Bonsu, Sandra (sister of church member in no. 49's church): 24 February 2005
75. Mensah Afriyie, Gloria (pastor): 1 September 2005
76. Mensah Afriyie, Gloria: 3 December 2014
77. Nana Dwamena Akenten II (Apenkrahene/chief of Apenkra): 19 September 2005
78. Obeng, Ransford (pastor): 12 September 2005
79. Obeng, Ransford: 9 December 2014
80. Opoku Danso, Eric (church member): 11 December 2014
81. Osei, Victor (pastor): 3 February 2005
82. Osei, Victor: 20 August 2005
83. Osei, Victor: 4 December 2014
84. Osei Brefo, Abigail (church member): 11 December 2014
85. Osei-Kuffour, Seth (pastor): 24 August 2005
86. Osei-Kuffour, Seth: 18 August 2013 (conducted by James Boafo)
87. Osei-Kuffour, Seth: 8 December 2014
88. Otu, Edward M. (pastor): 22 February 2005
89. Owusu, Kofi (Bamuhene of Apenkra): 19 September 2005
90. Owusu-Ansah, Edward (pastor/prophet): 13 December 2004
91. Owusu-Ansah, Edward; Addai, Felix & co. (pastors): 13 February 2005
92. Owusu-Ansah, Edward & co. (pastors): 15 September 2005
93. Owusu-Ansah, Emmanuel (pastor): 15 August 2005
94. Owusu Duah, Alfred (church member): 14 December 2014
95. Tawiah, Manfred (pastor): 12 September 2005
96. Yeboah, Francis (church member): 14 December 2014
97. Focus group discussion with pastors at Charisma Bible College: 5 September 2005

Techiman
98. Abrafie Koto, Nana Afia (queen mother of Techiman): 30 August 2005
99. Appiah, Elizabeth (wife of no. 7/101): 11 February 2005

100. Appiah, Emmanuel Kwame (evangelist, same as no. 7): 30 August 2005
101. Yeboah, Akosua (mother of 7/101): 11 February 2005
102. Konadu, Benjamin (pastor): 29 August 2005
103. Focus group discussion with pastors: 11 February 2005
104. Frempong Manso, Joseph (pastor): 29 August 2005
105. Owusu Ameyaw, David (pastor): 9 September 2005

Index

A

Accra, 5, 21, 52, 53, 82, 87n21, 101, 102, 158, 170, 172, 188, 207, 208
Addae, Samuel, 94, 108
Adubofour, Samuel Brefo, 33, 47, 55, 111, 112, 122n28, 145
African Independent Churches, 13. *See also Sunsum sore*
Afrifa, Francis, 153, 167, 169–80
age, 105, 138–40, 155, 163, 164, 172
akonkofoɔ, 10, 36–7, 45, 54, 57n15, 65, 68, 199, 201
Akyeampong, Emmanuel, 17, 18, 30, 33, 39, 40, 94, 95, 126, 127, 141, 204
Alive Bible Congregation (ABC), 1, 123n42, 157, 158, 161–3, 168, 178, 186, 192n14
Allman, Jean, 10, 11, 40–5, 55, 59n38, 155
Apostolic Church of Ghana, 1, 82, 88n30, 161
Appiah, Emmanuel, 168, 183
apprentice, 7, 105, 109, 171–4, 184–7
apprenticeship, 7, 22, 103–6, 151, 152, 154, 173, 184, 186, 187, 204. *See also* apprentice
approval, 5, 98, 99, 102, 115, 170, 180
social, 91, 98–100, 119, 120
Arhin, Kwame, 8, 31, 34–7, 56n3, 56n4, 57n7, 57n11, 68, 155, 184
Asamoah-Gyadu, J. Kwabena, 15, 34, 43, 49, 55, 58n25, 86n9, 99, 107, 126, 127, 145, 181
Asante, 4, 6–8, 10–12, 15–19, 22, 23n6, 24n8, 29–59, 63, 64, 66–70, 72, 74–6, 91, 92, 94, 95, 98, 105, 112, 119, 125–7, 129, 134, 141, 152, 154, 155, 181, 184, 187, 189, 190, 199–204
colonial, 12, 30, 39, 41, 42, 70
pre-colonial, 30–4, 39, 45, 56n3, 57n11, 63, 184
Asantehene, 31–4, 37, 39, 45, 53, 75
Asante kingdom, 8, 56n4
asofo (*ɔsɔfo*), 5, 23n6. *See also* pastor(s)

aspiration(s), 2, 7, 8, 13, 14, 18, 44–6, 50, 54, 57n16, 71, 97, 153–7, 163, 165, 173, 174, 176, 178, 186, 200
  aspiring groups, 29, 199
  aspiring people, 7, 10, 29
Assemblies of God, 44, 49, 51
Austin, Gareth, 31, 35, 36, 38, 41–3, 56n4, 57n12, 70, 82
authority, 5, 6, 8, 11, 16, 17, 19, 22, 24n11, 31, 33, 37, 38, 41, 44, 45, 48, 57n7, 65, 66, 83, 86n2, 91, 98, 99, 102, 105, 110, 112–14, 117, 119–21, 126, 129, 130, 133, 137, 138, 140, 145–7, 162, 175, 178, 181, 183, 185, 186, 188, 197–9, 202, 204
  charismatic, 24n11, 99, 102, 105, 146, 197
  religious, 16, 120, 126, 130, 138, 185
autonomy, 151, 166, 181, 185, 190

B

Baëta, C.G., 13, 42, 43, 58n19, 145, 146
Barber, Karin, 11, 137, 138, 199
belief, 4, 11, 14, 16, 30, 36, 55, 67, 68, 132, 141, 148n10
Berry, Sara, 30, 35, 71, 76, 85, 182, 198, 200, 201
Bible, 5, 53, 75–7, 84, 87n19, 93, 94, 103, 105, 108–10, 123n42, 125, 126, 133–9, 142, 144, 145, 147, 170, 171, 176, 185, 199, 210n980
Bible school, 1, 3, 5, 22, 52, 53, 98, 100, 103–11, 117, 119, 120, 135, 136, 152, 156, 157, 160, 161, 163, 168, 169, 173, 174, 177, 178

'big man,' 5, 8–10, 16, 19, 20, 22, 29–31, 38, 54, 56n1 63, 66, 68, 94, 121, 125, 142, 151–93, 200, 202. *See also* small 'big man'
'bigness', 5, 19, 20, 102, 135, 147, 152, 154, 178, 186–90, 197, 199–202
ɔbirɛmpɔn, 22, 30, 31, 37, 45, 54, 56n1, 57n8, 68, 187, 201, 203
blessing, 47, 70, 73, 101, 139, 146, 203
  God's blessing, 16, 20, 47, 64, 67, 69–72, 79
Bonsam, Kwaku, 127, 128
business, 9, 43, 45, 71, 75, 77, 95, 97, 98, 115, 122n22, 127, 138, 152, 155, 166, 167, 170, 171, 186, 198

C

calling, 9, 19, 81, 91–9, 104, 111, 113, 119, 120, 128, 170–1, 199. *See also* pastoral, calling
  divine, 92, 97, 120, 128
Calvary Charismatic Centre, 51–3, 108
careers, 2, 5, 6, 8, 12, 18, 19, 37, 44, 46, 79, 91–3, 96–8, 103, 104, 106, 107, 120, 152–4, 156, 165, 168, 169, 171, 172, 174, 179, 180, 184, 186, 188, 192n26, 193n26, 200–4
  pastoral, 2, 4–6, 8, 10–12, 16, 18, 55, 56, 85, 92, 94, 97, 119, 120, 138, 152–6, 158, 160, 168, 169, 171, 174, 177, 187, 189, 198–201, 203, 204
charisma, 99–103, 108, 109, 117, 120, 121, 146, 147, 177, 178, 210n98

charismatic
  Christianity, 4–6, 12–15, 17, 23n3, 29, 46, 49–55, 58n24, 64–6, 71, 76, 85, 114, 117, 128, 137, 148n25, 156, 168, 181, 185, 200, 201, 203, 204
  church(es), 1–3, 5, 9, 12, 14, 16, 23n3, 23n4, 47–53, 58n24, 64, 65, 69, 71, 73, 75, 76, 78, 79, 81, 84, 85, 86n13, 93, 105, 106, 110, 112, 115, 117, 122n21, 122n28, 125, 133, 135, 138, 142, 145, 153, 157, 170, 172, 175, 177, 182, 198, 201, 203, 204
  movement, 22, 23n3, 43, 47, 50, 51, 53, 70, 99, 122n11, 145, 167
chief, 11, 33–5, 37, 40, 41, 44, 45, 53, 79, 82, 112, 130, 132, 134, 153, 170, 179, 183, 187, 188, 197, 198, 200, 201, 207n4, 208n8. *See also* ɔhene
Christ, 14, 49, 67, 70, 77, 80, 81, 87n26, 88n27–30, 100, 122n14, 136. *See also* Jesus
Christ Apostolic Church, 3, 49, 88n30, 136
Christ Apostolic Church of Ghana, 82, 88n30
Christian Action Faith Ministries, 5
Christianity, 2, 4–6, 8, 12–17, 22, 23n3, 23n6, 29, 37, 39–41, 43, 44, 46, 49–51, 54, 55, 58n24, 64–7, 69–76, 85, 94, 114, 117, 127, 128, 137, 148n25, 156, 168, 181, 185, 200, 201, 203, 204, 207. *See also* charismatic, Christianity
church
  hierarchy, 5, 106, 135, 146, 147, 161
  service, 3, 5, 21, 22, 52, 104, 105, 118, 123n42, 125, 127, 131, 133–6, 142, 147n9, 160, 163, 192n26
Church of Christ, 80, 81, 87n26, 88n27–9
Church of Pentecost, 14, 44, 49, 51, 133, 161, 191n10
Clark, Gracia, 166, 181, 182
community, 5–7, 9, 16, 20, 22, 31, 38, 41, 46, 54, 63, 64, 66, 68, 69, 71, 74–7, 79, 82, 84, 85, 93, 116, 126, 143, 166, 167, 179, 186, 188, 190, 192n20, 199, 202
congregation, 1, 3, 7, 19, 33, 65, 71, 91, 98, 102, 113–17, 119, 123n42, 128, 129, 163, 174, 176, 178, 185, 186, 198, 201
continuity, 11, 14–16, 31, 38, 63, 203
conversion, 14, 15, 40, 41, 43, 44, 128, 166
Copenhagen, 93, 108, 123n36, 158, 160, 162, 163, 166, 167, 191n5, 193n29, 193n37, 207–8
cosmology, 17, 55
credibility, 7, 99, 103, 105, 107, 172–5, 184, 185, 187, 201

D
deliverance, 3, 22, 53, 125, 130, 134, 136
Denmark, 21, 93, 108, 156–63, 165–7, 174, 179, 183
dependency, 99, 110, 151, 152, 166, 185, 186, 190
destiny, 91–3, 97, 98, 119, 120, 121n10, 170, 199
devil, 127, 128
divination, 22, 125
Douglas, Mary, 12, 52, 55

dream, 92, 93, 97, 98, 100, 101, 103, 116, 120, 128, 129, 170
Duncan-Williams, Nicholas, 5, 48, 100

E
education, 8, 15, 36, 37, 39, 44, 50, 71, 75, 76, 84, 107, 127, 139, 155, 157, 199
elite(s), 7, 10, 35, 36, 45–8, 51, 53, 57n16, 70, 75, 154, 167
Engelke, Matthew, 15, 55
Englund, Harri, 182
entrepreneurs, 57n8, 68–9, 153, 186
entrepreneurship, 4, 7, 22, 43, 64, 151–3, 187, 204
  religious, 6
evangelist, 24n7, 51, 86n8, 107, 111, 147, 169, 175, 180, 210n71, 211n101
evil
  forces, 16, 22, 53, 128, 130–2
  power, 79, 82, 126–9
  spirits, 14, 34, 130–2

F
failure, 32, 43, 75, 81, 96, 162, 168, 200
Faith Convention, 52, 53
fake. *See* false
false, 22, 77–81, 85, 87n19, 87n22, 111, 112, 143, 144
family, 5, 14, 15, 21, 22, 33, 35, 36, 41, 43, 51, 67, 73, 75, 81, 97–100, 107–10, 112, 115, 117, 120, 127, 135, 145, 151, 152, 157, 158, 161, 163, 166–71, 174, 176, 178–86, 188, 189, 192n26, 197–200, 203
  extended, 7, 19, 35, 152, 184, 186

Family Chapel International, 51, 73, 74, 86n12, 86n14–16, 139, 142, 172, 173, 175, 177, 193n30
fate, 9, 92, 93. *See also* destiny
father, 75, 112, 113, 121, 146, 158, 161, 171, 172, 174–7, 185, 201
  spiritual, 99, 103–5, 110, 139, 169, 172, 173, 175, 176, 185, 187
fellowship, 3, 23n3, 49–52, 96, 97, 113, 121–2n11, 136, 155, 156, 161, 164, 165, 168, 183, 187
figure
  father, 146
  figure of success, 7, 10, 198, 204
formalisation, 91, 117–20, 197
Fountain Life International Christian Centre, 153, 176

G
genealogy, 99–103, 119, 120
  spiritual, 99–103, 119, 120
generation, 6, 23n3, 38, 44, 138, 143. *See also* age
genuine, 77, 78, 85, 111, 112, 130, 137, 148n16
Gifford, Paul, 5, 46–9, 55, 70, 71, 74, 86n8, 137, 148n25, 190
gifts
  gift-giving, 71
  spiritual, 1, 3, 106, 130, 147
god. *See also* man of God
  word of God, 2, 7, 78, 94, 95, 121n8, 125, 126, 130, 135–41, 169
graduation, 107, 109–11
Greene, Sandra, 12
Guyer, Jane, 71
Gyekye, Kwame, 64, 85, 92, 121n3

H
Haynes, Naomi, 15, 64, 71

healing, 3, 32, 43, 49, 53, 92, 94, 121n11, 135, 137, 143, 146, 203
history, 8, 10–12, 17, 18, 23n6, 29–59, 64, 68, 91, 118, 132, 157, 161, 193n36, 201
 historical context, 16, 63, 105, 200
Holy Ghost, 82, 125
 Holy Spirit, 49, 114, 128, 130, 133
hometown, 75, 76, 152, 153, 155, 158, 166–7, 170, 178–80, 183, 188, 189, 192n26
Hope Palace Chapel, 130, 131

I

Idahosa, Benson, 51, 100–2, 112
individual, 9, 10, 16–19, 22, 31, 32, 34–8, 41, 43, 45, 54, 63, 68, 71–5, 82–5, 92, 98, 109, 114, 115, 118, 121n3, 126, 130, 135, 146, 173, 181, 184, 190, 199, 200
institutions, 11–17, 19, 21, 39, 50–2, 55, 66, 71, 74, 107, 115, 117–19, 122n22, 146, 157, 161, 189, 200, 203, 204
 building, 117

J

Jesus, 14, 81, 84, 95, 143, 164, 177, 179. *See also* Christ
Jones, Ben, 12, 19

K

Kas-Vorsah, Joshua, 83, 94, 100, 102, 197, 198
kinship, 6, 20, 35, 41, 43, 181, 182, 189
Kirsch, Thomas, 99, 119, 129, 133, 146
knowledge, 2, 6, 7, 17, 18, 22, 30, 76, 78, 91, 93–5, 103, 105, 107, 113, 120, 125–48, 162, 169, 172, 178, 187, 190, 193n27, 198, 199
 of God, 95, 120, 139–41
 performance, 91, 136–45
Komfo Anokye (ɔkɔmfɔ), 31, 33, 56n6. *See also* priest
Kumasi, 1, 2, 8, 9, 21, 22, 34, 37, 39, 40, 50–4, 58n27, 58n29, 72, 73, 75, 76, 78, 80, 81, 83, 84, 87n23, 92, 95, 98–100, 104, 105, 107, 108, 110, 112, 115, 116, 118, 122n28, 125, 128, 129, 131, 134, 136, 139, 142, 145, 153, 154, 157–9, 162–73, 175–80, 188, 197, 207, 209–10

L

Le Meur, Pierre-Yves, 166, 185, 190n2
leadership, 1, 3, 7, 19, 45–7, 50, 72, 83, 91, 111–13, 122n11, 126, 147, 153, 158, 160–3, 177, 178, 188, 190, 198, 201, 202
legitimacy, 22, 38, 55, 64, 66, 85, 95, 98, 102–6, 108, 113, 120, 129, 143, 151, 152, 161, 162, 164, 166, 172, 184, 185, 188, 197, 198
legitimate, 6, 12, 20, 49, 69, 70, 81, 82, 84, 85, 102, 190
Lentz, Carola, 20, 24n11, 134, 135, 151–3, 155, 182, 188, 190, 197, 198
literacy, 37, 94, 110, 137

M

mainline christianity, 65
mainline churches, 47–9, 59n36, 65, 69, 70, 74, 98, 103, 121n11, 181, 199, 203

man of God, 3, 6, 11, 16, 19, 74, 92, 94, 101, 121, 127, 142, 143, 167, 181
   men of God, 1, 6, 79, 102, 103, 107, 165, 198
Marshall, Ruth, 13, 15
Maxwell, David, 4, 5, 12, 21, 59n39, 86n9, 147–8n9
McCaskie, T.C., 4, 8–10, 16–18, 24n6, 30–9, 44–7, 51, 55, 56n1, 56n2, 56n4, 56n6, 57n9, 57n15, 59n38, 63, 66, 68, 69, 71, 74, 92, 95, 98, 126, 148n10, 171
McCauley, John, 187, 189, 193n35
McLeod, Malcolm, 32, 33, 56n4, 56n6
Médard, Jean-François, 20
mediator, 7, 11, 32, 33, 56n2, 64, 113, 117, 127, 141, 152, 189, 197, 198, 202
   religious, 16, 199, 203
membership, 3, 99, 117, 118, 158, 160
metaphysical, 18, 30, 67, 135, 199
Meyer, Birgit, 13–15, 23n3, 55, 64, 70, 71, 128, 137, 181
Miescher, Stephan, 57n16, 95, 105, 111, 140, 154, 173
migration, 15, 157, 185. *See also* travel
miracles, 22, 53, 65, 91, 94, 95, 125, 126, 128, 130, 138
mobility, 8, 37–8, 57n8, 116, 154, 155, 185
   social, 4, 6, 7, 15, 16, 29, 31, 34–7, 46, 64, 152, 155, 167, 171, 186, 187
money
   fast, 78, 81, 82
   rapid, 68
moral, 4, 5, 10, 11, 37, 38, 63–6, 68, 69, 71, 78, 108, 128, 129, 176, 178, 190n2
   morality, 9, 10, 64, 78, 79, 81, 85

N

networks, 5–7, 18, 19, 21, 52, 76, 98, 99, 110, 116, 151, 152, 157, 167, 174, 176, 177, 180, 186, 189, 190, 199–202
Newell, Stephanie, 137–9
nhenkwaa, 37, 68
nkwankwaa, 10, 44–6, 154
nokware, 63, 65–8, 70, 77, 186, 200. *See also* truthful
Nugent, Paul, 48, 49

O

Obeng, Pashington, 17, 18, 30, 34, 94, 95, 126, 127, 141, 204
obligation, 35, 36, 41, 43, 132, 157, 167, 176, 178, 179
offerings, 32, 33, 67, 73–5, 79, 133, 167, 192n13
ɔhene, 11, 34, 182
'one-man' church, 5, 18, 66, 117
Onyame, 17, 32, 34
Onyame nnipa, 11, 74. *See also* man of God
Osei, Victor, 74–6, 139–45, 155, 172, 173, 175–7, 187, 190

P

past, 7, 11, 12, 14, 15, 18, 19, 37, 55, 71, 153, 165, 182, 189, 193n35, 200, 203, 204
pastor(s)
   complete, 91, 121, 146, 151, 198
   fake, 77–82
   false, 22, 77–81, 87n19, 112
   junior, 1, 110, 114, 133–6, 156, 165, 175, 177, 178, 185
   senior, 1, 3, 7, 18, 19, 80, 99, 101, 103–8, 110, 113, 114, 119, 120, 128, 136, 152, 154, 161,

162, 165, 166, 168, 173, 175, 184–6, 192n26
pastoral
  association, 50, 110, 117, 178, 187, 189, 193n31
  calling, 1, 22, 91–100, 103, 107, 112, 119, 120, 170, 199
  career, 2, 4–6, 8, 10–12, 16, 18, 55, 56, 85, 92, 94, 97, 119, 120, 138, 152–6, 158, 160, 168, 169, 171, 174, 177, 187, 189, 198–201, 203, 204
  work, 97, 105, 108, 121n4, 126, 135, 136, 152, 153, 156, 157, 168, 173, 174, 177, 186
pastorship, 3–8, 11, 12, 19, 21, 22, 63, 87n23, 91–123, 125, 133, 146, 151–6, 186, 188–90, 199, 201–2
patronage, 4, 8
Peel, J.D.Y., 12, 20, 58n17, 59n38, 193n39
Pentecostal. *See also* Pentecostalism
  churches, 23n3, 48, 79, 191n10
  classical Pentecostal churches, 16, 23n3, 49–51, 69, 80, 87n25, 88n30, 92, 152
Pentecostalism, 14, 15, 19, 21, 23n6, 43–4, 49–50, 64, 156, 185. *See also* charismatic, Christianity
performance
  access to spiritual power, 6
  performative, 126, 137
  of spiritual power, 4, 22, 91, 126, 130
politics, 7, 11, 14, 19–21, 46–9, 144, 145, 151–93, 200, 203, 204
position, 3–11, 16, 20, 21, 29, 34, 44, 45, 47, 48, 50, 64–6, 74, 76, 79–81, 91, 95, 99–101, 103, 105, 111–13, 117, 119–21, 122n11, 127, 129, 136, 145, 151, 153–6, 161–3, 167, 169, 177–90, 197–200, 202–4
poverty, 70, 74, 76, 85, 180

'refusal of poverty,' 71, 74–6
power. *See also* spiritual, power
  divine, 11, 173, 202
  join, 3, 4, 6, 18, 54, 151, 152, 154, 187, 190, 199
  source of, 17, 103, 112, 113, 126–8, 189, 200, 201
  supernatural, 9, 32
prayer
  meetings, 5, 83, 98, 136, 192n26
  praying, 1, 53, 64, 75, 76, 92, 94–6, 98, 104, 121n11, 130, 131, 137, 142, 152, 170, 172, 176, 179, 199, 203
preaching, 1, 21, 64, 67, 72, 73, 86n2, 94, 95, 101, 107, 110, 117, 125, 126, 135–7, 139, 142, 165, 169, 176, 179
preacher, 44, 73, 74, 87n23, 98, 102, 114, 136, 137, 147, 169, 186, 197
priest, 9, 11, 12, 23n6, 31–3, 46, 56n2, 66, 92, 98, 112, 127, 130, 198. *See also* Komfo Anokye (ɔkɔmfo)
  traditional, 16, 53, 93, 97, 98, 112, 127, 128
progress, 30, 37–9, 66, 70, 75, 77, 84, 106, 177
prophecy, 33, 43, 92, 102, 104, 130, 136
prophet, 1–3, 24n7, 43–4, 46, 47, 49, 53–5, 58n20, 77, 78, 80, 87n19, 87n22, 92, 93, 111, 113, 145–7, 148n16, 161, 163, 164, 170. *See also* pastor(s)
prosperity
  gospel, 22, 65, 70–2, 74, 79, 84, 202
  'sowing and reaping,' 67
protection, 22, 32, 36, 37, 43, 81, 104, 127, 173, 175–8, 185, 186, 201, 202
spiritual, 7, 53, 130

Protestant, 13, 69
public, 6, 8, 10, 30, 45, 47, 63–6, 70, 76, 78–80, 94, 98, 107, 108, 110, 128, 137, 145, 147n3, 154–6, 197
  debate, 64–6, 69, 77, 78, 84

R
Ranger, Terence, 8, 14, 59n38, 132
reciprocity, 33, 110, 167, 202
recognition, 6, 16, 20, 30, 31, 74, 99, 103, 106, 119, 120, 127, 144, 155, 166, 175, 180, 183, 185, 200, 201
regulation, 65, 66, 77, 117, 119, 120
religion, 4, 6–8, 12–15, 17, 19–22, 29–59, 65, 127, 200, 201, 203–4
religious expert
  religious leader, 7, 8, 30, 85, 99, 100, 102, 110, 112, 119, 120, 201
  religious specialist, 29, 33, 128
religious ideas, 29, 54, 64, 69, 203
religious movement, 12–14, 21, 45, 47, 55, 58n19, 132, 185, 202, 203
religious practice, 13, 41, 182, 183, 199
resistance, 95–8, 119
Resurrection Faith in Christ Ministries, 100
rich, 5, 10, 38, 46, 69, 75, 79, 180
  richness, 17, 70, 71, 74, 76, 79
rupture, 14–16, 22, 71, 181, 200

S
school leaver, 1, 58n16, 155, 171
Scripture Union, 50, 51, 155, 165, 168
sermon, 73, 86n12, 116, 133–6, 138, 144, 146, 168, 175
sincerity, 40, 66, 77, 78, 92, 98, 120

Skinner, Kate, 68, 75, 76
small 'big man,' 5, 8, 19, 66, 121, 151–93, 200
social media, 126, 137, 141–5
Soothill, Jane, 21, 69, 101, 102, 122n21, 148n11, 185
spiritual
  churches, 13, 42–4, 47, 49, 55, 80, 145
  growth, 76
  hierarchy, 102
  power, 2–4, 6–9, 11, 15–17, 19, 22, 29, 30, 32, 45, 56n2, 65, 67, 74, 78, 79, 81, 82, 91, 99, 101–4, 106, 107, 109, 113, 114, 120, 121, 125–48, 156, 163, 164, 176, 180, 185, 188, 197, 200, 201, 204
  realm, 7, 16, 17, 91, 95, 126, 127, 141, 189, 197, 200
  service, 115, 133, 134, 145, 152
  world, 17, 127, 141, 201, 203
status, 6, 7, 9, 11, 12, 16–19, 22, 29–31, 34, 36, 45, 48, 54, 63, 64, 68, 71, 81, 94, 106, 107, 109–11, 113, 114, 127, 135, 137, 138, 140, 141, 145, 148n25, 151, 152, 155, 157, 161–3, 166, 167, 172, 175, 178–89, 193n27, 200, 202–4
  social, 6, 8, 29, 103, 138, 155, 174, 188
stool, 36, 134, 135, 182–4, 193n36
straddling, 20, 184, 198
subordinate, 4, 10, 11, 41, 155, 171
  subordination, 6, 10, 11, 45, 46, 104, 106, 152, 185, 199
success, 5–7, 9, 11, 18, 30, 35, 37, 38, 48, 52, 53, 64, 67, 71, 75, 76, 85, 95, 98, 109, 116, 120, 126, 127, 130, 132, 143, 160, 162, 165, 173, 176, 179, 198, 201, 202

figures of success, 7, 10, 198, 204
Sunsum sore, 13, 43, 49
supernatural, 9, 12, 31–3, 56n2, 127, 146, 148n10

T

teacher, 95–7, 111, 121, 155, 156, 178, 191n3, 201
 teaching, 77, 93, 94, 103, 107, 122n22, 126, 173
 Techiman, 21, 96, 156, 168, 169, 180, 207, 211
 text, 76, 79, 126, 136–45
 tithes, 79, 84, 117–19, 122n11. *See also* offerings
 titles, 24n8, 29, 31, 43, 56n1, 63, 80, 83, 106, 109, 111–13, 148n16
 training, 9, 19, 22, 32, 33, 41, 50, 77, 91, 98, 103–11, 119, 120, 155, 156, 165, 173, 176, 187, 191n3
  informal, 104–6, 119, 120
 trajectory, 2, 6, 8–12, 16, 18, 22, 44, 91, 92, 97, 98, 121n4, 151, 153, 154, 157–80, 186–8, 200, 202, 203
 transnational, 116, 152, 156, 157, 160, 166, 167
 travel, 19, 71, 116, 156, 166, 170
 truthful
  pastors, 4, 22, 63–88, 129
  truthfulness, 6, 24n8, 63, 66, 67, 70, 78, 82–5, 109, 143, 162, 190

Tumi, 17, 18, 32, 126, 127, 132. *See also* power

U

Ukah, Asonzeh, 71–3, 86n7

V

Van Dijk, Rijk, 14, 15, 71, 167, 181, 182, 186
vision, 46, 76, 92, 93, 98, 99, 103, 144, 170, 175

W

wealth
 accumulation of, 30–2, 35, 37, 45, 49, 55, 68, 129, 200
 display of, 16, 54, 69, 74, 91
 distribution of, 8, 45
 legitimate, 81
Weber, Max, 14, 64, 99, 119, 120
well-being
 collective, 31
 welfare, 41, 64–6, 132
Wilks, Ivor, 16, 31, 44, 56n4, 56n5, 57n7, 57n8, 105
Wiredu, Kwasi, 66, 92, 93, 121n10
wisdom, 6, 7, 121, 134, 137–44, 172, 190
witchcraft, 14, 16, 41–3, 82
word of God, 2, 7, 78, 94, 95, 121n8, 125, 126, 130, 135–41, 169

Printed by Printforce, the Netherlands